"*Trance-Portation* belongs on every Pagan and occultist's bookshelf; it's destined to become a classic of the field. Diana Paxson's down-to-earth style speaks directly to real people with real problems—racing thoughts, distractibility, over-sensitivity—and lets them know that they, too, can achieve trance states that will enrich their spiritual lives."

—Deborah Lipp, author of *The Study of Witchcraft* and *The Way of Four*

"Diana Paxson has written a travel guide for trance and out-of-body experiences that will be a great help to anyone seeking to navigate the complex worlds that lie both within and beyond our internal landscapes."

—Michelle Belanger, author of *Psychic Vampire Codex* and *Psychic Dreamwalking*

"Diana Paxson has penned another great work. If you were a newborn to the world of the spirits, you can take her hand and she will teach you how to walk the paths of other realms. You will feel totally taken care of, all mishaps have been exposed and diminished, and only the safest ways to trance travel are in this book. She is a virtuoso of the practical yet totally blended into the mystical. A rare, rare find."

—Zsuzsanna Budapest, founder of Dianic Wicca and author of *Holy Book of Women's Mysteries*

"[*Trance-Portation*] is beautifully written and filled with both wisdom and practical advice. It should interest all practitioners of the Craft and help anyone who is having difficulty with things such as astral projection or trance magick."

—Eileen Holland, author of *The Wicca Handbook*

The Essential Guide to

Possession, Depossession & Divine Relationships

The Essential Guide to

Possession, Depossession & Divine Relationships

Diana L. Paxson
author of *Trance-Portation*

WEISER BOOKS
San Francisco, CA / Newburyport, MA

First published in 2015 by Weiser Books
Red Wheel/Weiser, LLC
With offices at:
665 Third Street, Suite 400
San Francisco, CA 94107
www.redwheelweiser.com

ISBN: 978-1-57863-552-8

Library of Congress Cataloging-in-Publication Data available upon request.

Cover design by Jim Warner
Cover photograph © Czajka / Mauritius, Superstock
Interior by Frame25 Productions
Typeset in Garamond Premier Pro

Printed in the United States of America.
EBM
10 9 8 7 6 5 4 3 2 1

To the memory of Niklas Gander

CONTENTS

INTRODUCTION

March 1991

"Who are you?"

"Grimnir..."

My friend Niklas stands before me, but that is not his voice. One of his eyes is hidden by an eye patch. When I look into the other, I see a whirl of stars.

Oh dear...

In His aspect as Grimnir, the Hidden One, Odin himself has come to the party. What do I do now? The rest of the kindred are following my instructions and pretending to give the "guest" a hard time. I recognize what has happened, but this is the first time I have had to deal with someone possessed by a god.

It had been such a simple plan.

I turn to Raudhildr, who is threatening Him with the spear dedicated to Odin. She has experience with possessory trance in another tradition, and despite my panic, her expression when she realizes just Who she is poking with that spear makes me laugh.

"Raudhildr, put the spear away, now! Fill the horn with mead and bring it here, now!"

When she brings back the horn, which I had decorated with symbols of Odin as a gift for Niklas, I begin to suspect that we have been set up by the god. For some time Raudhildr has been telling me that the Norse gods might like to work with us through possessory trance and I've protested that there is no evidence for the practice in the lore.

Clearly Odin thinks differently. He takes the horn and in one long swallow the contents go down. By this time, I've gotten the rest of the crew to shift from threats to hospitality. We escort the god to the high seat, where He settles down with a second horn of mead.

"High One, tell us about the creation of humankind—" comes the first question.

"We were walking along the shore . . ."

Instead of citations from the lore, the answers come from the perspective of the god. Some make people laugh, others bring tears. Finally, they are done, and I have to figure out how to get Niklas back again.

"My lord, the hour grows late. We thank You for your presence, but we need You to release this body now."

We pull off the eye patch and I ask Odin to give us back the medium under the name he uses in the pagan community, and then for that persona to shift to the one that goes with his name in ordinary life. To my profound relief, when we have reached that point Niklas goes limp and collapses into my arms.

We lead him to the dining room table where the feast is waiting. He asks how he got there, as the last thing he remembers was putting on the eye-patch as my dog came bouncing up the stairs, so we spend the next half hour explaining. He looks confused.

"I've done Drawing Down in my Wiccan tradition for years! I never completely lost awareness before."

Everyone at the table is discussing the ritual. They all think I wrote it with exactly this outcome in mind, but I'm thinking that I had better find out how this works. I don't know if possessory trance was part of Heathen practice before, but it certainly is now.

At the time this occurred, I had been a pagan for over twenty years and a consecrated priestess for almost ten. Since I began work with Odin and the Germanic traditions, four years had passed, and my group was already doing the work described in my 2012 book, *The Way of the Oracle: Recovering the Practices of the Past to Find Answers for Today*. I had read about Santeria, and had even written about possessory trance in my novel, *Brisingamen*. At various times I had felt the presence of various goddesses and spoken the words they gave me, but I had never experienced full possession, nor had I ever had to deal with someone who was possessed.

Odin's unexpected arrival at our ritual started me on a search through the literature of religious experience. It has been a long, strange trip, during which I have learned from people in a variety of traditions, and from more than a few gods. I have searched for ethnographic accounts of what happens in traditional cultures and contemporary research about how such states occur. To learn how to get people in and out of trance safely I spent many years working with the American Magic Umbanda House in Northern California, and I have learned how to step back and let my body be operated by a god.

My group and I are not the only ones to have discovered that possessory trance is not limited to people in traditional cultures. It is one of the oldest ways to get closer to the Divine. In some form, it is known in almost every human culture, and it is occurring, spontaneously or intentionally, in many spiritual communities today.

The idea that another personality can take over your body, displacing the person you think of as "you," is disturbing, and yet this dance with the Divine has been a goal of ecstatic religion for millennia: from the shaman dancing his animal allies to the early Christian speaking in tongues; from voudou initiates ridden by the loa to New Age channelers. American anthropologist Erika Bourguignon called it "possession trance" (Bourguignon 1976). Dr. Emma Cohen, an anthropology lecturer at the University of Oxford, identifies trance in which identity is transformed or replaced as "executive possession," as opposed to that in which invading spirits cause illness or misfortune (Cohen 2008, 1).

In traditional cultures, people recognize when someone goes into possessory trance. They understand the spirits that are coming through, and how to deal safely with both the medium and the Power. Most first world people who encounter the phenomenon have no context for such experiences. If we are going to explore possessory trance, we need to define some terms.

Trance

Trance is an altered state of consciousness different from consensus reality. The *Penguin Dictionary of Psychology* defines it as "a condition of dissociation, characterized by the lack of voluntary movement, and frequently by automatisms in act and thought, illustrated by hypnotic and mediumistic conditions"(in Lewis 1989, 33). In daily life we are continually altering our consciousness—from the attentive state in which one negotiates difficult traffic to the dissociation in which one drives long distances. The most common and profound shift is between waking and sleep. Usually, however, an altered state refers to a change in consciousness that gives one access to different perceptions or knowledge.

The content and interpretation of trance states are largely dependent on the cultural context. Such states can be used for relaxation, contemplation, spirit journeying, healing, oracular work, and deep meditation. A sequence of exercises for learning to cue and control such experiences is presented in my 2008 book, *Trance-Portation: Learning to Navigate the Inner World*. If you have no training or experience in trance work, I strongly recommend working through *Trance-Portation* or practicing some equivalent training to develop the necessary mental disciplines before you attempt possessory trance; however, you can work on exploring your own identity and developing a relationship with one of the Powers at any time.

Powers

The *Powers* are the spiritual beings that may speak or act through a human host. As I use this term, it is more or less synonymous with the Latin *numen,* defined as something to which one gives offerings or honor. In various times and places people have been possessed by gods, orishas, demons, and animal and ancestral spirits.

Medium

Possessory work differs from other forms of trance in that your person-identity is replaced by a personality that is identified by you and your community as a spirit or a god. The steps leading up to the possession may (and in my opinion *should*) be voluntary, but at some point the medium relinquishes control to the spiritual Power. Whether this transition is an exchange, a seduction, or a rape depends on the training of the person possessed, the nature of the Power, and the context and expectations of the culture.

Healthy Relationships

Even when we believe it is possible for a human to carry the personality of a spiritual power we cannot guarantee that it will be a positive experience any more than we can guarantee that every couple who marries will live "happily ever after." The medium may not have the strength and discipline to hold the energy. The Power, especially one coming from a tradition in which this kind of work has not been done for centuries, may not understand the limitations of the human partner. The community may not know how to take care of either the medium or the Power. Like Aslan in C. S. Lewis's *The Last Battle*, the Powers are not "tame lions." If we accept them as real we must accept that they have their own ways, preferences, and most especially, their own agendas.

Like a sexual encounter, a possessory experience is intimate and powerful, and it can have an equally intense impact. Just as sex is more rewarding in the context of a mature relationship, deity possession is most sustainable and productive when we approach it with the same care we would take in developing any other intimate connection. Actual possession, like coitus, is exciting; but in the long run what satisfies the god-hunger is the ongoing relationship with the Power.

Unlike a possessory ritual, this personal relationship is not dependent on the support of a community. For all these reasons, although I will be talking a lot about actual possession, we will be spending at least as much time on ways to develop a safe, sane, and consensual relationship with a spiritual power, starting with strengthening your own identity.

When I started collecting information about possession, the only books easily available were ethnographic studies and a few books about Santeria. T. K. Oesterreich's exhaustive study, *Possession: Demoniacal and Other* (Oesterreich 1930, 1966), provided a multitude of examples of possession in other parts of the world. Unfortunately, these works seemed to be based on the assumption that deity or spirit possession only occurs in third world cultures with unbroken traditions. The only first world examples available were accounts of medieval demon possession and contemporary psychiatric studies. Since then, many books on the Afro-Diasporic religions have appeared. From the Pagan perspective we have *Spirit Speak* by Ivo Dominguez Jr. and *Drawing Down the Spirits* by Kenaz Filan and Raven Kaldera. Erika Bourguignon, Emma Cohen, and Felicitas Goodman have studied possession from a cross-cultural point of view.

Given the potential dangers, why did I decide to write a book that might make it easier for the unwary to get in out of their depth?

My answer is that the meme is out there.

In the wake of emigration from Cuba and Haiti, information about possessory practices has diffused through American alternative religious culture. There has been a great deal of discussion regarding who can or should trance. In many traditions only those who have passed through the proper training and initiations are allowed to carry the Powers. But the Powers sometimes think otherwise. Wiccan covens are finding that their traditional Drawing Down may get them more than they expected. Some years ago I received an email from a couple who had been visited by Odin and Freyja at a baseball game.

The ecstatic nature of the experience is not the only way in which possessory work is like sex. Once people know that it is possible, they will be tempted to experiment. Even those who haven't sought out these experiences may find themselves being courted, or even seduced, by the Powers. Providing sensible information on possessory trance, like educating teenagers about sex, is a way to avoid unintended consequences from what is going to happen anyway.

I believe that we are wired to enjoy sex because it encourages us to reproduce. The fact that humans find pleasure in ecstatic religious experience suggests that such states also have a purpose. If we long for connection to God, or the gods, it is because there is Something out there to desire. In partnership with the Divine, we transcend our limitations. As the Powers expand our psyches we grow into our true selves.

This book will not make you an instant shaman, mystic, or trance medium. For those who seek to get closer to their gods, it will offer ways to satisfy that longing. For those who feel compelled to go further, it will provide guidelines for healthy spiritual relationships and techniques for opening up to possession or closing it down.

Possessory trance traditionally takes place in a group setting. This public dimension is one of the major points of difference between possession as a spiritual practice and as an identity disorder. Many writers insist that it should only be studied within the context of a specific tradition. I have several reasons for taking a cross-cultural approach. First, not everyone who is attracted to possession (or has spontaneously experienced it) has access to a traditional teacher or wants to change their faith. Second, by comparing practices from a variety of cultures we can get an idea of which elements and methods are fundamental and which are culture specific.

If possessory work is to move beyond the faiths with unbroken traditions, both the community and the mediums need training. Once core elements are identified, they can be incorporated into new traditions. Possessory work is, above all, a practice rooted in relationships—the relationship between the medium and the Power, and the relationship between the Power and the people. If you are already active in a group that is interested in possessory work, use this book as a class text, discussing the concepts and the results of the exercises. If you do not have a group but do have connections to a larger religious community, spread the word and try to put together a team, perhaps drawn from several complementary traditions. So that everyone starts with the same skill set, consider beginning by working through *Trance-Portation*. Even if you already have these skills, reviewing them will serve as spiritual conditioning. At the very least, find a friend who can act as your spiritual reality-checker. Do the checksum exercises regularly to chart changes. Start a journal in which you record your experiences.

The exercises will help the "god-hungry" who yearn for a more complete and personal relationship with Spirit, whether or not they engage in possessory trance. This book is also for the "god-bothered" who would like to avoid or control possession, and the "god wranglers" who are called to manage it in their communities in a productive way.

Part One

SELF-POSSESSION

Great gods cannot ride little horses.
—Haitian proverb

The pantheist believes that some part of the Divine is inherent in every individual and thing. The mystic loses his identity in those moments when his consciousness becomes one with the Divine Whole. The medium believes that divinity takes many forms. But even the gods (with a small "g") are very large. Before we can be possessed by Someone Else, we have to possess ourselves.

Possessory trance, like other practices involving the alteration of consciousness, thins the barriers between the self we think we know and the unconscious. We like to say that studying trance work can lead to "a first-class tour of your issues." If this is the case when we are studying internal practices such as meditation and journey work, possessory trance, in which we deliberately relinquish control, makes us even more vulnerable. The better we know ourselves, the easier it will be to tell whether what is speaking is one of the Powers or our own desires.

For this reason, the first part of this book will help you to question or even deconstruct some of your assumptions and certainties, to stimulate insight, and to seek reconstruction and self-knowledge. Some people spend years in therapy, exploring the questions asked here. Study this material with a group, or at least find someone to whom you can report on your experiences. If the tour of your issues becomes uncomfortably exciting, do consider working with a sympathetic therapist.

In the TV series *Babylon 5*, much of the action is shaped by the conflict between the Vorlons, who ask, "Who are you?" and the Shadows, who ask, "What do you want?" Both questions are important, and both answers are illuminating. Before we volunteer to relinquish our identity, we need to know what we want and who we truly are.

1

PERSONS AND PERSONAS

We all change. When you think about it, we're all different people all through our lives. And that's okay. That's good. You gotta keep moving, so long as you remember all the people that you used to be.
—Dr. Who

What Do You Want?

"I want," is one of the first things a child learns to say. What you want may not be what you need, but knowing what you want helps you to identify your priorities. In *Babylon 5*, Mr. Morden repeatedly asks the main characters this question, digging until he gets past the surface to the real desires.

Why are you reading this book? What attracted you to this subject? What do you want to know or be able to do by the time you reach the end? Write your answers in your journal and revisit them from time to time. But remember, there is no "right" answer, only *your* answer, and that is subject to change.

Bucket lists tend to include experiences, such as seeing the northern lights, that you desire because they are interesting or beautiful or fun. What would you want most if you knew you only had a year to live? Why? Try Exercise 1.1 at the end of this chapter and consider what your desires have to say about who you are.

In Exercise 1.2 you will be asked to list the things you truly *need*. We all require food, shelter, and contact with other people, but there can be a wide gap between the minimum amount we need to stay alive and an amount that makes life worth living. Western European culture is based on achievement and acquisition. Buddhism preaches non-attachment as a way to control the desires that bring suffering. How can we balance need and desire?

Many of us may find it particularly difficult to answer these questions because what we *need* is to be needed, to the point where our wants, if we can even identify them, show up pretty far down the list. Perhaps we first need to find out who we really are.

Who Are You?

We have considered what we want, but who is doing the wanting? Asking "Who are you?" again and again and rejecting each answer, as the Vorlon inquisitor does in *Babylon 5*, is a technique used in group psychotherapy to force people to strip away the masks that hide their true natures. It is a question with many answers, none of them complete but all of them true.

What Is Your Name?

In the late sixties, I would have found the question "What is your name?" challenging. At work I used my married name. I was still Diana L. Paxson in the science fiction community, but much of the time Mistress Diana Listmaker was my primary identity.

I worked with a group of mostly twenty-something men and women to found the Society for Creative Anachronism (SCA). One of the things we had in common was a deep desire to escape the culture we had inherited from the fifties. In the SCA, one could choose not only the period in which one was living but also the person one would be. On weekends, we lived in a community where we had a hands-on relationship to the food we ate and the clothes we wore, a defined place within a social structure, and a reasonable expectation that achievement would be recognized and rewarded. We did feel that the people who wore chain mail to work under their Oxford cloth shirts were taking it a bit far, but for many the Society "persona" felt more real than the individual described on their driver's license.

The term *persona* comes from the word for the mask used by actors in Classical Greece, and from there became a name for the part being played. It can designate a social role, such as mother, husband, minister, or doctor. For Jung, a persona is "a kind of mask, designed on the one hand to make an impression on others, and on the other to conceal the true nature of the individual" (Jung 1953, 190).

The persona is the public face, the individual a newspaper account usually describes, and we generally think of a person as the individual identified by his or her legal name. But what's in a name? Consider the questions in Exercise 1.4.

In earlier times, the name on the tombstone might well have been enough to describe you. Today, it is often only at the memorial service, when people from all the different professional and social communities to which the deceased belonged share their memories, that friends and family get a sense of who their loved one truly was.

What Is Your Role?

Often a name is tied to a particular role, but one may play multiple roles without changing one's name. Legally, our identity is tied to the DNA of the body we occupy from birth to death. But throughout our life our body changes, as do the roles we play. I am no longer the little girl who was crazy about horses, or the young mother, or the instructor in English 1-A. My memories of these people are a part of me, but they are not the person I am now.

Even in the present, we play many roles. Those who wear uniforms subordinate personal identity to the role of doctor or police officer. When going to a job interview we try to dress like the other employees. Wearing the costume, we adopt the speech patterns and conform to the corporate culture. We put on our best clothes to become an elegant participant at a ball or the opera, and take them off at a Pagan festival.

When most people talk about "roles," they are referring to acting. Greek drama emerged from religious ritual as a way for humans to vicariously experience the mythic interactions between humanity and the gods. The faces of the actors were hidden behind the masks. Today, face and body become the medium through which the character is expressed. So how does the actor "become" the role?

David Cole states that the actor makes a journey into the worlds of the imagination, an inner journey into her own psyche to find those aspects that correspond to the people and actions of the play. Then there comes a point in the acting process when a reversal takes place, and the images the actor has journeyed so far to find come rushing back upon her, using her body to become present to the audience. The actor experiences a state of double consciousness, in which she is fully the character she has discovered but at the same time is also herself, watching the performance as a removed spectator (Cole 1975, 1–57).

Is it possible to get too deeply into a role? Method actors have been known to stay in character not only all day when they are working, but throughout filming or the run of the play. A writer may start acting like the character whose point of view she is currently writing. Artists can be forgiven a lot of weirdness, at least if they are successful, but the same ease in identifying with another personality that enables them to portray a character convincingly can make family life difficult and put stress on a marriage. The better we are at taking on a role, the more important it is to be able to return to our core of authenticity.

What Is Your Real Face?

If our names and our roles do not define us, what about our bodies? Has anyone ever taken a photo of you that you accepted as what you "really" look like? Or a photo that looked like the person you would like to be? When you look in the mirror, whom do you see?

In *Till We Have Faces* by C. S. Lewis, the relationship between external and internal truth is explored:

> When the time comes to you at which you will be forced at last to utter the speech which has lain at the center of your soul for years, which you have, all that time, idiot-like, been saying over and over, you'll not talk about the joy of words. I saw well why the gods do not speak to us openly, nor let us answer. Till that word can be dug out of us, why should they

hear the babble that we think we mean? How can they meet us face to face till we have faces?

(Lewis 1956)

Before we can truly encounter the gods, we must learn to name ourselves. Only then will we have the strength to set the self aside and let the Other in.

Who Are You, Really?

When the Vorlon inquisitor asks Delenn who she is, she replies with a list of roles—Minbari ambassador, daughter of her father, member of the Grey Council, and the like. It is only when the inquisitor presses her to tell him what she would be willing to die for that she is able to define herself not by roles, but by deeds. Heathens are fond of saying "We are our deeds"(Wodening 1998). Though our bodies, our roles, and our names may change, the choices we make and the deeds we do reveal our essential identity.

Practice

Before you begin, get a notebook in which to answer questions from the exercises and record your experiences.

Exercise 1.1: The Bucket List

If you knew your life was going to end within the year:

- What would you want to see, and where would you want to go? What is it about each of these things or places that is important to you?

- Who would you spend time with? Who from your past would you want to see again? What would you say to them?

- What would you like to learn or do? Why? Why haven't you learned or done these things before?

- What do you wish you hadn't done? If there is anyone you have wronged, is there anything you could do to compensate for that wrong?

- Of the things you have done, which make you the most proud? Why?

When you have finished, ask yourself:

- What values are implied by these answers?

- What do I really care about?

- What makes life meaningful to me?

And, of course, if your bucket list is a long one—

- What am I going to do about it?

Exercise 1.2: Needs

Now make a list of the things you truly need. Write down the minimum resources that you require for each of the following categories:

- Shelter (size, location)

- Food, including special dietary requirements

- Health (medicines, treatment, exercise)

- People, relationships

- Spiritual (what feeds your soul?)

- How much money do you need to live?

- For what kinds of jobs are you qualified?

When you have made this list, start a new column and list the ideal for each category. For instance, if your minimum requirement for shelter is a two-bedroom apartment with a working kitchen and bathroom, your ideal might be a house with a yard and a room for each family member, space for computers, enough bookshelves, a kitchen with lots of cupboards, etc. Other than winning the lottery, what kinds of financial changes would enable you to live your dream? What is your ideal career? What would have to happen for you achieve it?

Exercise 1.3: Wants

Get a friend to ask you "What do you want?" ten times. Give a different answer each time.

Exercise 1.4: What's in a Name?

1. What is the name on your driver's license or state ID? Is it the same name as the one listed on your birth certificate? Why did your parents give you that name? In what ways does your given name represent or not represent the real you?

2. How are you addressed at work? What do your friends call you? What about your family? If any of those names are different, is the person they represent the same?

3. Are you involved in other groups or situations in which you are called by a name different from those given for questions 1 and 2, such as a nickname or an initiatory name? Was this name given to you by others, or did you choose it, and if so, why?

4. In the past, have you had other names that you no longer use? How do the persons those names represented differ from the person you are now?

5. List all of the names you currently use and describe the person that goes with each.

6. Choose a name that represents the person you would like to become. Why have you chosen each part of it? What does it mean?

Exercise 1.5: The People in Your Neighborhood

In the life you are living now, how many roles do you play? How many masks do you wear? If everyone you know came to your next birthday party, and each one was asked to say a word of thanks or praise (or blame), how many would be surprised by some of the things they heard?

Draw a picture representing yourself and surround it with circles indicating groups of associates or friends. How many of these circles intersect? For each group, write down what are you called, what you wear, and what you do.

Exercise 1.6: Who Are You?

Get a friend to ask you, "Who are you?" ten times in a row. Give a different answer each time. Which answer(s) are true?

2

THE SOUL PARTY

Much I owe to the Lands that grew—
More to the Lives that fed—
But most to Allah Who gave me two
Separate sides to my head.
—Rudyard Kipling, "The Two-Sided Man", *Kim*

Kipling's poem may have been a comment on Kim's double life as a European and a native of India, but as we have seen in the previous chapter, throughout our lives we go by many names, play many roles, show many faces to the world. These, however, are masks that we can put on or remove at will. What will we find if we try to answer the question "Who are you?" by exploring those parts of ourselves over which we have no control?

Body, Mind, and Spirit

In the last chapter, you looked into a mirror and asked whether the features you see there are really "you." One's features, after all, are used to prove identity as often as one's name. But a name can change and a face can be disguised. What about our body, the physical vehicle in which our consciousness rides around? In possessory work we relinquish control of our body, but it is the mind that becomes still while the body not only moves but may also perform feats impossible when the original owner is in charge. I have seen small women swing heavy swords while in trance and a man who walked with a cane dance vigorously.

Offering oneself as a vehicle is a service to both the Powers and the community. The partnership should be based on a contract that protects the horse as well as serving the rider. As you prepare to do this work, consider which health conditions may be a challenge and start thinking about how to deal with them. Mental health can also be an issue. Some kinds of problems—especially those involving dissociation, violence, or loss of control—may make possessory trance unwise, although it can be beneficial to develop a spiritual connection with a Power.

In Search of the Soul

The Egyptians believed that the soul lived in the heart. In traditional Chinese medicine, the physical soul is held to reside in the lungs, while the ethereal soul is located in the liver. Some Japanese traditions focus on the *hara*, the gut, as the focus of the life-force. In some systems based on the chakras, the solar plexus is referred to as the seat of the soul. The ways in which these organs respond to our emotions may explain the importance given them; however, in Western culture the consensus has been that if the soul has a location, it is somewhere in the brain.

There is evidence that many of our responses, including archetypal processes, are "programmed in." The extended consciousness through which we experience our existence rests upon deeper layers that can be linked to various structures in the brain. The areas that receive and process sensory input and process and store memories are all part of this complex system.

Analyzing the Psyche

In Western culture, the assumption is that a human has two components, the body and the soul. *Psyche*, the human spirit, is the root of the words for psychoanalysis and psychology. Today, we understand a great deal about the interlocking systems and organs that comprise the body, whereas some question whether there is even such a thing as a soul.

The physical body has many organs and systems, all of which must interact properly for a being to function. If the body is a composite, what about the psyche? Freud's structural model of the psyche identified three parts: the id, the superego, and the ego. The id speaks a physical language that includes all the deep, unconscious, and instinctual drives that evolution has given us. The superego is the voice of conscience, developing out of everything we have learned from our parents and our culture as we grow. The ego attempts to mediate between the id and the superego and the demands of the outer world.

The psychoanalytic tradition that is most relevant to a spiritually based exploration of the psyche is the one founded by C. G. Jung. As summarized by Michael Fordham (Fordham 1985), in this tradition the *Self* is the unified personality that incorporates a whole range of psychic phenomena, the *archetypes*. The *shadow* is the dark reflection of the conscious personality, embodying opposing values—aspects of the self that one does not acknowledge. The *anima* is the inner woman in each man, a primordial image that incorporates both his concept of the feminine and his own unexpressed feminine qualities, while the *animus* is the equivalent masculine image within a woman. These definitions are not exclusive, as they can combine or exchange elements or subdivide to appear as more specific, often mythic figures, such as the Maiden, the Wise Old Man, the Trickster, or the Hero.

All of these archetypes emerge from the collective unconscious, described by Jung as

> a second psychic system of a collective, universal, and impersonal nature which is identical in all individuals. This collective unconscious does not develop individually but is inherited. It consists of pre-existent forms, the archetypes, which can only become conscious secondarily and which give definite form to certain psychic contents.
>
> (Jung 1959, 43)

Whether we believe in the objective reality of the gods and spirits or not, the idea that their images are part of our human psychic programming may explain how someone who has never been exposed to the lore of a particular culture can spontaneously manifest the personality of one of its gods, as in the case of young man who had almost no knowledge of African culture when he was possessed by the orishas Shango and Ogun, and then spoke to a Lucumi elder, perfectly in character, about matters of which he had no knowledge (Fatunmbi 1991). On the other hand, it is possible that the orishas found him when his psyche was wide open, and grabbed the opportunity to use him as a messenger.

In the psyche, the psychoanalytic and spiritual models for the soul meet. *Psyche* comes from a Greek word meaning breath. In many languages, words meaning "breath" are used to mean all or part of the soul. The first breath marks our emergence as separate beings, the last, the moment when we leave the physical world.

Breathing is also one of the few essential physical functions that is both automatic and subject to conscious control. By slowing and deepening your breathing you can lower your blood pressure and seriously annoy medical personnel by manipulating an EEG. Controlled and patterned breathing is also one of the easiest and most effective ways to alter consciousness and move into trance. Exercise 2.1 at the end of this chapter will increase your awareness of the effects that breathing in different ways can have on consciousness. Practicing regularly will increase your control.

Soul Parts

Psychoanalysts are not the only ones who try to classify our nonphysical components. Many cultures have believed that we have not one but several souls.

Egypt

Ancient Egyptians identified five parts to the soul. The *Ib*, or heart, was the seat of emotion, thought, will, and intention. *Sheut,* the shadow that always accompanies us, was also held to contain some of its owner's essence. A person's name, the *Ren,* lived as long as it was spoken. The *Ba* manifested the person's essence in the world. The *Ka* was the breath that gives life, and thus the term that most closely matches the word for spirit in many other languages. It could be sustained by offerings. The *Akh* was a kind of ghost that could be created by the reunion of the Ba and Ka if the proper rites were performed and invoked to help living family members or to punish enemies (Allen 2003, 28).

Hinduism

In the Upanishads, *Atman*, the soul, is composed of five "sheaths." The outermost is the body, *annamaya khosha*, the "essence of food." As we might say, "You are what you eat." Second is *pranamaya khosha*, the vital breath. Third is *manomaya khosha*, which is the mind or will, followed by *vijnanamaya khosha*, the intellect or desire to know, and bliss, *anandamaya khosha* (Saraswati 1984).

Hebrew Kabbalism

Kabbalistic tradition identifies five elements of the soul, corresponding to the five worlds. Both *ruach* and *neshamah* are words for "wind" or "breath." As defined in the *Glossary of Kabbalah and Chassidut*, the five elements of the soul are the following:

- *Nefesh*: "creature"—the lower soul, relates to behavior and action.

- *Ruach*: "spirit," the emotions.

- *Neshamah*: "inner soul," the mind and intelligence.

- *Chayah*: "living one," the bridge between the first flash of conscious insight and its superconscious origin. Experiencing awareness of God as continually creating the world.

- *Yecidah*: "single one," the ultimate unity of the soul in God, as manifest by pure faith, absolute devotion, and the continuous readiness to sacrifice one's life for God.

Voudou

The concept of multiple soul parts is also found in Haitian voudou. The *ti-bonanj* represents individual consciousness, ego, and personal experience, and is the seat of moral action. The *mét-tét*, or "master of the head," is one of the lwa, the Powers that in theory are secondary to the Supreme Being but in practice are treated as gods. In the Afro-Diasporic traditions, a person's "head" is identified through divination and is usually similar in personality to the human. Although it would be more correct to say that the individual belongs to the lwa rather than vice versa, if the devotee cultivates the relationship, the lwa is always present. The *gwo-bonanj* is the divine spirit within a person. As Richard Hodges puts it, this is

> his life force, his invisible core; it is his vital spirit, his blood, his breath, his disposition, his intelligence. Its movements, its rises and falls are the invisible driving force behind the visible manifestation expressed by the man's body and his *ti-bonanj*. Finally, it is what a man's life amounts to, what he as an individual represents in eternity. For those who are his direct descendants, it represents their ancestry, and through them undergoes a kind of reincarnation.
>
> (Hodges 1995)

Germanic

We also find a rich lore regarding spiritual entities in Germanic tradition. In the Old Norse poem *Völuspá*, stanzas 17–18, we are told that the gods created human beings from the trunks of two trees, to which they gave the gifts of *önd*, which is breath and spirit, *odhR*, which I would define as ecstatic consciousness, and *lá, laeti, and litR*, appearance, movement, and health. Analysis of the Eddas and folklore reveal additional terms.

The physical body is called the *lich*, or *lyke*. However, we also find references to the *ham*, which can be translated as "shape" or "hide," which seems to refer to the astral or etheric body, an envelope encasing the physical form that can be detached and sent, sometimes in an animal shape, on journeys. The next level up includes the *Hug*, the part of the soul identified with personal consciousness, and *Mun*, meaning "mind," like the German *minni*, which carries with it connotations of feeling or preference as well as of mentation. Mythologically they are represented by Odin's ravens, Huginn and Muninn, usually translated as Thought and Memory. For more on Germanic theories of the soul, see *The Heathen Psyche* by Dr. Erik Goodwyn (2014), and "Heathen Full-Souls: The Big Picture", by Winifred Hodge Rose (/Idunna/ 67, Spring, 2006).

Allowing for the fact that these terms come from different cultures and languages and are neither completely equivalent nor really translatable, we can nonetheless see that many of the terms for soul parts fall into certain broad categories.

The divisions do not line up exactly, but clearly the idea that the body is paired with a soul which is itself composed of multiple parts is a popular one. The psychoanalytic model of the psyche identifies multiple structures below the level of the conscious self, whereas the religious models propose varying levels of superconscious soul.

	BODY	PERSONA	MIND	BREATH	GOD-SOUL
EGYPTIAN		Ba	Ib	Ka	Akh
HINDU	anna	mano	vijnana	prana	ananda
KABBALISTIC		nefesh	ruach	neshamah	chayah yecidah
VOUDOU		ti-bonanj		gwo-bonanj	
GERMANIC	Iá, laeti, litR	Hug	Mun	önd	odhR

Figure 1: Soul parts

Toward a Field Theory of the Soul

We think of ourselves as singular beings, but it can be argued that even in a "normal" state we are a system of associated parts. If this is so, then the dissociation necessary to allow spirit possession might be considered part of the spiritual ecology. Is it possible to present all these ways of looking at a human as a continuum? The following list is my own attempt to make sense of the possibilities. English is an inclusive language, and so I have adopted the terms that seemed most useful.

- *The physical body* consists of all the tangible physical elements, arranged into organs and systems. It takes in energy and transforms it into substance, can heal and repair itself, move, and reproduce. Patterns for some of the spiritual elements may be programmed in its DNA.

- *The etheric body*, also called the astral, energy, or subtle body, is an energy sheath projected by the physical body. This is a basic concept in magical traditions influenced by the Orient. Normally the etheric body surrounds the physical body, and can be perceived by some as an aura. In certain states it can detach and carry the consciousness elsewhere (out-of-body experiences), connected by the "silver cord."

- *Breath, the divine wind*, like the first two, is perceptible; but unlike them it is not a thing, but a process. Since the atmosphere is the breath of the planet, each breath links us to the life of the world. It is both a connection between the tangible and intangible parts and the catalyst that allows them to interact.

- *The unconscious* includes the emotional responses and array of archetypes inherited from our ancestors, stored or possibly accessed from a nonphysical realm through structures in the brain.

- *Memory* consists of the personal records, whether accessible or repressed, of events that have taken place during our lives.

- The *persona* is the face or faces we present to the world. The persona may not have been consciously created, but it is in essence voluntary—unless, of course, it is one of several alternate personalities created for protection.

- The *ego* is the Self, or core personality; the essential person who evolves by playing various roles.

- The *superego* is the rational intellect, formed by all that we have learned and admired, and, I would say, by our aspirations as well. Sometimes perceived as a separate voice advising or admonishing, this may be the part that Socrates called his daemon.

- The *God-soul* is what I believe is meant by the Hindu *anandamaya* or the Kabbalistic *yecidah*, or the ecstasy of *odhR*. This is the Divine Spark, the True Self into which we seek to grow.

Practice
Exercise 2.1: Mind and Body
Stand in front of a mirror and consider your body. Fingerprints or DNA would identify this body as the individual named on your birth certificate, but is this body really you? Compare photos of yourself at different ages. What has changed? What is the same?

Now, look at your body as a vehicle you are offering to loan to a god. Carrying one of the Powers can be strenuous. Now is the time to evaluate your physical condition and start getting into shape.

Exercise 2.2: Breathing
You know how to breathe, right? You've done it all your life. But unless you've had asthma or a choking episode or have trained in meditation, you've probably never paid much attention. However, breathing not only keeps everything going, it is one of the most useful cues for changing consciousness. By altering the depth and rate at which we breathe, we can cue both the psyche and the physical body to change.

If you are new to grounding and centering, you will find a more extended discussion of how it works in chapter 2 of *Trance-Portation*. Even if you are already experienced in trance work, doing this exercise in a deliberate manner may require more discipline than you expect.

Find a place where you will not be disturbed. Once you have internalized this process, you will be able to do it anywhere, but while you are learning (or reviewing) the skills, you will want to practice without interruption.

Standing in a balanced position, extend your awareness to about an arm's length outward in every direction. Move around a little and try to sense when your energy sphere is approaching a solid object such as a chair or wall, then, while maintaining this sphere of awareness, find a place that feels comfortable and stand still.

Preserving this awareness, sit comfortably and spend a few moments breathing normally. At first, paying attention to your breathing will make it harder. Relax, think about something else for a minute, and try again. How often do you breathe? How deeply? Do you breathe evenly?

Now, count as you breathe—in for four counts, hold for four counts, out for four counts, and hold for four more. Try for one second per count. If your inhalation or exhalation extends into the second four counts, that's okay. Do this for at least one minute, ignoring all other thoughts. You will end up taking about five complete inhalations and exhalations per minute. If you are distracted, resume counting until your total awareness is focused on the movement of your breath. If you need something to think about, visualize the oxygen entering your lungs, being absorbed by all the alveoli, reaching the bloodstream, and being carried throughout your body. How do you feel? This focused state is a good preparation for moving into trance, calming nerves, and dealing with anxiety.

Once you can do counted breathing dependably, experiment with slowing your breathing to two or three cycles per minute. How does that make you feel? If you close your eyes while you are doing this, you will find yourself moving into a very relaxed, passive state. What happens when you breathe in and hold your breath for a while? What is it like when you put off taking another breath after you exhale?

Now, speed your breathing past the one count per second rate. Breathe more shallowly to avoid hyperventilating, and skip the holds. How do you feel now? Faster breathing saturates your lungs with oxygen and can cause an adrenaline surge. If you have trouble keeping track, ask a friend with a good sense of rhythm to drum for you, or record your own drumming onto a tape and play it while you practice. Do this regularly. The ability to move into a receptive state at will is a basic skill in preparing for possessory trance.

3

IN SEARCH OF YOURSELF

*It is foolish to think that we will enter
heaven without entering into ourselves.*
—St. Teresa of Avila, *The Interior Castle*

Some say that the purpose of life is to discover who we truly are. If so, why would we want to voluntarily allow the persona we identify as our self to be displaced by another, even if we believe it to be divine?

Most religions hold that the purpose of our life is to become closer to God. Even Buddhism, which teaches that the primary goal is to eradicate suffering, makes that a step on the way to enlightenment. But where the mystic loses self-awareness in union with the Divine as a drop of water is lost in the sea, the medium becomes a vessel for a drop of divinity. In each case, the connection stretches our souls.

Many deeply desire such an expansion. "As the hart panteth after the water brooks, so panteth my soul after thee, O God. My soul thirsteth for God, for the living God . . ." says Psalm 42. Others fear it. "The Hound of Heaven" by Francis Thompson vividly evokes the poet's approach/avoidance relationship with the Christian God. Those who are "god-bothered" are very familiar with the patter of those pursuing feet. I was always one of the thirsty ones, but I have talked to people who spent years trying to close their ears to the call.

A "close encounter" with the Divine can be interpreted as evidence of sanctity or insanity, depending on the context. Whether we go to the gods or they come to us, the impact of spiritual experience is affected by the environment in which it occurs. Spiritual awakening is very different for someone who lives where the source, the symptoms, and the treatment are part of the culture than it is for someone in a setting in which neither he nor anyone else understands what is going on. Religious traditions that encourage such experiences have monasteries in which mystics can pursue their goal. But mystic union is essentially a solitary practice. Possessory work, on the other hand, requires a supportive community. Later in this book we'll be discussing what such a community looks like, and how it can grow.

Now that you have learned to think of yourself as a composite, it is time to put the pieces together. Whether you seek God or a god seeks you, connecting can be soul-shattering. The goal of this chapter is to prepare your psyche for possessory work by strengthening your sense of self.

Meaning

There are as many definitions of the Meaning of Life as speculations regarding the significance of the number forty-two. However, we do not have to agree on *the* meaning of Life, the Universe, and Everything. The question we do have to answer is, "What is the meaning of life to *me*?" Like *The Hitchhiker's Guide to the Galaxy*, possessory work can force us to reevaluate a lot of things we thought we knew. We have to get sane and centered before we voluntarily shake our sanity.

A study by psychologists from the University of Minnesota and the University of Virginia "defined meaning in life as the sense made of, and significance felt regarding, the nature of one's being and existence" (Steger et al. 2006). Their review of the literature cited elements such as a coherent life narrative, goals, and having a sense of value, purpose, effectiveness, and self-worth as characteristic of a meaningful existence.

The study asked whether people felt their lives had meaning and purpose. It did *not* ask what they believed that meaning to be. People whose lives have purpose are in general happier and better adjusted than those who do not, but despite the best efforts of philosophers and clerics the meaning of a life can only be defined by the one who lives it.

How would you define the Meaning of Life? Make a note of your answer.

Purpose

Is the goal of human life to perfect ourselves so that we may grow closer to God, or to achieve enlightenment by freeing ourselves from attachment? Or should we look at the problem in purely human terms, as a search for identity? One place to start is with your name.

Exercise 3.1 is based on an episode in Rudyard Kipling's novel, *Kim*. When this exercise is done by repeating a term such as "love" or the name of a deity, it is called "centering prayer," and it is a powerful method for connecting with the eternal Source beyond our surface realities. In European spirituality, this kind of prayer represents the Way of Rejection:

> It [the Way of Rejection] consists, generally speaking, in the renunciation of all images except the final one of God himself, and even—sometimes but not always—of the exclusion of that only Image of all human sense . . . The other Way is the Way of Affirmation, the approach to God through these images.
>
> (Williams 1953, 8–9)

Mysticism leads to the transcendence of all images and individuality. Only a very few enlightened beings live in a state of union all the time. It is a glorious goal, but as Jack Kornfield points out in *After the Ecstasy, the Laundry*, even those who attain mystic rapture still have to deal with consensus reality once they return (Kornfield 2001).

The Way of Rejection of Images is not the only path. As human beings in human bodies, most of us relate most easily to Spirit when it presents itself in a defined form. At the other end of the spectrum, the Way of Affirmation is responsible for some of the greatest works of art created by human culture. From Tibetan mandalas to the Parthenon, the perfect harmony of the images leads the mind to the harmony behind them. God is too big for the human mind to comprehend all at once. For many, it is easier to honor the Divine as revealed in the many aspects of creation rather than the overwhelming whole.

When we refer to God by a gendered pronoun we have already diminished "Him" by denying "Her." Polytheism takes the next step by seeing all aspects of the Divine as gods. In possessory work, we offer control of our bodies as a gift to these divine Persons, but they use our minds as well as our limbs. Not only the relationship but the work will be more successful if the medium is as fully realized as the Power.

Jung believed that the purpose of life was to discover and fulfill our deep innate potential. This journey of transformation he called individuation, a process that leads not only to an encounter with our true self, but with the Divine (Crowley 2000). I would agree that far from competing, the religious and therapeutic definitions of the purpose of life should be viewed as complementary.

Identity

So who is this individuated and fully realized Being that we are looking for? In the previous chapters, we explored the possibility that the person you think of as your Self is actually a collection of interacting entities. That doesn't mean you have no core identity—organizations and nations that are composed of many individuals can have a group soul. You also have an essence that both includes and transcends all its component entities.

Everyone has a story. Author and teacher Steven Barnes tells students to write a short essay on "how they grew up to be the person they are today. Because it is short, it will contain many of the basic building blocks of identity: events, beliefs, emotions, relationships, successes and failures" (Barnes 2014).

What is *your* story? Having deconstructed your identity, can you construct it anew? We choose our roles as we choose our names. Those who joined women's lib and other liberation movements of the sixties focused on breaking the molds into which they had been forced because of race or gender. To figure out who they are, adolescents form cliques that ban those they perceive as different. It is easy to point and say, "I'm not like *them*!" As women, or Hispanics, or members of any other group, we must do something harder—we must strive toward a positive definition of what we *are*.

In an episode of the second season of *Babylon 5*, "Comes the Inquisitor," relentless questioning forces Delenn beyond roles to actions. The meaning of her life is defined by the cause, or person, for whom she would sacrifice it. Our deeds give the lie to all our attempts to deceive ourselves or others. What we are is revealed by what we *do*.

Some acts, like getting married or buying a house, are carefully thought-out decisions, or should be. Others, like eating the last cookie or taking the elevator instead of the stairs, are habitual and unconscious acts whose effects are not visible until you step onto the scale. Some things cannot happen without a conscious decision, while others require a conscious decision to change. And then there are those sudden responses—braking to avoid hitting a opossum that scurries across the road, getting into the car at three in the morning to pick up a stranded grandchild—that are effectively instinctive.

My novels are thought experiments in which cause and effect can be made clear. Real life is harder. Often we don't realize we are being offered a choice until after we have made it. Although we cannot know the meaning of our own stories until they are finished, the more mindfully we choose the more likely it is that our stories will have a satisfying conclusion. Your responses to the exercises in chapter 1 are one place to start. Which of those roles and names did you choose? Which were given or forced upon you? Which do you wish to retain?

Now make a list of decision points in your life. Did a common value guide your choices? A repeated pattern? Were you aware that you had a choice? If you have made a succession of good or bad decisions, do you understand why? When you have looked at the big choices, consider the little ones. What decisions do you make every day and what are their cumulative results likely to be?

What do your deeds say about your deepest feelings? What things in your life have given you the greatest joy? List the work or activities that make you happiest. What were the moments in your life when you were most conscious of being in the right place and doing the right thing? Note whether these acts and moments were the result of conscious choice or instinctive action. Were any of them a surprise?

What are the things that you like about yourself and would like to reinforce? What are the habits and responses that have caused you problems, and what can you do to discourage them? Pay attention to the way you talk about yourself. Self-deprecating speech is a standard element in humor, but it can become an excuse, or worse, a guarantee of failure. Self-inflation has an equal potential to exasperate our friends and skew our relationship to the world. Remember that our unconscious minds believe what we say.

Based on your answers to the questions above, what do you value? Justice, compassion, security, adventure, creativity, order? List the things that are important to you, not because you think you ought to like them, but because they are the values that guide your choices.

For help in defining your values, try Mind Tools' helpful article, "What Are Your Values?: Deciding What's Most Important in Life," online here: *www.mindtools.com/pages/article/newTED_85.htm*. And to work out the relative importance of choices or values by paired comparison analysis, try Mind Tools' "Paired Comparison Analysis: Working Out Relative Importances," which can be found at *www.mindtools.com/pages/article/newTED_02.htm*.

Since your body is part of the community that makes up the self, this is a good time to consider its condition as well. Exercise 3.2 will help you collect data on your body, mind, and spirit that you can use for the regular self-evaluations (checksums) that will tell you how this work is affecting you.

Integrating the Elements

A marriage between two people who are secure in their own identities is more likely to succeed than one in which one or both partners have a poor sense of self and weak boundaries. In the same way, a relationship between a deity and a devotee will be healthier if the human partner has a well-developed identity before he or she gets involved with the god.

Create a display, collage, or scrapbook that represents the best things about you. Include a photo in which you look happy and smaller photos of people, places, or things that are part of your identity. Add the results of the self-analysis in Exercise 3.2. Use your favorite colors, symbols, scenes, and quotes. Label it with the name that best represents your identity.

The images you have chosen will help you with the next task, identifying and accepting all of your parts and integrating them into a coherent whole.

Begin with the name you put on your display. Why did you choose it? Do you need to expand it or make it more descriptive? How about adding your principal roles as titles? Now look at your body, but this time consider how your life has shaped it, and how it has shaped you. If you have scars or other marks, remember how you got them. Does your mental image of your appearance match what you see in the mirror? If you do not look like the person you believe yourself to be, perhaps your image of what that sort of person looks like needs to change.

Next, pay some attention to your ancestors. If possible, add pictures of them to your display. What stories have you heard about your grandparents? What do those stories tell you about the traditions of your family? Consider doing a DNA test to explore your ancestry. Read folktales from the country or countries from which your ancestors came.

Think about your gender. Sex is a biological fact bound into DNA, but gender is a way of relating to the world. Does your gender identification match your sex? By whose definition? Dress for a day in the clothing that most emphatically represents the gender that matches your sex. Then consider how a twin of the other gender would look and act. Make an opportunity to dress in the clothing of that gender. If neither gender role really expresses your essence, put together an outfit that does. Whatever you are wearing, take a few moments to extend that identity into your energy field, and change your body language to match. As you move around, think about what gender perceptions teach you about the world.

Include some images that represent your best memories. My display would include a photo of myself at the age of four, perched on a pony. What is the earliest thing you can remember? The best or worst? The strangest or most triumphant? Add your achievements—not just the conventional things you boast about in your Christmas letters, but also the little accomplishments that are important only to you. Find words to express the best things about you and the person you are striving to be.

When subjects burned incense to the emperor in ancient Rome they were not deifying the mortal man but strengthening his *genius*, the god-self hidden within. Light a candle and some incense in honor of your own genius, the spark of divinity inside. When you have completed this, do the self-blessing in Exercise 3.3.

Who are you, and where will you be when you find out? This passage from Lois McMaster Bujold's novel, *Memory*, describes how the process might feel:

> Who are you, boy?
>
> ... Who are you who asks?
>
> On the thought a blessed silence came, an empty clarity. He took it at first for utter desolation, but desolation was a kind of free fall, perpetual and without ground below. This was stillness: balanced, solid, weirdly serene. No momentum to it at all, forward or backwards or sideways.
>
> *I am who I choose to be. I always have been what I chose ... though not always what I pleased.*
>
> His mother had often said, *When you choose an action, you choose the consequences of that action.* She had emphasized the corollary of this axiom even more vehemently; when you desired a consequence you had damned well better take the action that would create it.
>
> He lay drained of tension, not moving, and content to be so. The oddly stretched moment was like a bite of eternity, eaten on the run. Was this quiet place inside something new-grown, or had he just never stumbled across it before? How could so vast a thing lay undiscovered for so long? His breathing slowed, and deepened.
>
> *I elect to be ... myself.*
>
> (Bujold 1996, 386)

Help for the God-Bothered

Knowing who you are may not be enough if the Powers keep knocking at your door. At the age of eighteen, River Devora, a talented psychic who now uses her abilities to aid in her work in the health field, "started struggling with involuntary possession by a variety of entities."

> They would usually come during the pagan rituals and smaller private circles I had started attending at that time. They didn't always speak English. A few were or claimed to be deities, some were the spirits of deceased folks, some I wasn't sure what they were. There were times when the possessing entities were helpful, providing healing, counsel, or prophecy. There were times they were opportunistic or even harmful to me, needed to be driven out, and left me feeling depleted or injured.
>
> It was a frightening time for me—I didn't feel like I had much control, and the folks around me were primarily coming from an archetypal Wiccan perspective and neither understood what was happening to me nor could they provide me with any practical skills for navigating the possessory episodes. Some folks thought I was crazy, some found me uncomfortably uncanny and avoided me (particularly if one of the entities speaking through me knew secret or private things about the other person that I had no way of knowing), and others treated me like I was some kind of magical saint or guru (which was the worst of the three, honestly). I was secretly afraid I was either crazy or broken, and I was very ashamed of the whole thing and wished it would go away.

Possible responses to unwanted possession include dispossession, warding, or release and training. Procedures to get a spirit to leave are discussed in detail in chapters 17 and 18. If possible, before expelling the spirit, helpers should find out who or what the entity is and what It wants. Sometimes promising a warded session in which the Power will be invited to come through and deliver Its message will relieve the pressure. The Power may require that you do this on a regular basis. If so, do your best to find training, either from a reputable group that practices possession, or from the Powers Themselves.

The rest of the time, invoke the persona you wear in the mundane world. Avoid colors or places that you associate with the Power. Reconnect with your physical body. Ground and center (if you do not know how to do this, you can find exercises and explanations in *Trance-Portation*). In the Afro-Diasporic traditions, initiates are put under the protection of the Powers by wearing necklaces in Their sacred colors. Lorrie Wood suggests making a necklace to represent your Self. Use your favorite colors. Select a special bead to represent each major aspect of your life and character. Also include beads that will help with grounding, such as black tourmaline or unglazed clay. When you put on the necklace, you are proclaiming that you are *self-possessed*. You can use the necklace as a rosary, touching each major bead to affirm your identity.

Practice
Exercise 3.1: Meditation on the Name

Stories about a young person's coming of age chronicle both the construction of the persona and the search for identity. The central figure in Rudyard Kipling's novel, *Kim,* is an Irish boy who has been raised as a native in India, where he survives by taking on many different identities. In the following passage, Kipling describes how contemplation of one's name can trigger a state of trance:

> A very few white people, but many Asiatics, can throw themselves into a mazement as it were by repeating their own names over and over again to themselves, letting the mind go free upon speculation as to what is called personal identity. When one grows older, the power, usually, departs, but while it lasts it may descend upon a man at any moment.
> "Who is Kim—Kim—Kim?"
> He squatted in a corner of the clanging waiting-room, rapt from all other thoughts; hands folded in lap, and pupils contracted to pin-points. In a minute—in another

half-second—he felt he would arrive at the solution of the tremendous puzzle; but here, as always happens, his mind dropped away from those heights with the rush of a wounded bird, and passing his hand before his eyes, he shook his head.

(Kipling 1901, 189)

Actually, most "white people" *can* do this, but at the time Kipling was writing it had not occurred to many Europeans to try.

Find a place in which you can sit comfortably in a balanced position for a little while without being interrupted. Relax, close your eyes, and begin to breathe slowly and regularly. In chapter 1 you considered your name, or names, with your conscious mind. Speak the name that you feel best represents the real you, then repeat it silently, again and again, and see where it leads you.

Exercise 3.2: Baseline for Checksums

On a scale of 1 to 5, with 5 being very good and 1 being poor, rate your:

- Physical health

- Energy level

- Immune system

- Stress level

- Concentration and focus

- Decisiveness

- Patience

- Connection to other humans

- Connection to Spirit

Exercise 3.3: Self-Blessing

Light a candle and some incense. Look at the following affirmations and fill in the blanks. Sit or stand in front of a mirror and read them aloud. Feel free to make additions and adjustments to the wording.

Think about how that name identifies you to the world.

>*My name is _____. It means _____. Blessed be*
>*my name.*

Think about thinking. How much of your self-concept is invested in your brain?

>*Blessed be my head, which holds my thoughts and memories and*
>*enables me to see and hear and move.*

Consider the expression in your eyes. What do they show? Remember the most beautiful things your eyes have allowed you to see.

>*Blessed be the eyes that see my image in this mirror, the eyes that*
>*are my windows to the world.*

Think about talking and listening. Remember the loveliest things you have heard. In the same manner consider every part of your body, appreciating what it does for you, remembering all the good things it has brought you, and giving it your blessing.

>*Blessed be the ears by which I hear these words, and the music of*
>*the world. Blessed be my hands, etc.*

List your major roles—relationships, work, etc.

>*I am a _____ May my deeds be blessed.*

Regulate your breathing.

> *I am energy. May this spirit shape be blessed.*
>
> *I am the heir of my ancestors* (name as many as you can), *who came from* (countries of origin). *May the instincts and archetypes in my unconscious be blessed.*
>
> *I am* _____ (gender identity). *May my* _____ (womanhood/manhood/other) *be blessed along with the* _____ (male/female/other) *within.*
>
> *I am all that I have met. May my memories be blessed* (think about a few).

Describe deeds that represent the best within you.

> *I am what I choose to do. May my accomplishments* _____ *be blessed.*

List your qualities and aspirations, such as hopeful, just, caring, etc.

> *I am* _____. *May my virtues be blessed.*
>
> *I am a child of earth and starry heaven. May the divine soul that is within me be blessed.*
>
> *I invoke my true Self, unity in diversity, constancy in change, the ever-evolving manifestation of my holy and eternal soul.*

Exercise 3.4: The Question

What is the Meaning of Life? What is the meaning of *your* life?

For further work on the Self, see Bruce Hood's *The Self Illusion: How the Social Brain Creates Identity* or Jennifer Ouellette's *Me, Myself, and Why: Searching for the Science of Self.*

Part Two

CHOOSING PARTNERS

Possessory work is a dance with the Divine. But what exactly does that mean? Many religions include the concept of a Divine Source that is beyond definition; however, despite theologians' best efforts to maintain monotheistic purity, most people experience Deity as a person, and as soon as we begin to personify the Divine, we have in practice become polytheists. One can experience the Divine Source, but one cannot "carry" it in a possessory ritual. Teachers such as Jesus and Buddha came close, but most of their followers need a human face through which to see the Divine.

This book is written from a polytheist perspective. For a brilliant demonstration of what that means, I recommend John Michael Greer's cat parable in *A World Full of Gods: An Inquiry into Polytheism* (Greer 2005, 82–84). If we are going to discuss possessory work, we need to begin with the assumption that Spirit manifests in many forms. Whatever the world may "really" be, we experience it as an array of discrete objects and beings. When I pray for help with a task, I call to the deity most likely to understand the problem, and I relate to that Power as a person. In a country whose legal authorities have granted personhood to corporations, that concept should not be difficult to understand. In fact, Divine Beings relate to us in ways that are much more personal than our relationships with corporations.

Interacting with a deity can be at least as intense as an involvement with a human lover. We may also relate to the Powers as parents or friends, employers or allies. Building an enduring connection progresses in stages as acquaintance leads to knowledge and knowledge to intimacy.

The most difficult stage in any relationship is the point at which we pull down our defenses, open the gate, and let the Other come in. Learning to sense the presence and hear the voice of a Power transforms worship into a profound and sustaining relationship. It can also be a preparation for possessory trance.

4

ABSOLUTES AND ARCHETYPES

In seeking absolute truth we aim at the unattainable,
and must be content with broken portions.
—Sir William Osler

Before we get involved with one of the Powers, we need to think about what those Powers actually *are*. Most of us have grown up in a culture in which most people believe that there is a single Supreme Being. Although both the United States and the European Union guarantee freedom of worship, statements about this right generally assume that behind all religions stands a deity who, if not the same as the Yahweh/God the Father/ Allah, of the Abrahamic religions, is a cat of the same breed.

However, if one looks at religion as it is actually practiced world-wide, it becomes clear that humans honor a variety of Powers, and even those who follow the Abrahamic religions are not always as monotheis-tic as they think they are. As a polytheist, I believe that divinity comes in many flavors. Furthermore, a look at folk practice shows that the Powers come in a continuum of "weight classes," as it were, that can be ranked according to degrees of personification and power, each of which is expe-rienced and honored in different ways.

The God Beyond the Gods
The concept of an Absolute, a Power so supreme it is without personal characteristics while at the same time being omni-everything, is found

throughout the world. It is Pure Being, primordial, ineffable, timeless, ungendered, and transcending all dualities.

The Hindu addresses it as *Tat tvam asi*: "Thou art That" (Chandogya Upanishad, 6.8.7). *Ehyeh Asher Ehyeh*, "I am that I am," is the answer given to Moses when he asks the Power that speaks through the burning bush to give Its name (Exodus 3:14). "I am all that which has been, which is and which shall be, and there is no man that hath lifted my veil" was the inscription in the temple of the Egyptian goddess Neith, Who may have originally been considered an androgynous Creator.

However, this affirmation of existence is only one way of expressing the paradox. The alternative is the apophatic definition ("neither is this thou"), as when John Scotus Erigena wrote, "We do not know what God is. God Himself does not know what He is because He is not anything. Literally God is not, because He transcends being" (Erigena 2011).

The medieval Christian called this being Deus. The Hindu name Brahman, from a verb meaning to grow, is a gender-neutral noun for the Absolute (Morales). For the Pythagoreans, it was Aiôn (Eternity) (Opsopaus 2002, 1), and Nous for the Platonist (Uzdavinys 2004). To unite with this Being (or state of being) is the goal of the mystic. Faiths that include this concept may call themselves monotheistic, but personally, I would describe them as "transtheistic," or perhaps "trance-theistic," since it is only in an altered state that the seeker can glimpse his goal. Although this level of Deity is by definition beyond personification, some reach it through contemplation of God-in-nature or devotion to one of the Powers. Others take the ascetic's path of rejection or negation of images, seeking to clear their road to the Truth that lies beyond material appearances.

The ecstatic state may be the fruit of intense and disciplined spiritual practices, or come upon the seeker unaware. For a single shining moment or a period of days the mystic loses all awareness of the physical world while her consciousness experiences ecstasy. The leap from the world of perception to that of pure intuition can be stimulated by contemplation of a religious symbol, reiteration of a mantra, or appreciation of the beauty of a lover or the natural world, but it leads to a place of transcendent knowledge in which the soul *knows* that Spirit is the Reality beyond and within all things. Studies of mysticism such as the classic work by Evelyn Underhill, *Mysticism*, include report after report in which terms such as love, joy, and bliss can only attempt to convey what was experienced.

The test of an ecstatic experience is in its impact. Contact with Deity at this level is a life-changing experience, leaving the mystic able to endure whatever else life may throw at him because he *knows* there is a certainty beyond all fears. Millions have dedicated their lives to this search. Not all succeed, but the practices of the various traditions are themselves worth exploring. Exercise 4.1 is one of the first steps on that road, as well as a basic mind-clearing skill that is useful in preparing for possessory trance. You will find a fuller discussion and more exercises in chapter 12 of *Trance-Portation*.

Sacred Geometries

In many traditions, the first division of the Divine is into a dyad based on polarity, as in the Wiccan Lord and Lady, the Christian God and Satan, or light and darkness, seen in the Zoroastrian Ahura-Mazda and Ahriman. Religions in which such a pair is basic to the theology are dualistic or ditheistic.

Just as three legs give the most stable support, dividing the Divine Being into three parts is even more popular. The Hindu *trimurti* consists of Brahma the Creator, Shiva the Destroyer, and Vishnu the Preserver. As defined by the Nicene Creed, the Christian trinity is God the Father, God the Son, and the Holy Spirit (although in practice the Virgin Mary is often a more popular third object of veneration). In Germanic tradition the world is created by Oðinn, the root of whose name is related to creative fervor, Vili, or "Will," and Vé, which is also the name for a place of worship. The image of the Triple Goddess—Maiden, Mother, and Crone—popularized by Robert Graves became a primary element in the Pagan revival, although the male principle is usually represented in Wicca by a single dying and reborn god rather than a triple masculine deity. For some, however, the Goddess becomes a simple replacement for the monotheistic male God.

Dividing up the Godhead makes the concept more comprehensible, but unless the Persons are addressed at the archetypal level, the arrangement seems to function more as a theological convenience than a focus for actual worship. God the Father and Jesus are fully personified, while the Holy Spirit is more of an experience than a being. Vishnu and Shiva have their own cults, but Brahma is rarely honored on his own. Oðinn exists in his own right as a fully functional deity, while Vili and Vé are unknown elsewhere in the lore.

Archetypes

An archetype expresses the basic identity that characterizes a class of objects. It provides a bridge between the abstract and indescribable Absolute and the personified deities with whom we actually interact. In works such as Plato's *Timaeus* and *Phaedrus* the Greek philosopher developed the theory of forms, or archetypes, which are the essential and eternal template for each thing that has an identity. Individual examples are mortal and mutable, but the original and ideal essence transcends time and space.

Jung used this concept for inherited ideas, thought patterns, and images that are wired into everyone's psyche as part of our collective unconscious. They include motifs such as the apocalypse, the flood and creation; events from the life cycle, such as birth, death, initiation, or marriage; and archetypal figures, in particular "the shadow, the wise old man, the child, the mother . . . and her counterpart, the maiden, and lastly the anima in man and the animus in woman" (Jung 1959, 114). The archetypal pattern is shared, but its manifestation for each individual is shaped by the conditions of life and culture. Jung found in this theory an explanation for the appearance of archaic mythological figures in the dreams of patients who could have had no exposure to these images in waking life.

Just as a survey of dreams reveals variations on certain images, students of mythology and folklore have identified motifs and figures that appear across a variety of cultures. Some of these similarities may be explained by diffusion, but others occur in cultures so widely separated by geography that unless the transmission occurred at a very early point in human history indeed, they must come from the collective unconscious. Trickster figures such as Coyote, Loki, and Exu are by no means the same Person, but one might say they hang out at the same bar. Working with an archetype may not have the same intimacy and power as working with a god, but it is a good way to access a particular vibration of energy.

In 1978 I was asked to create a coming-of-age ritual for a young woman friend. At that time I had never been to a Wiccan ritual, nor had I read Robert Graves; nonetheless, I had heard of the concept of the Triple Goddess, and it occurred to me that it might work as the basis for such a ritual. I invited all the Pagan women I knew and asked three of them to act as priestesses of the Maiden, Mother, and Wisewoman, leading a discussion of the social, physical, and spiritual significance of each phase of a woman's life. Although we were working at the archetypal level, the energy that came through with each figure was quite distinct, and the experience of working in a women's circle dedicated to the Goddess was unlike anything we had known in co-ed magical rituals.

I had also encountered the idea of working with archetypes in the Western esoteric tradition, where the Hebrew Kabbalah, and in particular the glyph of the Tree of Life, were developed into a system by which archetypal forms could be organized. The Tree is a diagram upon which ten spheres called sephiroth, are arranged, each of which represents a cosmic force or factor. Theologically, the sephiroth represent the different emanations from the Divine Source discussed above, which descend through the spectrum from the white light of Kether into the world of manifestation.

One way to work with the Tree is as a kind of cosmic filing system that allows you to sort and organize spiritual and mythic material from diverse sources. Magically, it provides a framework for focusing very precisely on a specific energy.

The original Hebrew system gave to each sphere a number, a name, and an order of angelic beings. When Greek and Hebrew texts began to be translated, a Christian and later an occult version evolved. The Renaissance humanist Giovanni Pico della Mirandola, who used syncretism as a way to look at the same thing from many different points of view in order to see it more clearly, melded Kabbalistic concepts with Platonic and Hermetic traditions. By the nineteenth century, the esoteric tradition had added to the Hebrew correspondences colors, symbols, planetary associations, and gods. Those listed in the appendix to Aleister Crowley's *Magick in Theory and Practice* include Egyptian, Hindu, and Greek deities. English composer Gustav Holst's orchestral suite titled *The Planets* evokes the astrological symbolism of this system.

The following passage from the chapter titled "The Descent of the Powers" in *That Hideous Strength* by C. S. Lewis shows what can be done with concentrated imagery:

> Something tonic and lusty and cheerily cold, like a sea breeze, was coming over them. There was no fear anywhere: the blood inside them flowed as if to a marching-song. They felt themselves taking their places in the ordered rhythm of the universe, side by side with punctual seasons and patterned atoms and the obeying Seraphim . . . Ransom knew, as a man knows when he touches iron, the clear, taut splendour of that celestial spirit which now flashed between them: vigilant Malacandra, captain of a cold orb, whom men call Mars and Mavors, and Tyr who put his hand in the wolf-mouth.
>
> (Lewis 1962, 235)

When I began to work with the Kabbalah in the early eighties, I expanded the list for each sephirah to include gods and goddesses from as many traditions as I could find (as well as adding music, magical tools, real-world experiences, and foods—I particularly remember the "primordial stew" we cooked for Binah). The advantage of this approach is that by combining many examples, all of which exhibit elements of the archetype, you can arrive at a concept of the essential energy, just you would look at a lot of Siamese cats to learn about the breed.

You will find a version of my classification in figure 2. Try going through the list and see how many deities you can add. Do Exercise 4.2: "Working with Archetypal Energy."

The instinct to categorize and create systems is clearly as deeply ingrained, at least in the consciousness of scholars, as any of Jung's archetypes. As Europeans discovered new cultures, mythologists with Classical educations did their best to force them into the same pattern, with a divine king and queen, and gods for each cultural function. For a discussion of how this was done with Germanic mythology, see Karl Litzenberg's *The Victorians and the Vikings: A Bibliographical Essay on Anglo-Norse Literary*

The Gods on the Tree

Number	Name	Meaning	Color	Astrology	Element
1.	KETHER	The Crown	White Light	Primum Mobile	

The Ancient of Days, White Tara seated upon the lotus,
High One, Just as High and Third,
Ptah, Brahman, Aion, Wakan tanka, Olodumare,
the supreme divinity of every mythology

2.	'HOKHMAH	Wisdom	Gray	the Zodiac	

Sophia (Stellarum), Metis, Athena, Ma'at
Uranus (the original sky father), Shiva as a hermit,
Hermes Trismegistus, Enki, Amon, Thoth,
Wotan the Wanderer, Merlin,
Gandalf and other archetypal wizards

3.	BINAH	Understanding	Black	Saturn	

The Great Mother, the Wisewoman, Nuit, Veiled Isis, Persephone of the
Underworld, Kali, Rhea, Cybele, Hekate, Heide, Cerridwen of the Cauldron,
Tiamat, Aditi, Spider Grandmother, Nana Buruku,
Saturn and Chronos, Kala (Shiva as Lord of Time); Odin at Mimir's well

4.	'HESED	Mercy	Blue	Jupiter	

Zeus/Jupiter, Poseidon, Thor, Odin as ruler of Valhalla, Nuada Silver-Hand,
Amon, Indra, Brahma, Obatala, Chango, all great kings and sovereigns;
Hera/Juno, Fricka, Eriu/Folta/Banba, Brigantia, Isis, Inanna,
all great queens and goddesses of sovereignty

5.	GEBURAH	Strength	Red	Mars	

Ares/Mars, Bellona, Tyr and the Fenris Wolf, Odin as a battle god, Taranis, the
Morrigan, Horus the avenger, Set the destroyer, Anat, Inanna as battle-goddess,
Durga, Varuna-avatar, Ogun, Oya, and all other war or battle deities, St. George,
Joan of Arc

6.	TIPHARETH	Beauty	Gold	the Sun	

Solar deities: Helios, Horus, Ra, Amataseru, Surya;
deities of healing and the arts: Apollo, Lugh, Isis;

Figure 2: The Gods on the Tree

Figure 2 continued

Defenders: Krishna, Mithras;
Sacrificed gods: Osiris, Dionysos, Balder, Odin as the Hanged God, Adonis;
Divine Kings: Rama, Solomon, Arthur

7.   **NETZACH**   **Victory**   Green   Venus   Fire

Deities of love and fertility: Shakti, Aphrodite, Freyja, Osun , Astarte, Hathor,
Inanna/Ishtar, Pan, Cernunnos, the Horned God, Diana of Nemi;
deities of the flame and forge: Hestia/Vesta, Brigid, Hephaestos/Vulcan,
Wayland Smith; fire deities: Agni, Loge, Pele

8.   **HOD**   **Glory**   Orange   Mercury   Air

Hermes/Mercury, Athena/Minerva, Anubis, Hanuman, Coyote, Odin
as lord of poetry, Brigid as patroness of poetry, Lugh the many-talented, Merlin,
Ellegua/Legba, Kokopelli and all other trickster, messenger, and way-shower
deities; androgynous deities: Avalokitesvara, Kuan Yin, Hermaphrodite.

9.   **YESOD**   **Foundation** Purple   the Moon   Water

Lunar deities: Selene, Lucina, Artemis, Sin, Aah, Soma, Chandra;
Generative deities: Aphrodite rising from the waves, Yemaya, Isis, Artemis as
midwife, Heimdallr, father of men; upholders: Shu (Egyptian), Atlas

10.   **MALKUTH**   **Kingdom**   Quartered   Earth
olive green,
russet, black,
lemon-yellow,
the Earth

Earth or fertility deities: Gaia, Demeter and Persephone, Saturnus and Ops,
Lakshmi, Corn Mother, Jordh, Nerthus, Nana, Oko;
cthonic, Underworld deities: Erishkegal, Inanna, Adonis, John Barleycorn

Relations. The French philologist and mythographer Georges Dumézil is best known for developing a trifunctional hypothesis that divides the deities in all Indo-European mythologies according to social caste. According to this theory, first function deities are in charge of sovereignty and magic, second function gods are warriors, and third function gods rule fertility and productivity (Dumézil 1958).

But the gods are not one-trick ponies. You will have noticed that some deities, like Odin and Isis, appear in different aspects under more than one of the sephiroth. The Norse god Freyr, whom Dumézil sees only as a fertility deity, was the patron of the Swedish royal house, while Thor the warrior was known as the farmers' god. In Germany, farmers left out a sheaf of grain for Woden's horse at harvest time.

From the spiritual point of view, the value of archetypal systems is that invoking or contemplating a group of deities along with other symbols relating to a particular kind of energy will create an extremely concentrated experience. In our Kabbalah study group, we spent a month on each of the sephirah, meditating on its meaning, wearing the appropriate color, and seeking relevant real-world experiences. The goal was to develop the particular kind of spiritual awareness it represented. As we shall see, this method of using colors, symbols, and associations is also an effective way to make contact with a god.

Figure 3: Thor, Odin, and Freyr from the Oseburg Tapestry

Practice
Exercise 4.1: The Stillness at the Center

This exercise builds on the breathing practice and energy work that you did in Exercise 2.2 in chapter 2. If you have not been practicing, go back to refresh your memory. Your goal at this time is not mystic rapture, although with sufficient practice this exercise can lead that way, but rather an internal quiet and receptivity that will at the very least help you to center yourself and relieve stress. This practice will also help you to clear your mind before invoking a specific Power.

Find a place where you can sit for a while without interruption. Check the status of anything that might cause anxiety, such as the faucets or stove. Minimize distractions by wearing comfortable clothing and sitting in a supportive chair (unless you are accustomed to sitting zazen).

Stretch every part of your body, and then find a balanced position in which you can be still for a long time. You may want to set a timer. Try three minutes the first time, and as you continue to practice, increase it.

Close your eyes, and as you breathe in and out, focus awareness on each chakra from top to bottom, linking yourself to the earth, and back again. Extend your awareness outward until you feel yourself sitting within a protective sphere.

Silently articulate your purpose, to seek inner stillness and experience the ground of being.

Count to regularize your breathing, and gradually lengthen the time you take for each breath. When you find a comfortable rate, maintain it.

This is the point at which your busy mind will try to distract you. As each thought intrudes, think, "Neither is this Thou." If you must have something to focus on, visualize flowing water, or the whirling glory of the starry heavens, or an unfolding multi-petaled flower, but as the mind slows even these images can be banished. If you feel yourself tensing, take a deeper breath, and as you exhale, relax.

Continue breathing and banishing awareness of your body, your surroundings, even your own identity, sending awareness further and further inward, seeking stillness. You may find light or darkness, or you may simply find a place of rest.

When the timer sounds, gradually increase the rate at which you are breathing, restore awareness to your limbs, and open your eyes. If necessary, eat or drink something to restore yourself fully to ordinary reality.

Exercise 4.2: Working with Archetypal Energy

The following is an exercise in syncretism. If the concept makes you break out in hives, you can skip this one—but before you do, at least read through the description to get an idea of how it works.

Think of an area in which you need inspiration and energy, and match it with one of the sephiroth. For instance, if you are working on communication, look at Hod; for your love life, look to Netzach. If you are facing a battle, consider Geburah, but if you need order in your life, go to Hesed.

Prepare an altar as your focus with a cloth and the correct number of candles in the appropriate color. You may wear that color as well. If you are not already familiar with them, look up the deities in figure 2. Make your own list with the names of the deities and the characteristics or powers that are relevant to your problem. If your sphere is associated with one of the planets for which Holst composed a piece, play the selection. Light the candles and sit down before your altar.

Count your breathing for a little while to get focused, and then read the names of the gods. Ask them to help you with your problem. Resume your counted breathing, thinking about the deities and opening your mind to any impressions or messages. When you feel the time is right, thank the Powers and extinguish the candles.

5

POWERS AS PERSONS

"I don't hold with paddlin' with the occult," said Granny firmly.
"Once you start paddlin' with the occult you start believing in
spirits, and when you start believing in spirits you start believ-
ing in demons, and then before you know where you are you're
believing in gods. And then you're in trouble."
"But all them things exist," said Nanny Ogg.
"That's no call to go around believing in them.
It only encourages 'em."
—Terry Pratchett, *Lords and Ladies*

If the search for the Divine Source relies on a negation of images, working with figures and archetypes might be called the Way of the Classification of Images. Increasing levels of Personhood leads to the Way of
Affirmation. This can, of course, take the form of Pantheism—"This also
is Thou"—in which we see the world and everything in it as an aspect of
the Divine; but it can also focus on images and symbols—"This also is
a *part* of Thee." The polytheist believes in many gods, although if he is
also a henotheist or a monolatrist he confines his service to only one of
them and believes that other Powers or Powers from other religions or
pantheons cannot or will not take an interest in him. This may or may
not be true. The kathenotheist, like the serial monogamist, works with
only one Power at a time.

Just as we cannot save "the Earth" but can only take steps such as recycling to improve one part of it, or serve "humanity" but can only feed individual people, rather than trying to connect to Spirit in general, most of us find it easier to use a face and a name. The Powers Whom we encounter as Persons include gods and beings that are honored like gods, deified humans, personal ancestors, and personal guardians and allies. For more on this, see chapter 10 of Ivo Dominguez Jr.'s *Spirit Speak* (Dominguez 2008, 183–95). These are also the categories of Powers Who may be carried or channeled in various types of possessory practice.

Type	Examples	Possessing?
The Absolute	Nous, Brahma, Ancient of Days	no
Geometries	Lord and Lady, Trinity	partial
Archetypes	war gods, love goddesses	partial
God-class	Odin, Aphrodite, Exu	yes
Aspects	Allfather, Ourania, Yangi	yes
Constructions	Lady Liberty, Fortuna	yes
Mighty Dead, Ascended Masters	Heracles, Washington, "Michael"	yes
Ancestors		yes
Allies/Guardians	fylgja, daemon, Power Animal	yes
Wights	local lake or forest	rarely

Figure 4: Levels of Deity

Gods

What do we mean by "gods," as distinct from "God"?

John Michael Greer observes that "gods are neither infinite, nor timeless, nor changeless. They are held to possess superhuman capacities of power and knowledge, but these powers aren't unlimited, and the gods themselves are subject to change like any other being" (Greer 2005, 55). As he points out in *A World Full of Gods*, most of the arguments against the existence of a single, all-powerful, all-benevolent God fall apart if one assumes the existence of many deities.

Even faiths that officially believe in an Ultimate Absolute Deity usually include some kind of personified Powers who act as helpers and with whom people can interact. In Hinduism, these are the devas; in West African and Afro-Diasporic religions, the orishas or lwa; and the archangels in Christianity (for saints and prophets, see page 57—the section on the Mighty Dead). In pre-Christian pagan religions, philosophers might contemplate the Ultimate, but everybody else simply honored the gods.

The Sanskrit *deva* and the Latin *deus* and *divus* ("divine") come from the Proto-Indo-European *d(e)y(e)w, meaning bright sky or daylight (Dumézil 1974, part 3, chapter 1). This root also gives us god names such as the Greek Zeus; the Latin Dis Pater, Jupiter, and Diana; and the Germanic Tiwaz (Tyr). The third century BCE Greek theurgist and Neoplatonic teacher Iamblichus tells us:

> Intelligent readers will understand from what has been said, that as the gods are spiritual essences, the partaking of them, or, in other words, of their irradiation, is analogous to the partaking of light. The luminance itself is no way affected, but the partaker is filled and pervaded by it.
>
> (Iamblichus 1911, chapter 3)

Thus, the gods could be identified as those beings who are from the heavens, and/or the radiant ones, those who are full of light.

The Greek *theos* (God) offers another option. In Plato's *Cratylus* Socrates says

> My notion would be something of this sort: I suspect that the sun, moon, earth, stars, and heaven, which are still the Gods of many barbarians, were the only Gods known to the aboriginal Hellenes. Seeing that they were always moving and running, from their running nature they were called Gods (Theous) or

runners (Theontas); and when men became acquainted with the other Gods, they proceeded to apply the same name to them all.

I take this to mean that the gods, whether or not they are associated with heavenly bodies, are always in motion, perhaps because they can manifest anywhere, or because their essence vibrates at a higher level than ours.

Another quality by which we can identify gods is Beauty; not the beauty defined by fashion, but the quality that can make the sight of a sunset or the sound of a symphony take one's breath away. We cannot define it, but when we encounter it, for a moment we experience a perfection beyond mundane comprehension. Iamblichus says,

> With these peculiarities there flashes out from the gods Beauty which seems inconceivable, holding the Beholders fixed with wonder, imparting to them an unutterable gladness, displaying itself to view with ineffable symmetry, and carrying off the palm from other forms of comeliness.
>
> (Iamblichus 1911, chapter 5)

The English word God comes from the Proto-Indo-European *guđán, which may come from a root ǵʰeu̯—"to pour, libate"—or from a root *ǵʰau̯—"to call, to invoke" (Watkins 2000), which would give us gods as "the beings to whom we call and make offerings." In Roman Catholic practice, the devotion owed to God is called *latreia*, which comes from the Classical Greek term used for a hired servant by Aeschylus, and for service to the gods by Plato (Scannell 1910). Gods might thus be defined as those beings to whom we owe service (although, as we shall see, a variety of relationships are possible).

Ivo Dominguez Jr. refers to Powers of this class as "Great Ones." They have personal names, although many of the names that have come down to us may originally have been titles such as Freyr, meaning "lord," and Freyja, meaning "lady," leaving us to wonder what the god's original "real" name might have been, or if each tribe or region had its own name and version of the same deity. Other god names relate to a primary attribute, such as Donar/Thunor/Thor for the god whose hammer strikes thunder from the clouds. The gods also have backstories—myths that recount their origins, deeds, and relationships—which may be referred to in prayers. When Jesus is addressed as a "personal lord and savior," he is being treated as this level of god.

To the "hard polytheist," god-class Powers are distinct and self-sufficient entities. However, Sandra Ingerman offers another perspective:

> I was at a workshop many years ago where I was teaching . . . people how to merge with a helping spirit that they work with to get understanding. I was doing a demonstration of what that would look like. And one of the helping spirits that I work with who I write about in my books is the Egyptian goddess Isis. So I had merged with Isis in this group, and I told the group that they could ask Isis whatever questions they wanted and she would answer them. One of the participants in the group asked Isis, "Can you see all of our power animals and teachers sitting in the room here?" And Isis gave a really interesting response. She said that we give the spirits a form by giving them a name, but that actually the spirits don't have a particular form. We give them a form.
>
> People who journey see bear as a power animal, or [they see] eagle, or some people have Jesus, Mary, or Buddha as a teacher. In reality, they don't have these names or personalities. But it's our need from a human perspective to be able to know that we have this bear or eagle or Jesus with us, but the spirits who work with us actually have a formless energy, which gives them the unlimited potential to create the healing that we need on a personal level and on a planetary level.
>
> (Simon 2011)

It might also be observed that these forms serve as filters to protect us from a reality that would otherwise overwhelm us. Although those who have a particular devotion to one deity may call on him or her for help in every area of life, most of the time we ask for help from the deity Whose specialty the problem is, just as, although there are times when one must go directly to the president of a company, even when one gets her attention, her response will generally be to refer the request to the appropriate department.

For our purposes, let us define gods as radiant, active, beautiful beings with their own personalities, histories, and interests to whom we relate through acts of worship.

Aspects

Even subdividing divinity into individual gods may not be enough when we are talking about possessory work. The gods are very big, and our psyches are small. We need to recognize that only a portion of a Divine Persona can come through. Because the gods are fully realized persons, they, like we, have many aspects. This is one reason why they often have numerous bynames, epithets, or paths. The Greeks recognized that Apollo of Delphi was not quite the same as Apollo Lukeios. Exu has nearly a hundred paths in addition to the aspects in which he accompanies other orishas. Exu Yangi, the earthen head who watches the door, is a different personality than the absinthe-drinking Marabo, or Tiriri who calls the other orishas in.

We think of Aphrodite as the love goddess, but in Judy Harrow's *Devoted to You: Honoring Deity in Wiccan Practice*, Maureen Reddington-Wilde opens her discussion of the goddess with the following:

> Aphrodite, sea-born, Cypriot, Heavenly One, Common One, Golden One, Dark One, War-like, Prostitute, Protector of Marriages, Nurse, Grave-Digger, Fair-Sailing One, Laughter-Loving. By all these names and many more, and by whatever name you wish to be called, we honor you.
>
> (Reddington-Wilde 2003, 159)

Odin has more bynames than any other Germanic deity—according to English archaeologist Neil Price, over two hundred (Price 2000).

Some refer to his appearance, but more often they have to do with his powers—glory, wisdom, or destruction. His epithets refer to him as a god of war, of commerce, of magic, and of wandering. He is the riddler and the giver of dreams. For more on this, see "Eighty-One Names of Odin" (Paxson 2009).

In part one, we explored the concept of persona. Exercise 5.1 will start you on the first steps to learning about the personae of the gods and where they come from.

Constructed Gods

Do the gods create us, or do we create them? Is the Divine immanent or transcendent? To both questions I would say yes. While I personally believe that the Divine Essence, manifesting in Spirit and in the universe, is our source and origin, I also believe that the human mind has a lot to do with the ways in which the gods appear.

In *Applied Magic* Dion Fortune states that

> A thought-form built up by continual visualizing and concentration, and concerning which a strong emotion is felt, becomes charged with that emotion and is capable of an independent existence outside the consciousness of its creator ... Exactly the same process ... takes place when a number of people concentrate with emotion on a single object ... Whenever such continuity of attention and feeling has been brought about, a group mind, or group Elemental, is formed which with the passage of time develops an individuality of its own, and ceases to be dependent for its existence upon the attention and emotion of the crowd that gave it birth ... When this process has been repeated regularly over considerable periods, the images that have been built up remain on the astral in exactly the same way that a habit-track is formed in the mind by the repeated performance of the same action. In this form the natural force remains permanently concentrated. Consequently subsequent worshippers need be at no

great pains to formulate the simulacrum; they have only to think of the god and they feel his power.

(Fortune 1962, 19)

As we will see when we get into the discussion of how to develop a relationship with a deity, what a god looks like and says about him- or herself can be different from the description in the book of myths. Go to a museum and you will see how images have changed over the centuries. Modern Pagans find that Hermes or Odin are quite happy to help with computers, while Ogun can take care of an automobile. Whatever the gods are "really," the ways in which they appear to us are shaped both by ancient tradition and the insights being shared in the community today (the "unverified personal gnosis," or UPG, that becomes a group belief). This is probably where our lore about the gods came from in the first place. Are we making these images up? It may begin that way, but when enough people have the same image of a given deity (and, presumably, the god approves), the image acquires an independent existence.

For example, when I began to work with the Norse goddess Frigg in the nineties, people in my group saw her wearing white and pale blue. Some years later, a post from a Santeria initiate on the East Coast was forwarded to my friend Lorrie. He wrote that a female Power who was dressed in pale blue and white and whose name was something like "Frig-gah" had appeared to him in meditation and helped him with a problem. Coming from a faith with an elaborate tradition of how to make offerings, he wanted to know the proper way to thank her. This man had had minimal contact with heathenry, and in any case I don't think we had shared our view of Frigg with people on the East Coast at that time. There are two possibilities: either our visualizations of the goddess were strong enough to affect Frigg's wardrobe, or those really are her preferred colors (although I do have another friend who has "seen" her in a red power suit).

The same principle governs the creation of deities. The Roman pantheon was full of gods and goddesses who appear to be personifications of virtues, such as Concordia or Fortuna. It is unclear whether they were perceived as persons or abstractions, but they certainly received offerings. Following this example, many modern Pagans honor the goddess of Liberty, as seen in the iconic statue, visualizing her torch bringing light to all the dark corners of the national psyche. Any aspect of divinity with a name and image can be addressed as one does a god. The older and more widely worshiped the Power, the stronger and more effective a possession is likely to be.

The Mighty Dead

Next to the gods in power are the eponymous tribal ancestors, heroes past and present, saints, prophets, orishas, and Ascended Masters believed to have once been human who are now clearly something more. In Latin, there was a distinction between *deus/dea*, referring to gods and goddesses of divine descent, and *divus/diva*, the term for humans (such as the emperors and empresses) who had been deified after they died ("Divus" Britannica.com). Such divinities were in some cases more popular than the true gods on the assumption that although less powerful, they were more likely to listen to prayers from their descendants or those who lived on their lands.

Although they are treated as other cultures treat gods, the orishas of Africa, such as Shango, who is said to have been the fourth ruler of the city of Oyo, are officially held to be humans whose virtues, or sometimes whose sufferings, raised them to mythic status. Their *patakis*, or teaching tales, include stories set in both the human and mythological world. This dual nature creates a precedent for adding contemporary culture heroes such as Elvis, Martin Luther King Jr., Kennedy, and Princess Diana to the altars.

The practice of interpreting the gods as deified mortals is called after the Greek philosopher Euhemerus, who considered all myths to be history in disguise (Spence 1921, 42). This approach allowed Snorri Sturluson to write about the Norse gods without running afoul of the Church. He euhemerized the gods in the *Ynglinga saga* at the beginning of his *Heimskringla*, a history of the Norse kings, where he tells how Freyr inherited Odin's rule and after his death received offerings.

When all the Swedes marked that Frey was dead, but that good seasons and peace still continued, they believed that it would be so, so long as Frey was in Sweden; therefore, they would not burn him, but called him the god of the earth, and ever after sacrificed to him, most of all for good seasons and peace.

(Sturluson 1990, 11)

When Saxo Grammaticus wrote his history of the kings of Denmark, he included the story of the wise king Fróði, who also continued to receive offerings after he died. There were several kings of Denmark whose names sound like titles of Freyr. Were they local deities believed to have once been men, or were they humans who became deified and identified with their god?

In Greece men sacrificed at the tombs of the legendary heroes and raised them to the status of demigod. In the North, the distinction between the dead and the gods could be unclear. Anyone who claims descent from someone in the British royal line can also claim descent from Woden. Viewed thus, the gods *are* ancestors. But not all of the Mighty Dead are heroes. In the Celtic lands, the dead may become part of the host of Faerie. In Scandinavia, ancestors become the *alfar* and *disir*, the male and female guardian spirits of the family line. In the Christian traditions, especially the Catholic and Orthodox, this role is played by the saints. However friendly we may become with our gods, there is also a sense of awe, a recognition that they are an order of magnitude greater than we, whereas we can address the saints, heroes, or legendary ancestors as highly respected friends.

Personal Ancestors

Closer still are the dead who might be expected to take a personal interest because we are their relatives. These are people whose graves we can visit, whose names we remember. In some shamanic traditions, ancestors are among the helping spirits. The dead mother to whose grave mound the young hero goes to ask counsel in *Svipdagsmál* or who intervenes from heaven in fairy tales is a familiar figure. Ancestor spirits still guard us today.

In *Grandmother Moon,* Zsuzsanna Budapest tells how her grandmother's spirit kept her from being killed during the Hungarian Revolution.

With the rise of the Spiritualist movement, our personal dead became popular sources of inspiration and counsel, and they are often quite willing to speak through a medium. At a New Age convention I once picked up a button that read JUST BECAUSE THEY'RE DEAD DOESN'T MEAN THEY'RE SMART; but my experience with the dead who speak through seers in oracular sessions has been that in most cases they are more open-minded and supportive than they were when they were alive.

Religions may change, but the instinct to honor our dead is still strong. A collection of silver-framed photos with a vase of flowers is an ancestor shrine. After 9/11, the wall around the site of the Twin Towers became a backdrop for shrines. Pagans who have been unable to talk to their parents about religion for years can find in stories about their dead relatives something to share, and many who report on their near-death experiences mention seeing their loved ones waiting to welcome them.

In her book *Divine Horsemen: The Living Gods of Haiti*, Maya Deren describes the Haitian ritual in which the *gwo-bonanj* of a departed relative is called back:

> A year and a day following the death of a person, the family undertakes to reclaim his soul from the waters of the abyss below the earth and to lodge it in a govi where it may be henceforth invoked and consulted in the event of illness or other difficulties and so may participate in all the decisions that normally unite the members of the family in counsel. Thus the aid of his knowledge, the disciplines of his moral authority, and the inspirations of his intelligence are reincorporated as a functioning force in the reality of his family's daily life.
>
> (Deren 1953, 46)

The *govi* is treated as a holy icon and given offerings. If this service brings results, it will continue, and as those who knew the person in life die off, the spirit will become in effect a demigod, and possibly eventually be identified as a "path" or aspect of his head lwa.

Although many families have traditions that honor the ancestors, the worship is often implicit rather than focused. See Exercise 5.2 for suggestions on how to work with your ancestors of the flesh and spirit in a more intentional way.

Allies and Guardians

The final level of Power that may sometimes speak or act through us, as well as communicate *to* us, is the inner ally or guardian spirit. Today the concept is most familiar from Native American traditions and shamanism, in which the shaman works with and may take on the persona of an animal ally in trance, but animal totems or helpers are familiar from European folktales and Norse folklore, in which the *fylgja*, or "follower," appears in animal or human form. The Aztec call this being the *nagual* or *tonal*. It appears in English folklore as the familiar spirit. Among the Classical Greeks, the *daemon* filled this role. Note the daemon is not a "demon" in the sense of an evil spirit. Our confusion results from the fact that early Christian theologians identified any Power other than the Trinity, the saints, and the angels as being by definition demonic (some still do).

The most famous example of a relationship with a daemon is of course that of Socrates, whose belief in the entity that communicated with him was so vivid that he was accused of teaching the youth of Athens to believe in new daemons instead of the gods of Athens. He himself questioned this voice that spoke to him through dreams and divination and from within. His eventual conclusion was that this was the Muse of Philosophy, also identified with Eros and the soul.

According to Iamblichus, everyone has a daemon whose job it is to govern our spiritual development:

> As soon as the soul chooses him for leader the daemon immediately comes into charge of the completing of its vital endowments, and when it descends into the body, unites it with the body, and becomes the guardian of its common living principle. He likewise himself directs the private life of the soul, and whatever the conclusions we may arrive at by inference and reasoning, he himself imparts to us the principles. We think

and do just such things as he brings to us by way of thought. He guides human beings thus continually till through the sacred theurgic discipline we shall obtain a god to be guardian and leader of the soul.

(Iamblichus 1911, chapter 17)

Wights

Most traditional cultures are animists, believing that anything with an identity has a spirit, which in some cases can take a human form. This includes spirits of nature such as trees, waterfalls, mountains, and stones, and those who inhabit man-made objects such as mills, boats, cars, and homes. In Japan, they are called the *kami*. The traditional word in English is "wight." Making offerings to these beings is an ancient practice. I would have said that they do not possess, but I have heard of a situation in which a storm spirit grabbed a medium and sent her sprinting for the nearest body of water, shedding clothing as she ran.

Practice
Exercise 5.1: Surveying the Field

The connection we make with a Power through possessory trance is a relationship, and anyone who has ever gone looking for someone to date knows how hard finding a good match can be. If you are already active in a specific tradition or faith community, you will probably want to work with a Power from its pantheon. If you are eclectic in your practice, or your tradition does not support this kind of work, you can look more widely. While most Powers function best within their own cultural context, there are some, such as Isis, Brigid, and Kuan Yin, who have cheerfully adapted to a variety of spiritual environments.

Read up on the myths of at least three cultures. No matter which tradition you work in, seeing how gods and goddesses from different pantheons interact and behave will help you to understand which elements are specific to the deity and the culture and which are more generally characteristic of Powers. You can start with works that include myths from many cultures, such as that of Edith Hamilton, but be aware that many older retellings are colored by nineteenth-century interpretations. Once you focus on a particular culture, look for good recent secondary sources, and eventually primary sources as well. You can also, of course, find a great deal of information on the Internet, but there's a lot of UPG out there. Read critically and look for sources with respectable bibliographies.

A sample of available secondary and primary sources follows.

Germanic

Edda, Snorri Sturluson (13th century). Translated and edited by Anthony Faulkes. New York: Everyman, 1987.

The Poetic Edda. Translated and edited by Andy Orchard. New York: Penguin Books, 2011.

Norse Mythology: A Guide to Gods, Heroes, Rituals, and Beliefs. John Lindow. New York: Oxford University Press, 2001.

Our Troth, Vol. I. The Troth. N.p.: Lulu.com, 2005.

Greek

The Penguin Book of Classical Myths. Jenny March. New York: Penguin, 2009.

Metamorphoses. Ovid (8th century). Available at classics.mit.edu/Ovid/metam.html.

Celtic

Celtic Mythology. Proinsias MacCana. London: Hamlyn, 1970.

Ancient Irish Tales. Edited by Peete Cross and Clark Harris Slover. New York: Barnes & Noble, 1936.

Egyptian

Egyptian Mythology: A Guide to the Gods, Goddesses, and Traditions of Ancient Egypt. Geraldine Pinch. New York: Oxford University Press, 2004.

Graeco-Egyptian Mythology. Tony Mierzwicki and Donald Kraig. Stafford, UK: Megalithica Books, 2006.

Eternal Egypt. Richard J. Reidy. Bloomington, IN: iUniverse, 2011.

Native American

American Indian Myths and Legends. Edited by Richard Erdoes and Alfonso Ortiz. New York: Pantheon, 1985.

Hindu

Dictionary of Hindu Lore and Legend. Anna L. Dallapiccola. New York: Thames & Hudson, 2002.

Mahabharata. Translated by Kisari Mohan Ganguli (1883–1896). Available at www.sacred-texts.com/hin/maha/.

Exercise 5.2: Honoring the Ancestors

Part One: Make a Family Tree

Gather as much information about your family as you can, including talking to older relatives, and construct a family tree. Make it the centerpiece for an ancestor altar. Add photos of those relatives you particularly wish to honor and other decorations such as flowers. You may also include photos of people from your extended family, close friends, and ancestors of the spirit (writers or teachers or others) now departed whose work helped to make you the person you are—or you can give them an altar of their own. Picture frames with mats that have spaces for a number of pictures are a convenient way to organize the collection.

Light the candle and say the names, offering your love and respect. You may also use a prayer such as the following, adapted by Ember Cooke from my original.

> Our mighty Mothers here we honor
> from womb to womb since world's beginning,
> and Fathers of the flesh and spirit,
> sacred seed itself renewing,
> mindful Mentors, wisdom winning,
> sacred Skalds and holy Heroes,
> kind Companions, comfort bringing,
> faithful Friends and helping Healers.
> Beloved Dead who came before us,
> ancestors, be with us always.

Part Two: Have Dinner with the Dead

Once you've done your research and created an altar, have dinner with the Dead. Dig out the old family recipes or research the food of the lands from which your forebears came. Move the photos to your dining table and cook a traditional family meal. Set places for yourself and any (living) family members who are joining you and put out another plate for the ancestors. During dinner, tell stories about the people in the photos. Then sit for a time in silence, listening for whatever messages they may give you in return.

A dinner of this kind works well on Hallowe'en, All Souls' Day, or All Saints' Day. It is also good to honor your ancestors on Thanksgiving and at Yule and other holidays with a strong family tradition.

6

DIVINE RELATIONSHIPS

And didn't you know me, Pallas Athena the daughter of Zeus,
Always standing beside you, and guardian in all your labours? . . .
Well, here I am again to make plans for you!
—Homer, *The Odyssey*

A connection with one of the Powers can become as intimate and as long-lasting as a love affair, and it should be approached with the same care. Sometimes, of course, it is the Power Who chooses us, and we may or may not be able (or want) to say no, but however the relationship begins, it is we who decide how to respond.

A divine relationship may be "much like a marriage commitment while still liking and respecting all the other people in your life" (Harrow 2003, xii). In some traditions a medium is only allowed to carry the Power to whom she is initiated, whereas in others someone with training can bring through whatever Power is called. Like those who practice polyamory, people who get involved with more than one deity have to apportion time and energy (and altar space) so that everyone gets His or Her due. But whatever the nature of the connection, if it is to become a rewarding relationship it needs to be tended and developed.

Getting to Know You

In the last chapter you were asked to start reading mythology. Now it is time to choose a Power. If you are not already involved with a particular god or spirit, this will help you to find one who seems compatible. This is not a permanent commitment. The Power you work with while you are developing these skills may become a part of your life, may stay with you for a while and then pass you on to another deity, or may remain connected only while you are working with the material in this book.

When you choose a Power, review your issues. Are you attracted to this being because He or She has dealt with the same kind of problems you have? For instance, a man with an autistic child might work with Obatala, who is the patron of handicapped people because when he had the job of creating human bodies he got drunk and made some of them with deformities. It is good to choose a Power who can understand your problems, but that can make it harder to distinguish between that Power's opinions and your own.

People connect with the Powers that will become their close companions in many different ways. Geoffrey Miller unexpectedly encountered Anubis while he was trying to meditate on the Greek god Pan (Miller 2003, 4). My first significant encounter with Odin occurred during one of Michael Harner's shamanic workshops, when we were instructed to seek a teacher in human form. I was already interested in the religion of the North, but I knew enough about Odin not to go looking for him on purpose. If I had realized that agreeing to become His student was going to turn into a permanent relationship I might have said no, but then I would have missed some of my life's most rewarding experiences.

Although Odin is my primary Power, with his encouragement I have learned how to work with a number of others. If you are already close to one of the gods, you might find it easier to understand the process if you use these exercises to develop a relationship with a different one.

Here are a number of considerations that may help guide your choice:

- Culture—the Power comes from a tradition you are already practicing, a culture with which you are comfortable, or one that strongly attracts you.

- Similarity—the Power is like you in gender, personality, apparent age, or interests.

- Polarity—the Power attracts you because He or She has strengths and characteristics that complement and balance your own.

- Sympathy—you are strongly moved by elements in the Power's myths.

- Synchronicity—you keep finding references to the Power, or encountering His or Her symbols.

- Connection—the Power appears in your dreams, or you feel His or Her presence everywhere. Associated music or colors become very attractive.

See Exercise 6.1 for a process that may help you decide which Power(s) to pursue.

Background Check

Browsing though different pantheons and mythologies is something like going to a mixer where you meet a lot of people. Now it's time to develop a relationship. How do you prepare?

If you were dating someone from a different culture you would want to know as much as possible about his or her upbringing, language, and customs. The same rule applies to getting friendly with a Power. To know that Brigid is a goddess of poetry, healing, and goldsmithing means little unless you understand what those things meant to the people who first worshiped her.

Time, money, and time to read are limited, so how do you choose? The Internet offers a lot of free material, but quality and credibility vary. Start with websites that have reading lists and footnotes, especially those citing works written by people in the culture and time period you are looking at. If a number of sites recommend the same work, it might be worth investigating. You can also find reading lists on the websites of organizations devoted to particular traditions. Read as much as you can, including history, ethnography, and educational books about daily life in the culture. That background will help you to evaluate material on contemporary practice.

The following websites have reading lists for some of the cultures that seem to be of the greatest interest. Look for sites that reference books by reputable scholars, or you can compare lists and list the major ones they agree on—websites come and go.

- Celtic: IMBAS Reading List—*www.imbas.org/imbas/readlist.html*.

- Greek: Temenos Theon's Hellenic Reading List—*www.temenostheon.com/books.html*.

- Kemetic (Egyptian): The Twisted Rope, "Kemeticism"—*thetwistedrope.wordpress.com/kemeticism*. (Not that the works of Wallis Budge are accessible and inspirational; however, some of his conclusions and translations are questioned by scholars and modern Kemetic practitioners.)

- Germanic: The Troth—*www.thetroth.org*.

- Afro-Diasporic: Questia, "Santeria"—*www.questia.com/library/religion/other-practices/santeria*. This list mostly covers studies of contemporary practice.

Altar Work

Once you have some background, it is time to invite the Power into your life. In romantic terms, this might be the equivalent of asking someone over for dinner and conversation.

Make a place in your house for an altar. It should be big enough to accommodate an image, a candle, and the other items that you will inevitably end up collecting. If you have small children or cats, find a space that cannot be easily reached (unless your altar is to Bast or Freyja, in which case access by cats is a feature). If all else fails, try a box shelf attached to a wall. Another way to keep things safe is to make a shrine from a cardboard box, painted or covered with shelf paper and lined with cloth, with a door that closes. A box can also be used to make a folding travel shrine.

Figure 5: Box shrine for Kuan Yin

Begin with an altar cloth in an appropriate color or combination—either those prescribed by tradition or a color or pattern that you strongly associate with the Power. For instance, if your Power is strongly involved with the natural world, try green or a print with leaves or flowers. Look on the Internet for a good picture or statue. Add a glass container for a votive candle or tea light in an appropriate color. Include a cup or dish for offerings.

With time, you will undoubtedly add things. Miniature tools or weapons and images of animals associated with the Power are common choices, as is a vase for flowers. Be aware that as your ability to "hear" the Power improves, you may find yourself impulse buying—and the impulse is not your own. If you get a strong sense that Osun would really love a gold-plated bud vase for her altar, ask her to bring you wealth to pay for it.

Figure 6: Home Odin altar

Once your altar is in place, start working with it. Light the candle and offer a small portion of food or drink. This could be a cookie, an apple, or a shot glass full of alcohol. If possible, it should be something known to appeal to the Power or the culture, such as mead or beer for the Norse gods, wine for the Greeks, or rum for most of the African powers. (Do not offer alcohol to Obatala or Kuan Yin.) The Afro-Diasporic faiths have a rich tradition of food and drink for each orisha (in some cases, for each path of each Power). Gods from other pantheons tend to be less particular. It can be interesting (albeit expensive) to simply go into a good liquor store and see what appeals. If you have nothing specific, offer whatever you are drinking or a glass of clean water.

Explain that you are making this offering to honor the Power, and ask for a blessing. Sit quietly and watch the flicker of candlelight on the Power's image. Do the features seem to move? Think about the stories you have been reading. Ask the Power to teach you what they mean. Relax, slow and count your breathing, and let your mind drift. Note the ideas that appear. After a few minutes, breathe more quickly and return to ordinary consciousness. Write down any insights that came to you. If you have trouble staying focused, work through the exercises in chapter 4 of *Trance-Portation*.

At this point you should also start looking for or working on a piece of jewelry or some other wearable item that represents the Power. This could be a pin or pendant, perhaps of a sacred animal or plant, or a necklace of beads in the right colors. Wear it when you do your altar work and meditations. With time, the simple act of putting on this piece will initiate the process of aligning your energy with that of the Power.

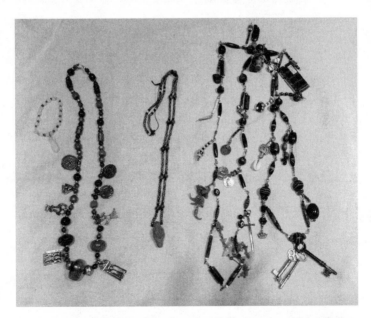

Figure 7: Kuan Yin working bracelet, Odin ritual necklace, daily Nana necklace, ritual necklace for 24 paths of Exu

Invitation

Once you are comfortable with sitting with the Power, you can move on to more formal invocation and praise. The simplest format is to simply chant the name of the Power or a simple phrase, such as "Hail Hermes, ward my way."

If prayers survive from the culture in which you are working, use them as models. For instance, the pattern for the Homeric hymns is as follows:

I begin to sing of (*name*), son or daughter of (*name*),

who (*one of the myths about the deity*).

And now, (*description and epithets, statement of request*).

And so, farewell, (*name and epithet*),

And now I will remember you and another song also.

For an online translation of all of the Homeric hymns, see Theoi Greek Mythology, "Homeric Hymns 5–33"—www.theoi.com/Text/HomericHymns3.html.

A late Icelandic poet opposing the conversion to Christianity began with an invocation to Thor as giant-killer, likening the giants to the priests. The Germanic pattern for an invocation was to list the Power's achievements and then make a request.

A formula for invocatory prayer can be summarized as,

Hail (*best-known name*), (*descriptive epithet*),

Child of (*parent*), lover of (*spouse*)

You who dwell in (*name of hall*),

You who (*summarize several relevant deeds*)

With your (*characteristic tool or weapon*)

Come swiftly to aid me

As I (*summarize problem being addressed*)

(Or, I hail you and welcome you to my home.)

If these forms feel awkward, use blank verse, rhymed couplets, or whatever inspires you.

Anyone who has been to a ceremony in one of the African traditions knows that songs are a very effective way to connect worshiper and deity. Collect music that reminds you of the Power. My playlist for Odin includes everything from Wagner's "Entry of the Gods into Valhalla" from *Das Rheingold* to the Doors' "Riders on the Storm" and Frank Sinatra's "My Way."

Better still, write original songs in praise of your Power. A song with a complicated tune and many verses is good for praise. A chant with no more than four lines and a repetitive melody can induce trance. You will need both. You can borrow a tune for the praise song, but the tune for the chant should be original, or something so obscure you are unlikely to hear it unexpectedly. We had to deal with this issue when my friend Lorrie wrote a trance song for Freyja to the melody of Beethoven's "Ode to Joy," which at the time was also her cell phone's ringtone. Exercise 6.2 includes guidelines for incorporating prayers and songs into a weekly practice.

The Powers will also appreciate pictures, sculpture, beadwork, and any other art they inspire in you. I do not know whether creative people are more likely to be attracted to this practice, but people who get involved with the gods often take up some form of art or craft.

Your Place, Not Mine

There is a point in many romantic comedies when the couple looks into each other's eyes and murmurs, "Your place or mine?" When I lose or suppress awareness of my body in order to journey to the world of the gods in meditation, I am going to "Your place." Possession, in which I invite the Power to occupy my mind and body, is an invitation to "mine."

Journeying or otherwise shifting one's focus from our world to that of the Power through vision or visualization is an example of "kataphatic prayer." This is the Way of Affirmation of Images, in which we use words and symbols to illuminate various aspects of the Divine. In Christianity, this way is often considered inferior to the Way of Negation of Images discussed in chapter 4, but because when we are practicing polytheism we are already experiencing the Absolute through its many manifestations we consider such practices an excellent way to connect with the Powers. For more information and exercises for learning this skill, see chapters 5–8 of *Trance-Portation*.

Creation of the Scene

Contemplation of sacred images, especially complex paintings filled with imagery such as the Tibetan thangka (scroll paintings), can be a very powerful practice. Medieval religious paintings and sculptures were also used in this way, and the meditations on the Stations of the Cross are still part of Roman Catholic practice today. You will already have collected some images for your altar. Now is the time to go back to the books or the Internet and gather more. In Exercise 6.3 you will find suggestions for using images to visit the "world" of the Powers. In the first part, you will meditate on the meaning of an image. In the second, you will deepen your contemplation until you can enter the world of the picture and participate in the action. This latter is a technique best known to European culture from the *Spiritual Exercises* of Saint Ignatius of Loyola.

Journeying to the Astral Temple

By this time, you should know a fair amount about the Power and the culture from which He or She comes. The next practice involves creating your own path working or spirit journey to visit Their Otherworld. The structure of such a journey can include the following stages.

Visualize a Starting Point

After you have found a comfortable position and relaxed and slowed your breathing, one popular way to start is by visualizing a familiar place outdoors. This should be somewhere you have visited often enough to remember not only its appearance but also its sounds, smells, and textures. It should be a place where you feel safe and happy. Some people who journey regularly like to create an astral "base camp" furnished with tools and garments for their travels.

Find a Path

Once you are focused, look around you for a path or doorway. When I first began this work, I would start from my bedroom, where I visualized an additional doorway in my closet that opened to a downward staircase. If you are starting from an outdoor location, find a pathway or trail that leads into a forest and begins to go downhill.

When I journey, the path through the forest leads to a plain whose center rises the World Tree, an image found in many cultures that serves as a central axis and point of reference. It is visible from everywhere and will help you find your way back if you get lost. It is important to make a note of the landmarks as you journey, as you will want to retrace your steps on your way back home.

Travel to the Country of the Gods

When you reach the plain and the World Tree, look around you for different kinds of terrain. Select the one that matches the homeland of the Power you are seeking and move toward it. If you are working in a tradition that has a well-defined "map" of the Otherworld, use that to build up your image.

Find the Power's Home

Once you have reached the right landscape, use the images from your research to locate the kind of palace, temple, or place in nature where the Power you are working with is likely to be found. You might look for Hecate in a Greek temple or at midnight at a triple crossroad. Freyja seems to divide her time between Sessrúmnir, her house at Folkvangar in Asgard, and Vanaheim. One would look for Ogun at his forge in the jungle, Isis in her temple or the papyrus swamps of the Nile Delta, and Coyote in the mountains of Arizona or California.

Look for the Power

When you have reached the place, see if the Power is at home. Sometimes one needs to pass through several levels—gateway, mudroom or portico, interior space, and finally the altar room or high seat. I find it useful to look for a light source, such as a hearth fire, altar flame, or shaft of sunlight, and visualize the image of the Power limned in light which then solidifies until I see the god in full color.

Conversation

If you have been reading your journey onto a tape, this is the point at which you will leave a gap of three to five minutes. This is the time for you to articulate any questions you have brought with you and listen for the Power's reply. At first it may be enough to simply be in the Power's presence. Repeated journeys will make it easier to hold on to the vision and hear the words.

Return

When you feel that the interview is over, thank the Power and retrace your steps from the building through the landscape to the plain. Stop to reorient yourself at the World Tree, and then take the path up through the forest and back to the place from which you began. Take a few moments to settle back into your body. Breathe more quickly, move, and open your eyes.

You may find it helpful to write out your journey and record it onto a tape, leaving an empty space at the point at which you are communicating with the Power. Guide yourself by playing the tape each time you journey until you have memorized the sequence.

Practice
Exercise 6.1: Speed Dating

If you have not already chosen a Power to work with, identify three deities that interest you:

- One who is like you in ways such as gender, the age at which s/he is usually portrayed, or personality;

- One who is very different, but attractive;

- One who is a bit outside your comfort zone.

Draw or download from the Internet an image of each Power.

On three successive nights, light a tea light in front of one of the pictures. You can also offer a glass or cup with a drink of something appropriate. Contemplate the picture and reflect on what you know about Him or Her. Focus on the details of the picture, then close your eyes and reproduce the image in your mind. Repeat this until you can see the picture with your eyes closed. Chant an affirmation such as

> Holy (*name*), I greet you.
> (*Name*), I honor you.
> (*Name*), I ask your blessing.

Keep a notebook beside your bed, and when you wake up the next morning write down any dreams. During the day that follows, watch for things that remind you of the Power.

During the week after you have done this, continue to record interesting events and insights in your notebook. At the end of the week review what you have written. Can you see a pattern? Continue working with whichever Power has made His or Her presence most apparent.

Exercise 6.2: Date Night

On the same day each week, light your altar candle, make an offering, say the prayer you have written, and sing your song. Once a week, read one of the myths, folktales, or patakis in which the Power appears. During that week meditate on the story. What are the motivations of the beings involved? Is there a lesson to be learned? What relevance does this story have to your own life? (If at first there seems to be none, expand your meditations to include family and community.)

Exercise 6.3: The Family Album

When you visit the home of someone in whom you are interested, a photo album left out on the coffee table will inevitably attract your attention. Looking through the pictures can tell you a lot about the individual. You can get the same kind of information by looking at pictures of the gods.

Go back to your books and the Internet and scan or download as many images of your Power as you can. Look for pictures of statues or portraits and illustrations from mythology books or the grand mythological paintings from European museums. Add the portraits to your altar and spend some time contemplating each one. How similar is the image to the way you see the Power? What do the artists' interpretations of the figure tell you about how the Power is viewed by others? What symbols accompany the figure? What can you learn from those associated symbols?

Now take a painting of a scene from one of the myths and expand it so that you can see the details clearly. Relax, slow your breathing, and contemplate the picture. Close your eyes and reproduce it in your imagination. Look again and find more details. When you have thought about the significance of the elements in the scene, try to imagine what lies beyond the borders of the picture. If you could see past the left side of the picture, what would it look like? If you were standing there and looking toward the scene, what would you see? Continue to do this until you can close your eyes and see the scene around you. Now look for motion. Let the figures come to life and watch the event unfold. When the exercise has come to a conclusion, turn away, and let the images fade. Begin to breathe more quickly, open your eyes, and return to ordinary consciousness.

Think about what you saw. How did it make you feel? Did it leave you with new insights into the meaning of the story being portrayed? When you have done this with a few paintings, try imagining additional scenes for which you don't have an illustration.

7

TERMS OF ENDEARMENT

The infinite abyss can only be filled by an infinite and immutable
object, that is to say, only by God Himself.
—Pascal, Pensée #425

The search for Something, or Someone, that will fill the abyss that Pascal references above is the "god hunger" that impels many of us to seek an intimate relationship with a spiritual being. Some friendships are for life, while others last while the friends share a goal. In the same way, although spiritual involvements may deepen into a lifetime relationship, sometimes we work with one Power to deal with a particular issue and then move on to another. There are also times when one god hands a devotee over to a different deity.

For many, working through the material in the previous chapter along with the training presented in part four will be sufficient preparation for carrying that Power in possessory trance. However, if your real goal in learning possessory work is to get closer to a Power, you will find in this chapter examples and information that will help you.

There are many ways to relate to the Divine. Some traditions emphasize faith and some focus on works. Some people, like Linus in the *Peanuts* cartoons, feel that the most essential quality in worship is sincerity, while others, like the Romans who believed that if a mistake was made in a ceremony the ritual had to be started over from the beginning, require strict adherence to the rules. Furthermore, Powers that come from living traditions are accustomed to being treated in specific ways.

Learn all you can about the ways in which any Power you are interested in is or was worshipped. The Powers may tolerate ignorance, but when information is available not making an effort to find it is less forgivable. If you are working with Someone who has not been honored in centuries, you may have to explain why you cannot sacrifice a hecatomb of heifers in your backyard. That said, unless the Power is one of the more wrathful deities (whom you might want to think twice about getting involved with anyway), if you do your best and are respectful, most, like Kuan Yin, who reproved the monks who rejected the meat offered by the ignorant peasants, will accept offerings in the spirit in which they were made.

Interaction with a Power can play out in a number of ways. In her introduction to *Devoted to You*, Judy Harrow described the four "Pagan henotheists" who contributed accounts of their practice to the book. She described herself as a "serial henotheist" who worked closely with several deities at different stages in her career, "depending on which issues were focal for me at that time."(Harrow 2003, xii). Alexei Kondratiev and Maureen Reddington-Wilde were Celtic and Hellenic Reconstructionists, respectively, while Judy and Geoffrey Miller honored their deities within Wiccan ritual structures. Harrow also observed that Geoffrey and Maureen

> perceive the Gods as self-aware entities that exist independently of humankind, while Alexei and I tend to perceive them more as metaphors through which humans try to comprehend patterns of energy and meaning that are ultimately beyond our ability to define. Maureen writes about using rituals that Aphrodite will recognize from ancient days, because that's the most likely way to attract her presence. In contrast, I believe that Mother Nature is always present, and that the only thing that changes in ritual is my awareness of Her Presence.
>
> (Ibid., xiii)

These are all valid concepts of deity; however, it is very hard to embody an abstraction. As we move toward possessory trance, we become increasingly aware of the Powers as persons to whom we can relate in many ways.

Relationship Models

As the Greeks are so fond of pointing out in their plays, the gods are stronger than we are. Whatever the relationship, the human will be the junior partner. They are certainly *bigger*, and the better we grow at perceiving Their presence, the more we realize that the only way to connect is to lower our barriers and let Them in. Just as the Powers appear to us, for the most part, in human form, our relationships with Them are modeled on the ways in which we relate to other humans. Of course, not all human relationships are healthy ones. If our work with a Power is to be productive we should model it on positive human interactions.

Before you go further, take a few moments to consider your own relationship history as described in Exercise 7.1 at the end of this chapter.

Child to Parent

One of the most popular models for relationship to a god is that between a father or mother and a child. God the Father is the senior deity in the Christian pantheon. In the Afro-Diasporic religions, one is known as the "child" of one's head orisha. Iamblichus refers to men as the children, nurslings, and pupils of the gods. (Iamblichus 1911, chapter 10). In Wicca, it is common (though neither universal nor required) to have a patron or matron deity, or one of each with whom you work as a pair. A deity does not have to be a father god or a mother goddess to take this role.

A child–parent relationship with a Power will inevitably be colored by the way you relate to your own parents. Someone who had a kind father or a nurturing mother will find it easy to believe in a loving deity. Those whose parents were harsh may react to the strong personality of a Power with rebellion or fear. On the other hand, there are those who find that the love of a parental Power makes up for early deprivation.

In comparison to the Powers we are all no more than children, yet in every human culture parents strive to raise their children to become strong and self-reliant adults. I cannot believe that the gods wish anything less for those whom they love. If They are sometimes hard on us it is because as good parents They are pushing us to achieve our full potential.

Lover to Beloved

Another popular relationship is that of lover and beloved. Given that sexual union is the most ecstatic connection that most people ever know, it is not surprising that so much mystical poetry, from the Song of Solomon onward, uses not only romantic but erotic imagery to describe the relationship. The first flush of connection, especially, can inspire a rapturous enthusiasm like the beginning of a love affair, when everything you see and hear reminds you of your beloved.

Especially in cultures in which marriage is the only permissible relationship between adults of different genders, this relationship can result in a spiritual marriage. Catholic nuns become brides of Christ, walking down the aisle dressed in white and receiving a ring. Shamans and other spiritual workers may acquire spirit wives or husbands through visions or dreams. The spirit spouse acts as a tutelary spirit and helper (Espin and Nickoloff 2007, 1315b).

In polytheistic religions, priests or priestesses may have relationships or be considered spouses of their gods. In *Flateyjarbók*, a medieval collection of Icelandic sagas, we find a temple in Sweden where

> the image of Frey had been made so powerful that the devil spoke with men out of the carved idol, and a young and beautiful woman was given to Frey to serve him. It was the inhabitants' belief that Frey was alive, as he seemed to be in some respects, and they supposed that he would need to have marital relations with his wife. She mostly had to take care of Frey's temple sanctuary and everything that belonged to it, along with Frey.
>
> (Waggoner 2010, 35)

In the *Jómsvíkinga* saga, Haakon Jarl of Hålogaland has a temple to a goddess called Thorgerda Hölgabrudhr, who aids him in battle and is known as his wife.

In Appendix A of *Divine Horsemen*, Maya Deren describes the practice of loa (divine energy) marriage as reported by Milo Rigaud, in which a male devotee may marry Erzulie, or a female one of the male loa, such as Dan-ba-lah, Ogou, or Guédé (Deren 1953, 263). The loa may demand that this marriage take place before the devotee marries a mortal spouse. The ceremony is modeled on a civil marriage; a contract is drawn up and signed and vows are exchanged, followed by a reception in which all of the loa join in.

The terms of the contract generally provide that the loa will protect and provide for the spouse, and that the spouse will serve and honor the loa. He or she may promise to spend one night a week in a separate bed with his or her divine mate. Such contracts must be written carefully, if necessary with the help of a mediator, to prevent either party from making unreasonable or impossible demands. In fact, I would recommend negotiating the contract with the Power through two different mediums in separate sessions, as well as speaking to the Power through the bride or groom.

In recent years the devotional path of god-spouse has been appearing in pagan traditions. Beth Lynch, who is a wife of Odin as well as a seeress, provides some excellent advice on her blog, "Wytch of the North":

> A deity marriage comes to pass as a result of 1) years of devotion on your part that naturally and gradually turn into something deeper and more intimate, or 2) a deity's sudden decision to actively pursue and court you—which is, believe me, an obvious and undeniable state of events. If this happens to you there will be no need to consult a seidhkona or reader; there will be no room for doubt left in your mind . . . Like a human marriage, a deity marriage will transform your life, not only in the dreamy-blissful ways you're envisioning, but also in practical terms: your existing human relationships may fall apart under the strain of your new commitment and you may be called upon to endure hardships, loneliness and poverty for the sake of your Beloved. And *unlike* human marriage, for

its very existence a deity marriage requires that you remain open, constantly, to your divine Spouse.

(Lynch 2013)

The path of the lover or spouse is usually modeled on the way such relationships work in the devotee's society. In the past it was assumed that the divine spouse would be of the opposite gender. But gods have same-sex relationships in many mythologies. Today, when equal access to marriage is becoming so widely accepted in our human society, the assumption that a divine marriage is heterosexual may change.

Just as your relationship with your parents affects a relationship with a parental deity, how you relate to a Power as a spouse or lover may depend on your romantic history. For some, previous positive relationships make it easier to connect in this way with a god. Others may turn to a god because of disappointment with humans. Whatever your motivations, you will need to put the same effort into maintaining your divine relationship as you do in mortal romances. You may not have a separate bed to sleep in, but you can establish a "date night" on which you focus on your god.

To Lynch's comments I would add that if you feel you are called to make this kind of commitment to your Power, first do some serious thinking. If previous romantic relationships with humans failed, was it because you always belonged to the god, or because you don't yet know how to deal with commitment? If you have a human spouse, do you both understand the rules of polyamory well enough to manage what is, in effect, a dual relationship? And can you accept that your divine Beloved has other lovers?

Friend to Friend

A third model for a divine relationship is *philia*, that of friend to friend. As C. S. Lewis points out in *The Four Loves,* while lovers gaze at each other, friends stand side by side. This is not to imply that a god-friend considers himself the god's equal, but that the relationship is one of mutual respect and often of commitment to a shared goal.

In the *Eyrbyggja saga* 4, a chieftain called Thorolf Mostrarskegg is called *vinur Thors,* the friend of Thor. When the king pressures him to convert to Christianity, he inquires of "Thor, his dear friend [*ástvin*], whether he should reach a settlement with the king, or go away from the land and search for another destiny [*ørlög*] for himself." We are not told exactly how Thor gives his response, but the answer is that Thorolf should go to Iceland. When he arrives he throws overboard the carved pillars from his high seat that had been in the temple and claims the land where they come to shore. Another Old Norse word for one's god is *fulltrui*, the fully trusted one. In this case, Thorolf trusts Thor to advise him. They move to Iceland together, and Thorolf continues the relationship in the new land.

Hávamál 44, in the *Elder Edda*, offers advice on keeping up a friendship that is as valid for a god-friend as it is for a human one:

> If you have a friend you know will be true,
> and from him you will get good,
> share your mind with him, and gifts exchange,
> and fare to find him often.

Interestingly enough, St. Teresa of Avila made a similar observation: "Mental prayer in my opinion is nothing else than an intimate sharing between friends; it means taking time frequently to be alone with Him who we know loves us" (Teresa of Avila 2008, 44). Whatever the nature of your relationship with your god, the connection will fade if you do not pay attention. Pour out a libation or put flowers on the altar. In your meditations, share your joys and fears. Open yourself to the help that the Power can give.

Be aware, however, that divine friendships, like human ones, may have rocky moments, especially when there are obstacles in the work you are doing together. In medieval Spain, saints were known as the "friends of God." After being bucked off her horse on her way to one of the monasteries God had told her to found, St. Teresa of Avila observed, "Dear Lord, if this is how you treat your friends, no wonder you have so many enemies" (Ibid.). Fortunately, when you have this kind of relationship, arguments with your divine friend are not only acceptable, they are expected.

The success of this relationship also may be affected by previous experience. How many people do you still know from your childhood?

From college? How often do you see them? How many best friends have you had? Often friendships fade because one or both friends move away or move on. If your friendships often end in quarrels or disillusionment, you need to do some serious thinking about what you are looking for in a relationship.

Sometimes we idealize new friends and are disappointed when they turn out to be only human after all. It is as easy to project your illusions onto a god as onto a man, and although a god may purposefully show himself to you in a guise you will find attractive, the Powers have their own agendas, and the relationship is much more likely to change you than it is to change the god.

Servant to Master

The servant to master category covers relationships that are by definition unequal. No matter how positive and supportive the connection may be, the Power is giving the orders and the devotee obeys.

Employee to Employer

Somewhere between the relationship between friends and that between master and servant lies that of the trusted worker and the boss. It is common for those who are involved with a god to say that they "work with" the deity. Sometimes the "work" is the effort you are making to improve or heal yourself with the help of the Power. Some people, however, have a definite sense that they have been recruited to do specific jobs, which can be anything from saving the whales to bringing beauty into the world. Sometimes the Power releases the employee when a particular task is done. For others, the reward for a job well done is . . . another job.

This kind of relationship is likely to be especially attractive to those who seek meaning in their lives. In Lois McMaster Bujold's novel *Paladin of Souls*, Ista, who has already had a rocky relationship with one god, asks another, "What can the gods give *me*?" the answer is "Why work, sweet Ista!"(Bujold 2003, 170), a response that makes every god-bothered person who has read it hoot with laughter. When a god comes into your life, the first question is often "Why me?" Powerful as the gods may be, for some things they depend on human hands and voices. Knowing why the Power wants you gives you a purpose.

One specific type of employment is as a priest or priestess of a particular Power. This may be a temporary relationship, as when one takes the role of a goddess in a ritual; short-term, as when one spends a year working with a god in an initiatory sequence; or permanent, involving a formal ritual of dedication, as in a Christian ordination or an Afro-Diasporic head-washing.

Soldier to Commander

A more formal version of the commitment of servant to master is the relationship between a soldier and commander. It is generally established by formal oaths that may bind the "soldier" to a term of service or forever. This model is particularly popular with Heathens who vow to stand with the gods at Ragnarök.

This is the path of the spiritual warrior who is willing to make whatever sacrifice is required by his lord. Its great advantage is that once you have made the commitment, you no longer have to waste time trying to triage obligations. The god's orders come first. However, "God wills it!" has been the slogan of more than one crusade. Orders can be misinterpreted even in a human chain

ALLFATHER ODIN WANTS YOU!

Figure 8: Uncle Odin Wants You

of command. Those who follow the god-warrior's path must work even harder than usual to understand the true will of their gods.

Servant to Master

In ancient Greek, the concept of *latria* referred to the service that humans owed to the gods. To serve the gods was to live a good life, and part of one's duty was to the community of which the gods were a part. But a servant, though he may be part of the household, is not permanently linked by blood. The servant chooses to serve, is compensated for her labor, and may one day leave.

This is a useful model for those who need to work with, or for, a specific Power for a certain period. In some traditions, those with the required training and preparation can act as mediums for whatever Powers are needed in a ritual without being formally dedicated to Them. The title of *servitor* may be given to those who watch over mediums in trance for the Powers to make sure they have food, drink, and whatever else they need. Service freely given is all the more rewarding because it is voluntary.

Slave to Master
The concept of devotion to a god as slavery is an ancient one, expressing total devotion as well as awareness of the difference in power between humans and gods. In Romans 6:18, new Christians are told that they have been freed from slavery to sin and are now slaves of God. In recent years some pagan spirit workers have begun to use the term "god-slave" to describe their relationship with their deities, meaning that they will do whatever they think their Power requires of them without argument or delay.

In an essay titled "Terms of Service: A Little Polemic About Being a God-Slave," Galina Krasskova gives her perspective:

> I am a *godatheow*, a godslave. Most of the spiritworkers and shamans that I know are also godslaves—outright owned by their Deities. It goes with the territory . . . I belong, like property, to a Deity, in my case Odin. I have committed myself to this and I am content with this status quo. Yet at the same time, it is technically non-consensual, and if I ever decided I wanted to leave this relationship, I would not be permitted to do so. Within the bounds of this relationship I have a significant freedom, but I am not free in the way one unbound might be. My place is to serve.
>
> (Krasskova 2009)

This is, as Krasskova herself recognizes, a disturbing metaphor, but for some it seems to be the only way to express the totality of connection.

She also points out that the terminology of BDSM (bondage/dominance/sadomasochism) can be helpful in illuminating a complex dynamic in which submission is not self-hatred but a total offering.

This sense that one has no choice in the relationship is like a lover's belief that his love is fated, an explanation for attractions unexpected, perhaps inconvenient, but irresistible. God-slave is not, in my opinion, a relationship that should be sought out, but in some cases it may be the only term that seems to describe what is happening. I should observe, however, that other divine relationships may also lead to a sense of total and permanent connection, in which the presence of the Power is a fact as undeniable as sight or hearing. Mikki Fraser defines this state as being "god-owned," in the sense that children are in a permanent relationship with their parents but still have free will (Fraser October 22, 2013).

Living with Love

The downside of using human relationship models to explain our relationship to the Divine is that the very experiences that make such comparisons possible may bring with them trauma as well as joy. What all the models seem to have in common is love. Sometimes it's tough love, and if the Powers give us a job to do their love may not be disinterested, but one of the great rewards of sharing our consciousness with a patron deity through trance is sensing the love that Power feels for His or Her devotee. Perhaps the most fundamental requirement for establishing a positive relationship with a Power is the willingness to believe that you are worthy of love.

Practice
Exercise 7.1: Human Relationships

Take a few minutes to consider the following questions:

- What is your relationship history?

- How did/do you get along with each of the following: mother, father, siblings, lovers, spouse, friends, employers?

- Is the relationship ongoing? If not, how did it end?

- Who are the most important people in your life now, and why?

- What relationships are missing in your life?

- Which of your relationships have been the most rewarding?

Exercise 7.2: Divine Relationships

Now that you have thought about various kinds of relationship with the Powers, what would you consider the advantages and disadvantages of each model?

If you are beginning to work with a Power, can you tell which kind of relationship is developing?

Exercise 7.3: Identifying the Relationship

As you explore the myths, you will realize that the Powers are multifaceted as well as multidimensional. For example, the goddess Brigid is a tribal goddess who leads her people to victory, the generous saint who gives her father's goods away to feed the hungry, and the candle-crowned bringer of light at the end of winter. Thor is the mighty slayer of giants, the loving husband of Sif and the father of Thruth, and clever enough to outwit a dwarf. Athena is the teacher of crafts, the companion of heroes, and the defender of the city.

Visualize the Power as He or She appears in each story you read. How does each image make you feel? Does the image of Brigid feeding the hungry make you want to help Her or ask Her to feed you too? When you think about Athena, do you want to learn weaving or wisdom? Identifying the stories and aspects that attract you will help you understand how you might relate to the Power, at least for now—if the relationship deepens it will inevitably evolve.

8

COMMUNICATION

Now this began with me from my childhood; a certain voice, which always, when it comes, turns me aside from that which I am about to do, but never impels me to do anything. It is this which opposed my mixing in politics, and I think very wisely.
—Socrates, in Plato's *Apology*

Good relationships depend on good communication. Prayer and contemplation can elevate the spirit, but the relationship becomes infinitely more rewarding once information starts coming back down the line. For centuries the god-hungry have cried out to what seem to be deaf gods, while the god-bothered have begged them to be still. The ideal, I think, is to learn how to listen, and to do so often enough that we neither forget how to hear the gods nor force Them to come after us.

Listening to the Powers is one of the skills on the possessory continuum. One develops an awareness that the Power is near, a sense of emotion and perhaps of direction. Next come coherent thoughts or words that you feel are not your own, and you can remember the gist of the communication and make notes afterward. Once this kind of communication is well established, you can try writing down the input. This is easiest if you are a touch typist and can set up a computer file and type away without worrying about going off the page. Essentially, you are taking dictation in the same way as a court reporter or stenographer, for whom the words flow in through the ears and out through the fingertips.

The state in which a Power uses your senses to produce words is related to the fervor of inspiration in which an artist or craftsman looks up after several hours of intensive work and gazes in astonishment at the beauty that has been created by his hands. Sometimes the Power simply seizes the human consciousness, as in the stories of the prophets. Sometimes one is forced to let go by overwhelming need. But the experience is much more rewarding when it is the result of a trained and willing partnership.

To return to a metaphor used a little while ago, practices such as these are not so much a matter of choosing "Your place or mine" to get together as they are of getting on the phone or meeting somewhere in between. They are another step on the continuum that leads to full possession. They are found in almost every religion, are highly rewarding, and can be safely practiced by an individual working alone.

But where do such voices come from?

Angels or Illness?

In Samuel 3, the boy is awakened by a summons that sounds as if it has come from his master, the priest Eli. After this has happened three times, the priest decides the voice must be that of God and instructs Samuel to answer. When he does, a relationship begins that results in Samuel becoming the spiritual leader of Israel.

Until the modern period, auditory hallucinations, in which one hears words without any external stimulus, were believed to be of spiritual origin—depending on their subject matter, demonic or divine. Socrates was guided by his daemon until his death—some might say *to* his death, since his daemon did not tell him to flee his trial and execution. Joan of Arc heard, and later, saw, saints who told her that she must lead the armies of France against the English and told her how to do so.

Psychology has mostly focused on what happens when such hallucinations are associated with illness. While it is true that auditory hallucinations can accompany mental illnesses such as schizophrenia, and in some cases counsel violence, many otherwise ordinary people hear voices that cause them no problems at all. A growing number of "voice-hearers" whose experiences have not been negative are now beginning to band together to help each other deal with and learn from the phenomenon (Smith 2007).

But what if the goal *is* to hear voices or receive words? I would propose that just as our visual senses open our awareness to the Divine by allowing us to see not only objects but also Beauty, perhaps our inner monologue can also function as a mechanism for receiving ideas that originate outside ourselves.

Eloquent Locutions

One of the great spiritual conversationalists in the Christian tradition is St. Teresa of Avila, who began by avoiding prayer. Eventually, however, God started talking to her, and apparently He refused to stop:

> The words are very distinctly formed; but by the bodily ears they are not heard. They are, however, much more clearly understood than they would be if they were heard by the ear. It is impossible not to understand them, whatever resistance we may offer. When we wish not to hear anything in this world, we can stop our ears, or give attention to something else: so that, even if we do hear, at least we can refuse to understand. In this locution of God addressed to the soul there is no escape, for in spite of ourselves we must listen; and the understanding must apply itself so thoroughly to the comprehension of that which God wills we should hear, that it is nothing to the purpose whether we will it or not; for it is His will, Who can do all things.
>
> (St. Teresa of Avila 2008, 25)

What does a god sound like? Author Daniel B. Smith tells the story of Richard K., who suffered from hearing a variety of voices for over twenty years. However, he says that one of the voices was different: "It is like a sign. It is like an impression in my soul. I listen to the impression and I give words to it. I verbalize the impression" (Smith 2007, 87). This voice makes Richard feel better, and he interprets it as the voice of God.

Many modern theologians feel that "what (Divine voice-hearing and other religious experiences) can't withstand is the popular assumption that in being investigated and described by science, as they have been for several centuries now, religious experiences have lost their claims to spiritual veracity" (Smith 2007, 91). I would say that although our culture as a whole may be living through a period of "spiritual hearing loss," many of those involved in new and alternative religions are looking for "spiritual hearing aids." Helping people to find such aids is one of this book's goals.

Learning to Listen

To begin, we have to convince ourselves that the universe is not random, that there are Beings that want to communicate with us, and that we can perceive their meaning. One way to start is to seek synchronicity.

A method of prophecy used in ancient Israel was to articulate a question and then go outdoors and take the first object that the eye fixed upon as an omen. The seer shifted perception to interpret the scene symbolically, a response often expressed in poetic terms (Porter, in Loewe-Blacker 1981). Another method of prophecy is bibliomancy, in which you let a book (preferably a substantial one) fall open and without reading touch a paragraph. Now look at what you have picked and see if it gives you insight into your question. You can do the same thing by tuning the radio to a popular music station and seeking inspiration in the title or words of the song playing at that moment. Part of the process involves seeing something as significant. The other part is connecting what you need to know to what you have seen.

When you have had the experience of identifying an omen and later finding out that your interpretation was correct, you may begin to notice that those moments give you a unique sense of certainty. Once you have some confidence in your ability to receive information, you can begin developing ways to "hear" the Power you are working with.

T. M. Luhrmann, whose first book, *Persuasions of the Witch's Craft: Ritual Magic in Contemporary England*, was a fascinating study of how Pagans learn to think magically, has continued to explore religious experience in *When God Talks Back: Understanding the American Evangelical*

Relationship with God, a study of the Evangelical Christian Vintage movement, which teaches people how to hear God. As a comparative study I find it fascinating. The god that the Vintage Christians are learning to listen to is not the one Who talked to me, but the skills are the same.

For the Christian brought up to believe in a single supernal God, the idea that you can have a personal relationship with this all-powerful Being takes some getting used to. As I stated in chapter 4, my feeling is that God as an Absolute is best contacted in the state of consciousness in which the human is not aware of his or her *own* personal identity, much less the personality of the Power. To talk to the Christian God, I think you have to dial down the bandwidth to receive a more limited aspect of Him, or better still, address your prayers to God the Son. Polytheists don't have this problem. We already recognize that we can only interact with a part of the Absolute. The god-class beings discussed in chapter 5 have personalities that we can relate to.

As described by Luhrmann, members of the Vintage movement learn, through sermons, books, and talking to other members, how to differentiate the thoughts, mental images, and sensations that are placed in their minds by God from their own. They "use their own experience of how conversation happens and how they relate to trusted friends to pick out the thoughts and images in their minds that are like those ordinary moments, but different in certain ways" (Luhrmann 2012, 47).

Vintage members, like the followers of many other religious traditions, are told to go to a private place, address their prayers to God, and open their minds to receive an answer. Luhrmann observes that for many, the first thoughts or insights they identified as coming from an outside source appeared when they were praying for other people.

This is a phenomenon that we have often noticed in oracular practice, when the seer perceives images or information relevant to the questioner that she could not have known through any ordinary means. Some of this information seems to come through telepathic contact with the questioner, but it is often followed by insights or instructions perceived and expressed with a certainty that is quite different from the way in which the seer would normally speak.

Mikki Fraser describes his own experience in learning to listen as follows:

> I think one of the hardest things to do in learning to "hear" is learning how to shut down your own ego and expectations when listening. I think sometimes people can trick themselves into hearing or seeing certain things, because it's what they expect to hear or want to hear. It takes practice to open up and just let things flow (and sometimes you don't get an answer, and sometimes that *is* the answer).
>
> The other thing I've had to do, is to get a more solid idea of what my own inner dialog sounds like, again, so you can learn to differentiate between what your voice sounds like, and what someone else's voice sounds like. There is always the trap of influencing what you'd like to hear over what actually is being said to you. I find that god/spirit voices flow much more unpredictably than my own voice and often feel stronger or more intentional. Try to learn to trust your instincts and go with your first impression instead of second-guessing yourself.
>
> (Fraser October 14, 2013)

Practicing Exercise 8.2 at the end of this chapter will help you to let the ideas and images flow.

You can tell when you achieve inner stillness, no matter how briefly, but how do you distinguish between your own inner monologue (or dialogue, if you talk to yourself), and the words or thoughts of a Power? Think back to the discussions in part one. To identify what is *not you*, you must know yourself.

You should already have a diary, journal, or blog. Reread some of the entries from your earlier writings. Can you identify a particular tone or voice? Everyone uses characteristic vocabulary, turns of phrase, and sentence structures. If you find it hard to identify your own style, write a description of an event and ask a friend to do the same. Compare the two versions.

Differentiating source from style can be a challenge, since the Power will be drawing on your data banks and vocabulary to communicate with you. The other way to identify the source of an idea is to examine its content. By now you should be pretty familiar with the culture and personality of your Power. Do the ideas and words you are getting when you ask Him or Her for guidance seem appropriate? This can be tricky, since some Powers have moved with the times and can express themselves in contemporary slang as well as in archaic language. But the concepts and attitudes that come through should be consistent with what you know of the Power. As Fraser points out, another test is to ask whether what the Power is saying is what you expected (or wanted) to hear. My experience has been that when I ask a question to which I know the answer, I get told in no uncertain terms not to waste the god's time.

Another way to test for validity in a communication is by getting a second opinion. When you receive what feels like a spiritual communication, whether through meditation or as an unexpected insight, write it down. If you know other people who work with the same Power, ask if they think the communication sounds authentic. Remember, however, that most Powers have many aspects. If the person you are asking works with a very different "path" of your Power, he or she may not recognize even a valid communication as real.

Finally, as a follower of the Heathen traditions, I believe in personal responsibility. No matter Who you think is talking to you, through the agency of an oracle, a possessed medium, or your own head, *you* are responsible for evaluating and deciding what to do with the information.

Divine Dictation

Once you are getting fairly consistent results by simply listening, try taking dictation. By writing down the words as you receive them, rather than as you remember them, you will simultaneously cut out a step that could allow your own style or ideas to alter what you hear, and create a full record of your experience.

This kind of writing actually takes two forms. The first, automatic writing, is a form of possession in which the hand (or the cup on a Ouija board) feels as if it is being moved by some other force or being. The human does not know what is being written until afterward. The second form is more like taking dictation, in which you record the words you hear within. When done with paper and pen it can be hard to interpret, as the pen can run off the edge and looking at the paper to begin the next line can break your focus. If you are a touch typist, trance writing on a computer is far more effective, so long as you keep your hands in the correct position. For an analysis of the process, see Exercise 8.5.

When I begin to perceive words, I type them just as I would if I were taking dictation. Fortunately, the communications often come in bursts with pauses between them so that I can catch up. I type with my eyes closed, not worrying about typos or punctuation, until the god brings the session to a close. Then I can lift my hands and open my eyes, shaking my fingers and breathing more quickly to return to ordinary consciousness.

Most of the time I may have to fix a few typos, but the text is perfectly clear and requires no editing. Occasionally I find that at some point my hands got out of position and part of the message is now in code. Rather than assuming I was not meant to read that part, I have found that if I can identify one word and figure out what position my hands were in when I typed it, I can move my hands to the opposite position, type the wrong text, and see it come out correctly spelled. For instance, say my hands have moved one key to the right of where they should be, resulting in "upi ,idy jsbr (syormvrz" instead of "you must have patience." I only have to move my hands one key to the left of normal, and type "upi ,idy jsbr (syormvrz" as I read it off the page, to translate it back again.

Following is an example of a dictated transmission from the website *Odin Speaks*, which is a collection of dictations from Odin taken down by several different people.

> Of course I call—I am always calling! One of my names is Omi, "Far Crier," after all. The question is, who can hear? Some hear me often, some never. Some create an image in their minds to worship. Sometimes I can speak through it, and at others they are creating messages in my name. But that has been the case in every religion.

Your modern machines provide a good analogy—if you focus the channel properly the reception is good; if not it becomes fuzzy, and you have to guess at the original message. If it is too fuzzy, you will give up in disgust or despair. But all the time the station is putting out the same signal. It is not the message that is distorted, but the transmission. There are differences also in the machine receiving. Some have the capacity to express and perceive every nuance, every vibration high or low, whereas in others, only the loudest or most perceptible tones will come through. The message is there, but you do not get all of it because you do not have the sensitivity to receive it. And yet again the message may be received, but the sound equipment is incapable of expressing it adequately. Some systems may be better on the high notes or low ones—what I say now is badly transmitted because this "receiver" does not have the concepts or vocabulary to completely describe what I am trying to say. In any case, the point is that the message begins, is transmitted from the source, complete and whole, but reception varies.

As to the calling, what I desire is individuals who will get the message out. They do not have to be "dedicated" machines. I do not want slaves or automatons. And despite what I have said earlier, the most faithful receptors are not always the best. Seeing how the message changes, or better still, engaging in dialogue with someone who can question or argue, teaches *me*. For this I will say, the message is always clear in origin, but it evolves with time.

I call always, and I accept those who hear me, and some I seek out because their abilities are needed. Do they need to be crazy? As in crazy wisdom or dysfunction? The former I can use, the latter I can pity, but I cannot show mercy. Sometimes the machine that picks up my call is too fragile to bear the volume. I am sorry for it, but I cannot alter the call, for there are some who will hear only when I "transmit" at full volume.

And yet the spirit is eternal and survives its lifetimes, and learns, and the soul that failed in one life may yet return to hear and understand the call in another.

(Odin "On His Nature and Purpose," Source One)

This method is useful for recording journeys as well as direct conversation. Here is an example written by someone preparing for an initiation to Exu who was doing a series of journeys to speak with some of His principal paths:

2/29 Laroye

Friday to Saturday, February 29th, the extra day that evens out the years. A very liminal time, a sacred day. I come to the crossroads that lie within. Candles are burning there, red and black. I see a figure standing there, leaning on a stick. The flicker of candlelight plays across his face. Sometimes he seems to smile.

"Axé baba, I have come to see you. Do you have a word for me?"

He puffs on a cigar. The smoke wreathes his face.

"A word? Only one word? What good would I be if I stopped there? I got many words, as many words as there's ears to hear. I have one word for the king and one for the beggar, one for the man an' one for the woman. Are they the same words, are they different? It wouldn't do you no good for me to tell you. Even when the word's the same it's changed by those who hear. What do you hear? You have to listen more than you speak.

"I'll make you a net to catch the word. Write another story about the road, about a messenger, about how words may unite or drive apart. Offer to me always before important meetings where there's many opinions.

"You gettin' too tired to listen. Come see me again, we'll talk more."

He strides off and I turn away from the crossroads and from there to my own house and room.

"Axé, Baba."

(Filly, November 19, 2007)

Discernment

Once you start getting results with these methods, you will have to address the question of quality control. How can you know Whom you are *really* talking to, and whether you should believe in what is said?

As a writer, I know just how much effort it takes to get the right words onto the page. I wrestle with the concepts, try different phrasing, delete and replace, move clauses, and change punctuation until it looks good enough to get on with—and the next time I look at that passage, I'll probably change it again. When I am doing automatic writing and have a good connection, the words flow through me in complete sentences. I may have to pause between clauses, waiting for the next chunk of text to come through, but when I open my eyes and reread what is on the screen, the phrasing is elegant and sure. Furthermore, even when some of the communications cover things that I already know, I would not say them in that way, if at all. Whoever is speaking may be mining my data banks for vocabulary, but the perspective and phrasing are in a voice that is not my own. And then there are the ideas that would never have occurred to me at all.

When you reread what you have written in trance, apply the test of common sense. If the information you are getting is rational, illuminating, and appropriate in content and style to the Power you think you are talking to, you can probably go ahead and accept it. When in doubt, ask the opinion of someone else who works with the Power.

Mikki Fraser has some additional suggestions for distinguishing your voice from that of a Power:

> Don't be afraid to question what you heard and put it to the test. You won't be more impious for doing so, and the gods understand that our human interaction with them is complicated. I would recommend you do that A LOT in the

beginning. If a god tells you something is going to happen and it doesn't, or gives you advice that completely backfires and contradicts what they said, it could have been your own subconscious talking, not a god. And that's ok, this stuff isn't easy.

You could even establish a test if you wanted to. It could be something as stupid as "Hey, Jupiter, I feel like what you had to tell me today was important. If I heard you correctly, could you give me a sign of seeing a white feather today?" Stupid example, but you get the point. And if you establish a sign, try to let go and not think about it all day (it doesn't prove anything if you're actively trying to make your sign come to pass!). And once you get your answer, stop asking the same question. That doesn't annoy just humans. If you can figure out a way to plug in, in which you're having a success rate, that will help you build confidence in what you're hearing, and things will move more smoothly.

Also, I would suggest extreme caution for people that suffer from schizophrenia, MPD [multiple personality disorder], or any similar diseases. There is nothing to say that those conditions and hearing spirits are always mutually exclusive, but if you are suffering from a condition like this I would be very careful to differentiate between voices and definitely have a solid "test-system" intact before even attempting to try this.

I would also say this: If by following the advice, or listening to the words of what you think to be a spiritual being, you start to make horrible decisions that negatively affect your life, start separating you from your human friends and family, or it similarly impacts your life and free will in a negative way, STOP LISTENING TO THEM. I am personally of the belief that if a being has your best intentions at heart, it won't rip apart your life to no purpose, and it will never fuck with your free will . . .You may not be a "GOD" proper, but we all possess the divine spark and we all have the right to our free will. Sometimes you do have to stand up for your own free will, and just because you think a god told you to shove a cactus up your ass, it doesn't mean you have to say, "Ok! How far?" Sometimes the spirits might just be checking to see how far they can push you before you'll actually stand up for yourself.

It's also important to remember that not everyone in the spirit world is automatically your friend. There are just as many assholes out there as there are down here. There may be beings out there who might just try to screw with you to see how far they can push you. I think that this is where having a patron God or Goddess should come in. Loki is my bouncer (I know, some of you reading this might think that's a scary thought, but it's true) and I have another patron who serves the same function. Since I am a pretty open person, I ask them to keep away beings that may not have my best interest at heart. If whatever is trying to talk to me doesn't even get through security, we aren't talking.

And never fall into the trap of believing that when people are talking about "hearing" gods, that we all hear them as clearly as if we were talking to a human being. I've been doing this a long time, and I'm still always second guessing myself. I'm totally floored every time I hear something correctly and what was said comes to pass, and I still ignore advice I should have listened to because I thought I was hearing them wrong, or think that I'm hearing them right and I'm misunderstanding the context. It's never easy, but it gets better with practice.

And don't feel bad if this is something you never master. Gods are NOT humans, and they talk to us in many more ways than just words. For some of us it comes in words, for some it comes in pictures, for some it comes in feelings, or even just experiencing nature. Life is the Gods' language. Words are simply just one of the alphabets.

(Fraser October 14, 2013)

Practice
Exercise 8.1: Seeking Omens

Articulate a question. Ask the Power you are working with to give you an answer through three omens that day. Try walking outside, bibliomancy, and radiomancy. Watch out for colors, numbers, or symbols that you associate with your Power. At the end of the day, write down everything you can remember. Did any of your experiences strike you as being significant? Did you get an answer to your question?

Exercise 8.2: Words in Water

Sit down in a safe, private place and ask if the Power has a message for you. Ground and center, breathe, release all thoughts. Visualize a flowing stream, and listen for the sound of running water. Focus on the sound and note what impressions come into your mind. Listen for words. When the impressions cease to come, resume awareness of your body by moving, speeding up your breathing, and opening your eyes. Write down everything you can remember.

Exercise 8.3: Remember When

Choose one of the myths in which your Power appears, and visualize it as a movie you are watching. Ask the Power for comments on the meaning of the event, or how it affected Him or Her. When the sequence is finished, return to ordinary awareness and write down what you learned.

Exercise 8.4: Dream Work

Before going to sleep, put a notepad beside your bed. Visualize your Power and specify a question or topic. Think about it as you go to sleep, and the moment you wake up write down whatever you can remember of your dreams.

Exercise 8.5: Dictation

The Process

1. *Saturate*: Review all you have been learning about your Power to saturate your awareness with His or Her appearance and nature.

2. *Ward*: Choose a time and place when you will not be interrupted. Secure the place in which you are working physically and psychically to create a safe space.

3. *Cue*: Create a conducive environment. Light a candle or incense to signal your intention to make contact with the Power.

4. *Prepare for recording*: Set up a computer file or position paper and pen. Sit down in a comfortable chair.

5. *Open up*: Follow the procedure through which you have trained yourself to become receptive—relax, breathe, etc.

6. *Articulate*: Call on the Power. Articulate the question you want to discuss, or ask for guidance with some problem and write this down. Position your hands correctly on the keyboard and close your eyes.

7. *Receive*: Repeat your question mentally, then wait, quieting your inner monologue. When ideas that seem to develop or answer your question start coming to you, write them down.

8. *Return and evaluate*: When no more input is coming, lift your fingers from the keyboard or put the pencil down and open your eyes. Read what you have written. Are these ideas that you have had before, or do they seem to be new thoughts? Is the style different from the way you usually express yourself? Do the ideas make sense? Are they appropriate for the personality of the Power you called?

9

DEVOTION

She's playing in my heart. Whatever I think, I think Her name. I close my eyes and She's in there, garlanded with human heads. Common sense, know-how—gone, so they say I'm crazy. Let them. All I ask, my crazy Mother, is that You stay put.
—Ramprasad Sen

Relationships, with Powers as with humans, can exist on many levels. For some, the connection has a time limit. Others find themselves in the kind of relationship that Mikki Fraser describes as being "god-owned," in which

> much of your life-work ends up revolving around the work of and for this God, your personal energy is strongly "touched" by them, and your personal gifts and lessons in this life are ones only that God can teach you. Being God-owned, in my opinion, resembles being someone's child or partner more than it does being a slave. For me, it means that I still possess the free will to ignore the advice or request of the God who holds ownership over me, just like a child may be in a relationship of shared "ownership" with their parents, but still might ignore or disagree with their parents at times (even if it's to their detriment!).
>
> (Fraser October 22, 2013)

As the connection with your Power develops you will probably be looking for ways to deepen it. Whether you eventually decide to make a formal or permanent commitment to the Power or not, practices such as those which follow are time-tested ways to solidify and maintain a positive relationship. They can also help to prepare you for possessory trance.

Relationship Readiness

Before you engage in intensive devotional work, much less take an oath to a Power, you need to think about why you want to do this and whether you are ready to take on such a commitment. Devotion to a Power should be approached with the same common sense and care as one would (or should) use with any other committed relationship.

Pay special attention to your expectations, history, and obligations. Unrealistic expectations can go both ways. Committing to the Power may not bring you the peace, joy, status, or prosperity that you expected. Conversely, what you thought was going to be a pleasant addition to your spiritual work may turn into a consuming passion. Past involvements, with both humans and Powers, will affect the way you react to this one. If you have not already done so, your god may force you to confront your issues and face your demons. You also need to consider whether your devotion to the Power will conflict with already existing obligations to a spouse, children, or employer.

Work your way through the questionnaire on relationship readiness at the end of this chapter. Even if you have already gone so far down the devotional path that return seems not only impossible but unthinkable, the questions will lead to self-knowledge.

Bhakti

In Hinduism, one of the many ways of worship is "bhakti," the Way of Devotion. In the *Bhagavata Purana*, nine forms are listed:

1. *śravaṇa* ("listening" to the scriptural stories of Kṛṣṇa and his companions),

2. *kīrtana* ("praising," usually refers to ecstatic group singing),

3. *smaraṇa* ("remembering" or fixing the mind on Viṣṇu),

4. *pāda-sevana* (rendering service),

5. *arcana* (worshiping an image),

6. *vandana* (paying homage),

7. *dāsya* (servitude),

8. *sākhya* (friendship),

9. *ātma-nivedana* (complete surrender of the self).

(Haberman 2001, 133–34)

All of these are ways to improve one's connection with the Divine. Internal meditation on the chosen deity is especially popular. Some Christian mystics have identified with Jesus so completely that they manifested the stigmata of his wounds.

One of the most notable exemplars of this path was the eighteenth-century Indian poet Ramprasad Sen, whose love for the Great Mother is celebrated in his poetry. Eventually he left home and work to live as a wandering poet, singing Her praises, and in the end followed Her image into the Ganges for its yearly cleansing and was drowned. In his work he praises and argues with the Goddess in Her many forms, but especially as Kali.

The Crowley Method

In *Liber Astarte,* Aleister Crowley lays out a program for "Uniting himself to a particular Deity by devotion" (Crowley 1988, 183). The purpose of this method is to become absorbed in the Deity, not to be physically possessed ("Your place" rather than "mine"). This being a work by Crowley, a master of language who sometimes seems to be drunk on his own words, the instruction takes almost twenty pages, but the major points can be summarized as follows:

1. Choose a deity suited to your own highest nature, preferably one who partakes in some manner of love.

2. Worship with rites based on the culture of the Deity, while affirming His identity with "all other similar gods of other nations, and with the Supreme of whom all are but partial reflections."

3. Choose a place for devotion that is private, safe, and speaks to the heart.

4. Install an image. If the Deity is not one who can be portrayed, have an empty shrine.

5. Furnish the shrine from the table of correspondences in *777*.

6. Create an invocation that includes the following:

> First, an Imprecation, as if a slave unto his Lord.
>
> Second, an Oath, as of a vassal to his Liege.
>
> Third, a Memorial, as of a child to his Parent.
>
> Fourth, an Orison, as of priest unto his God.
>
> Fifth, a colloquy, as of a brother with his brother.
>
> Sixth, a Conjuration, as of friend with his Friend.
>
> Seventh, a Madrigal, as of a lover to his Mistress.
>
> And mark well that the first should be of awe, the second of fealty, the third of dependence, the fourth of adoration, the fifth of confidence, the sixth of comradeship, the seventh of passion.
>
> (Ibid., 184–85)

7. Purify and consecrate the shrine.

8. Set a schedule for worship, at least once a day and once during the night. This may be at a set hour or as the spirit moves you.

9. Use Wand and Cup rather than Sword or Pantacle. Wear the robe of one's grade or a robe appropriate to the deity and culture.

10. Use the correct incense for the Deity and archetype.

11. Practice the ritual, especially physical movements, until you can do it smoothly.

12. Make your ritual original and personal.

13. Engage in real-world activities that the Deity would like, and avoid those He would hate.

14. Do not do or say things your Deity would hate.

15. Recognizing that people are busy, the essence is

> And we bear witness that this which followeth is the Crux and Quintessence of the whole Method. First, if he have no Image, let him take anything soever, and consecrate it as an Image of his god. Likewise with his robes and instruments, his suffumigations and libations: for his Robe hath he not a night-dress; for his instrument a walking-stick; for his suffumigation a burning match; for his libation a glass of water? But let him consecrate each thing that he useth to the service of that particular Deity, and not profane the same to any other use.
>
> (Ibid., 187)

16. Repeat the invocation inwardly as often as possible.

17. Seek to perform the ritual inwardly, "For in the brain is the shrine, and there is no Image therein; and the breath of man is the incense and the libation" (Ibid.).

18. Make every thought, word, and act into an act of devotion.

19. Limit reading to the holy books of Thelema, or to books that have nothing to do with devotion or the god.

20. Focus one's meditations precisely.

21. Meditate on all examples of love (*or, presumably, on the virtues appropriate to your deity*).

22. Visualize conversations with your Deity.

23. Turn your meditations into a spell.

24. Create a Mantra or Continuous Prayer by including the name of the Deity in a short, rhythmic sentence, and repeat it subvocally constantly.

25. Alternate active invocation and passive waiting.

26. There may be periods of mute contemplation/awareness.

27. There may also be periods where you feel nothing. Continue the practices and be patient. If you go back to normal life you will have to start over.

28. Let your oath give you the discipline to resist the temptation to quit.

29. Thinking you have succeeded can be as deceptive. Continue with your routine.

30. You will experience many flickers of ecstasy before you are carried away by inspiration and you get a full response.

31. Don't mistake the symbols for the reality.

32. Things that have similarities are not identical.

33. Keep the aspects of your Deity and His qualities in balance.

34. Stay healthy.

35. If focus and consistency prove impossible, give up and work on discipline and training for awhile.

36. Use the method of Rising on the Planes.

37. Create a talisman to represent the Deity and sacrifice it to symbolize giving up shadow for substance.

38. Meditate on or dramatize legends or events from the Deity's story.

39. Unless the Deity is savage, do not try constraint and cursing.

40. You may get better results by working with a Deity opposite to yourself in nature.

41. Balance discretion and aspiration in making this choice.

42. There are more advanced methods.

43. Don't declare your Deity to be "sole God and Lord" no matter how ecstatic your experience.

44. Be discrete and selective in what you tell others of what you are doing. True sacrifices in one's heart are better than outer sacrifices. Spill your own blood if blood is required. Blood can attract evil.

45. There is a further sacrifice of which nothing is to be spoken.

46. Self-mutilation is abominable. It might bring success, but it bars further progress and is more likely to lead to madness than union.

47. Do not withdraw from human affections while seeking the love of your god.

If many of these suggestions seem similar to things said in this book, it is because, like Crowley, I am drawing from the Western esoteric tradition, which itself owes a great deal to Hindu and Kabbalistic traditions, and even the *Spiritual Exercises* of Saint Ignatius of Loyola.

Commitment

Devotion to a Power may lead to a formal commitment. In some religions, a formal ceremony of dedication is required for a newcomer to the faith or for coming of age in the religious community, as in Christian confirmation or a Bar Mitzvah. The god-marriage discussed previously is such a commitment. Mystery religions often have a degree system that involves dedication to a specific deity.

In Santeria, those who wish to become members of a house first "receive" Elegua and the Guerreros, Ogun, and Osossi and Osun, and they take on obligations toward them. Getting their *collares,* or necklaces, completes their initiation as members of the religion. Those whose heads are claimed by an orisha may continue with the *kariocha,* an elaborate and expensive process requiring up to three years of preparation (although if divination indicates an immediate need for the orisha's protection, the process may be speeded up). The initiation ceremony culminates in a three-day feast at which the orisha is "seated" in the head of the neophyte (Canizares 1999, 28–33). Many parts of this ritual are secret. I have been told that at times even the initiate must keep her eyes closed, and in fact she will not learn what was going on until her training is complete and she is called on to assist at someone else's initiation. Traditionally this is the first time that the neophyte is possessed. The ritual also includes a divination in which the initiate is given predictions and taboos.

In voudou, initiation is not required for possession. In fact, it may be the remedy when possessory experiences cause problems. The head washing, and the training that precedes and follows it, deepen the initiate's understanding of the loa, condition him to respond to the songs, and expand his psyche so that the human and the Power can coexist more comfortably. The ceremony does not always give the initiate the ability to enter possessory trance. Although modern dancer Katherine Dunham was initiated in Haiti, she never became possessed. However, the priests concluded that her ability to dance indicated the approval of the gods (Burt 2013, 4).

Even in a possessory tradition, the ability to be possessed is not the inevitable or only effect of initiation. The primary purpose is to formalize and solidify the relationship between the devotee and the Power.

Anatomy of an Initiation

Dedication to a Power can be public or private. In either case the process is much the same; however, a public initiation ceremony, like a wedding, also changes your relationship to your community. Following are the basic elements.

Making the Decision

Although I have seen Heathens overwhelmed by the emotional impact of a sumble (a Viking ritual that includes a formal series of toasts) spontaneously raise the horn to vow themselves to Odin, impromptu dedication is not recommended. If the group has a responsible leader the oath will probably be challenged, and the young man advised to study the lore until he understands what he is getting into.

Sometimes, the Power will make His or Her presence known with sudden and overwhelming force, and you can only accept what has happened and make whatever alterations in your life are required. For others, awareness that a permanent change has occurred dawns gradually. You realize that every piece of clothing you have bought in the past year is in the colors of your god. His altar is taking up an increasingly large

Figure 9: Altar for initiation to Nana

space in your room, and to feel His presence you have only to say His name. At that point, the decision regarding whether to dedicate becomes moot. A formal ceremony is not necessary, but it can help you manage the relationship, and if your god has work for you to do, it will clarify your status in your community.

In Afro-Diasporic traditions, the Power to whom one is initiated may be determined by divination and/or by personality. When you find a girl who is feminine, flirty, and loves pretty things and parties, the cowries as well as everyone who knows her will probably agree that she is a child of Osun. In some cases the personality is so congruent that the individual is very nearly an avatar of the deity. Pagans take a less predictable road, and it may take some time before the omens, dreams, encounters in meditation, and the like add up and you realize that you have been attracted to, or in some cases stalked by, the same Power all along.

Before you commit to an initiation, negotiate the terms of your relationship. What does the god want? What do *you* want in return? Common sense should guide you in setting the parameters. The advice of someone with experience in these matters will help you avoid extremes. Discuss the obligations you are taking on and consider modifying them to a level consistent with your lifestyle and resources (or increasing them to a level that will challenge you). If possible ask someone who also works with your Power to confirm what the Power has told you. If the response is significantly different from what you are getting, get a second opinion from someone else, preferably from a different group or community.

Discuss this decision with your family or significant other. Dedication is a job as well as a relationship. Serving your Power will take time and physical and spiritual resources that might otherwise be spent on people. You may not see your relationship as a god-marriage, but devoting yourself to a Power will inevitably bring a third Person into your life with whom your spouse or lover will have to deal. A spiritual relationship can be far more profound than simply sleeping with another human. Look at works on responsible polyamory, such as Dossie Easton and Janet Hardy's *The Ethical Slut: A Practical Guide to Polyamory, Open Relationships & Other Adventures*, for advice on making sure the needs of all parties are met.

Not all initiations are to specific Powers. Consecrations of clergy, for instance, may include a commitment to serve the religion and the community in general, or a whole pantheon of gods.

Training

The amount of time that elapses between the decision and the actual ceremony depends on the tradition, how much background you already have, and your resources. Santeria initiations can cost thousands of dollars. Pagan ceremonies are usually more modest, but to honor the Power properly will take some kind of investment. The crucial element, however, is the training.

The prospective initiate should spend at least a year in preparation, or more if the work the Power has called you to do involves mastering specific skills. The topics covered here are an outline, to be expanded and fleshed out in consultation with the elders in your tradition and others who are dedicated to your Power. Read everything relevant you can find. Work on self-knowledge, explore the place of the Power in your religion, and develop your own devotional practice. Use the practices described in chapter 7 to establish a dependable connection with your Power and communicate regularly. Work out exactly what your commitment will mean. What taboos or service does the Power ask? What are you willing to give? Negotiate. As you are preparing to dedicate yourself to the Power, He or She is moving closer to you. The commitment runs both ways.

If the ceremony is going to be public, you will also need time to prepare ritual robes, gifts for those who are helping you, and other items. Fortunately, much of the handwork can be done as part of your devotional practice.

Preparation

During the day or days immediately preceding the initiation you will be getting your mind and body ready to receive the Power, and the ritual space ready for the ceremony. You may be required to go on a special diet. The night before the ritual may be spent in a consecrated space. You will almost certainly take a purifying bath immediately before the ceremony, and dress in new or clean garments.

At the same time, the ritual space is being cleaned and decorated. Ideally this should be done by your helpers, although scrubbing a floor can be an act of devotion. You should certainly help set up the main altar to your deity. You may prepare some of the foods that can be made up ahead of time, but the final cooking and serving will have to be done by others. Think of your situation as analogous to that of the bride in a big wedding, and plan accordingly.

The Ritual

If your tradition has a format for initiations, your elders will go over the procedure with you and make sure you understand the meaning of each element, although there may be parts that are kept secret until the time comes. If you end up writing the ritual yourself, it should include the following elements.

Blessing the Space

Before the ritual begins the space should be formally purified, blessed, and warded in a manner appropriate to your tradition or the culture of the Power.

Invocation

In some traditions other Powers, such as quarter guardians or other deities in your Power's pantheon, may be invoked or invited to come and bear witness. In the American Magic Umbanda House, at this point all the other orishas are invited to bless the initiate. In other traditions, they may be invited to the party afterward. Here, or just before the actual dedication, the Power to whom the initiate is being dedicated should also be invoked.

Consent and Dedication

Next, the person conducting the ritual should formally ask if the initiate still wants to make this dedication. Once this has been done, the initiate may take a formal oath or repeat the vows that have been agreed on. These should be recorded so that the initiate will remember what he has sworn. Members of the community bear witness.

Transformation

An initiation is a Mystery, in the sacred sense, and consists not only of words said but of things done. The unconscious speaks a symbolic language, and actions will reach a level of the spirit that is beyond words. The presence of the Power may be further invoked by prayers or by the songs with which the initiate has been conditioned to make the connection. The initiate may receive a sanctified item of jewelry. In possessory traditions, the head is washed with sacred herbs, or herbs may be rubbed into a slit in the scalp after the head is shaved, literally "opening the head" to the orisha. This part of the ritual may be performed in private, witnessed only by other initiates or elders.

Affirmation

When the initiation has been performed, the initiate is dressed in new garments and presented to the community. The initiate may be given a necklace or other piece of jewelry to wear from then on. In a possessory tradition, by this time she is usually possessed by the Power Who may dance or bless the guests and join in the feasting.

Integration

After the ceremony, give the initiate some time to internalize and integrate what has happened. In Santeria, initiation is followed by a yearlong novitiate, during which the *iyawó*, or "bride of mysteries," must wear white and limit mundane activity. This period is essentially a spiritual childhood, during which the novice grows into her new identity. Depending on the tradition, the initiate may be given taboos or obligations, or make promises for future activity (see "Maintaining the Relationship" below).

Private Initiations

Unlike a marriage, which requires witnesses as well as the couple involved, all a dedication requires is the devotee and the deity. Fulfill the requirements for training, preparation, and purification. Invoke the Power and take your vows. Especially if there are no human witnesses, I would recommend writing down what you did and the exact wording of any promises you made. Many honor the occasion by blessing a pendant or ring that they will wear all the time from then on.

Some get a tattoo, which is what I ended up doing. Since then I've met others who have gotten a valknut tattoo (also known as the "insert spear here" mark) as a sign of dedication to Odin. Favored sites seem to be the solar plexus, the heart, or between the shoulder blades. When supported by witnesses from the community, getting a tattoo becomes a sacred act, especially when the work is accompanied by chanting or singing.

Maintaining the Relationship

Initiatory traditions recognize the need for outward actions to sustain the inward transformation. Unless the dedication includes a specific time limit, this is a lifetime commitment, so organize your life for the long haul. No relationship will survive without regular communication, so a good place to start is by setting up a schedule of regular practice—a daily offering, a weekly date night, or at the very least, an anniversary celebration. You will find some useful ideas in the exercises provided at the end of the chapter.

Reestablishing a Connection

One thing that can go wrong in a spiritual relationship is the loss of contact. When you pick up the psychic telephone, do you get an "out of service" signal on the line? Consult with people with experience in god wrangling, even if they are from other traditions. Ask someone who works with your god to inquire on your behalf. If necessary, invoke the Power into another priest and discuss the situation.

Moving On

Sometimes relationships, even with gods, do fade. Have you, or your life, changed to the point where it is time to simply say thank you and move on? Sometimes one Power passes a devotee on to another. I know of a case where Freyr turned one of his men over to Odin, and another in which Odin withdrew to allow a female devotee to switch allegiance to Freyr. While meditating, Jessica saw Freyr hold out his hand to her and panicked, snapping out of trance. She figured it was a one-time event, but

I couldn't read my Runes, and for two weeks straight every
time I threw them down Ingwaz was always in a prominent
position face up. I developed a writer's block, and in a *bede*
[bidding] to Odhinn, in place of Odhinn's name I said Freyr's.
Minor trances found me on the same hill—every single time.
I became confused, angry, scared, and yes, even broke down
a few times. Everything I knew seemed turned upside down
and topsy turvy. I performed a blot to Freyr, but this did not
seem to be enough. In his own way, Freyr had made it clear
that he did not just want to be a deity to whom I gave blot or
invoked over a mead-horn.

(Blalock 2003, 21)

Eventually Jessica realized that Odin had led her through the changes
she needed to make, and "the next time I tranced, I didn't run" (Ibid.)

Taking Some Time Off

On the other hand, you may be enduring something like the "dark night
of the soul," in which for a time the devotee feels cut off from his god. If
the mystic perseveres, the connection is usually eventually restored at a
higher level. A spiritual counselor provides reality checks for the mystic's
experiences. Having someone like this with whom you can share your
feelings will help you get through periods of deprivation without despair
and periods of joy without megalomania.

Balancing Your Relationships

Another issue in a long-term relationship with a Power is the effect that
this dedication can have on your human relationships. Even if you discussed the situation with your nearest and dearest before your initiation,
the reality may be challenging. Honor requires that you give everyone
his or her due. A three-part negotiation may be required.

As you monitor what you are giving to the Power, consider also what
the Power is giving to *you*. Can you take your troubles to your god and
get good advice? Do your meditations and workings bring you peace
or joy? Is there a purpose to your relationship? Even those who start as

lovers need to move beyond the mutual admiration society stage to take their place as a couple in the community. The Powers love those They claim, but affinity is not enough to justify a relationship. Admittedly, this opinion is based on my experience with a very goal-directed god, but I believe that the energy raised by interaction with a Power needs to be put to work or the relationship becomes sterile.

Practice
Exercise 9.1: Relationship Readiness Questionnaire

If you believe that you are being called to dedicate yourself or to enter some kind of formal relationship with one of the Powers, before you commit yourself, answer the following questions:

- Why do you want to get into a formal relationship with a Power?

- Is the Power already part of your life? Do you communicate easily and regularly?

- What is your vision of a life in which you have such a relationship? What will you do, and what will the Power do for you? How will a formal relationship affect your status and reputation in your spiritual community? If your community disapproves, do you still want the connection?

- What do you want from a divine relationship? Make a list of requirements.

- Have you had human relationships that followed the same model as the one you are developing with your Power? Were they successful? If not, do you understand what went wrong and how to fix it? If you have never had this kind of relationship with a human, why do you think it will work with a Power?

- What is your psychological/emotional status? Do you think this relationship will solve your problems?

- What is your physical condition? Is dealing with health concerns a major part of your life?

- How are things going in your work/career? Will spending time and money in spiritual activities compete or interfere?

- Does your family support your decision to follow this spiritual path? Do you have children whose needs might take precedence over the work you do with your Power? If you have a mate, does he or she realize that the Power will be an invisible partner in your relationship?

- Do you or have you had relationships with other Powers? If current, do They approve of the new connection? Have you sworn any oaths that would limit your ability to enter a new spiritual relationship?

Exercise 9.2: Nine Ways of Working

Adapt the nine forms of bhakti to work with your Power:

1. Each night, read a relevant myth, poem, or article.

2. Write one or more songs or chants in praise of Him or Her. Collect songs by others and sing them.

3. At a specific time each day, stop what you are doing and focus on the Power.

4. Do the work of the Power in the world, such as housecleaning for a goddess like Frigg, or volunteering at a wildlife refuge for Artemis.

5. Place an image of the Power on your altar and contemplate it. (This can be combined with other practices on this list in a daily ritual.)

6. Celebrate the strengths and qualities of the Power. Offer honor.

7. Do things *for* the Power, such as making beautiful items to put on His or Her altar.

8. Hold the Power in your mind as you go about your daily activities. Share your pleasures and pains.

9. Open your mind and offer yourself to do the Power's will.

Exercise 9.3: Approaching the Aspects

This weeklong meditation sequence is inspired by an exercise created by Mikki Fraser for working with Loki in his forthcoming work, *Playing with Fire.*

Identify seven aspects of your Power. Some gods have paths or bynames; others have a variety of functions. Choose a color to represent each aspect. Each day, light a candle and meditate on the facet of the Power's identity that this aspect reveals. Write down what you learn.

Exercise 9.4: Dining for Deities

Hold a dinner party for your Power. Choose appropriate foods or a menu from the culture (ask the Power what He or She would like when you meditate). Set the table with cloth and napkins in the Power's colors. Put an image nearby. Invite friends who also work with this Power or those to whom you would like to introduce Him or Her (for instance, when you are planning an initiation). Sing a song and bless the food in the Power's name. As you eat, tell stories about the Power's deeds, past and present. This is not a possessory event, but an opportunity to share the presence of the Power Who means so much to you.

Part Three

THE DANCING FLOOR

If you build it, he will come.
—*Field of Dreams*

In the film *Field of Dreams*, the hero sees a baseball diamond and hears, "If you build it, he will come." Not only does the baseball diamond attract the spirit of Ray's father, it brings the spirits of great ballplayers of the past. If instead of a baseball field we build a dancing floor for the gods, They too will come.

In part two of this book you developed your relationship with the Powers and your ability to hear them. On the principle that before you invite the dancers you must first build the ballroom, while you continue to strengthen these skills you can create and train a community to welcome the Powers when you, and They, are ready for Them to arrive. If your tradition already includes possessory trance, the material that follows will help you to place your practice in a wider cultural context.

It has taken first world scholars a long time to accept that in a traditional setting, possessory practice can play a healthy and useful role. In recent years, psychologists have wondered about the relationship between possession and personality or identity disorders.. In her comparison of multiple personality disorder and possession, Deborah Golub identifies a number of differences between a dissociative disorder and the way possession works in traditional cultures. In these cultures, possessory trance is considered normal, healing, and resocializing rather than pathological. The ability to go into trance is encouraged. The medium is well adjusted in everyday life and the spirits only appear within a formal ritual context. The spirits themselves are viewed as separate beings who belong to the culture and act in characteristic ways. Possession occurs within a ritual context, in which the spirit is formally invited. When possession takes place within the parameters of the culture it is not considered pathological. Treatment or healing is required only when possession occurs in uncontrolled ways, and any uninvited or recalcitrant spirits respond to traditional methods for expulsion. Repeated possessions in a ritual space may be part of a cure (Golub 1995, 299–302).

What does a possessory ritual look like? Who gets involved, and what do they do? What role do possessory traditions play in their parent cultures? In the chapters that follow, we will be examining possession in a variety of settings to identify principles and practices that we can use as a guide.

10

POSSESSION IN THE PAST

Your God never talks to you, but we have a god who converses with us.
—Indian villager (Oesterreich 1966)

Today, we are most familiar with trance possession as it is practiced in the Afro-Diasporic religions, but if, as I believe, the ability to let a Power temporarily occupy one's body and replace one's personality is a natural human function, then we ought to find evidence that it occurs and has occurred in cultures all over the world.

Pagan Europe

The gods of Olympus play an active role in *The Iliad* and *The Odyssey*; however, when they wish to communicate with their devotees, they almost always take a human form, as when Athena comes to Telemachus in the form of Mentor, a family friend. The goddess, "her bright eyes glinting," says that she will "play the prophet and tell you what is in the minds of the immortals." When she is finished she disappears, and Telemachus "understood what it all meant, and he was amazed, for he believed her to be a god" (Homer 1937, 18). Although the assumption is that the goddess is taking the shape of a mortal, the conversation is characteristic of the way Powers speak through people in trance. I have always wondered if in these incidents, a god has briefly taken over a human body instead.

Certainly the Greeks were familiar with a variety of trance states. The best-known example is of course the oracle at Delphi. It is clear from the writings of Plutarch, who served as a priest at Delphi, that the prophetic priestess was controlled by Apollo (Plutarch 1936, 347–501). The many prohibitions and purifications by which she was prepared for trance were intended to free her from distractions and make her completely receptive.

However, the majority of the Delphic oracles whose texts have survived are not expressed in the first person. The only times that the god seems to answer directly are when the question affects Delphi itself, as when the town was threatened by raiding Gauls (quasi-historic question 231), and the answer was "Let the offerings and everything else stay where they are at the Oracle. I and the white maidens will attend to this" (Fontenrose 1978, 344). The "white maidens" were presumably the spirits of the snowstorm that Apollo used to block the passes and prevent the Gauls from reaching Delphi. Interestingly enough, although I have carried Apollo in other contexts, when I do oracular work in the Greek style, the experience is more like channeling, in that I speak the words that are given to me, not in the persona of the god, but as direct statements, while simultaneously carrying on a conversation with the god in my head.

Another possible example of god possession from the earlier period in Greece is the ecstatic rites of the maenads of Dionysos. Possession by the spirits of nymphs, Pans, satyrs, and the like are also possibilities. Certainly the maenads saw visions. The primary Greek term for divine inspiration is *enthousiasmos* (origin of the modern English "enthusiasm"), from *entheos,* to have a god within. The first-century Neoplatonic philosopher Iamblichus writes at length about possessory practices in *Theurgia*:

> Either the divinity possesses us, or we our entire selves become the god's own, or we are active in common with him. Sometimes we share the ultimate or last power of the divinity, at another time the intermediate, and sometimes the first. At one time there is a bare participation of these raptures; at another there is also communion; and sometimes, again, there is a complete union. Either the soul alone enjoys, or it has it with the body, or else the whole living individual shares it in common.
>
> (Iamblichus 1911, 7)

In the rites described by Iamblichus, the possessed individual spoke in an unusual manner, sometimes musically, or with intervals of silence. Movement or dance was harmonious, and the body might appear to be "lifted up or increased in size, or borne along raised in the air." The possessed were also impervious to pain.

In Greek esoteric practice, the two major types of operation seem to have been the animation of statues and a mediumistic trance in which the theurgist experienced the god. Preparation included fasting, sleep deprivation, and prayer, and the experience itself was triggered or facilitated by the presentation of "symbols and tokens" that established a contact between a human being and god, the use of cues such as the sound of the bull roarer, and drugs or perfumes and incenses. Music, dance, and rhythmic sounds or motions might also be used. According to Proclus,

> Human beings receive the divine spirit and are possessed by it. Some mediums experience this kind of thing spontaneously, either at certain times or irregularly, but always "just like that." But others stimulate themselves to enthusiasm by voluntary action. Some mediums are completely ecstatic and possessed and no longer aware of themselves; others remain conscious to an astonishing degree, so they can apply the theurgical experience to themselves . . . When the medium is in total trance, it is absolutely necessary for someone "sober" to give assistance.
>
> (Luck 1989, 213)

Like the Greeks, the Norse had tales in which people realize that a god has visited them only after he has gone, as in this story from the *Saga of Olaf Tryggvason*:

> King Olaf was at a feast at this Augvaldsness, and one eventide there came to him an old man very gifted in words, and with a broad-brimmed hat upon his head. He was one eyed, and had something to tell of every land. He entered into conversation with the king; and as the king found much pleasure

in the guest's speech, he asked him concerning many things, to which the guest gave good answers . . . In the morning the guest is nowhere to be found, but the king's cooks report that he had given them some meat for the feast. Then the king ordered that all the meat should be thrown away, and said this man can be no other than the Odin whom the heathen have so long worshipped; and added, "but Odin shall not deceive us."

(Sturluson 1990, VII:61)

There is also the episode in *Heidhreks Saga* in which the hero challenges Gestumblindi to a riddle game with Gestumblindi's life as the prize. Gestumblindi prays to Odin, and it is Odin who takes his place in the game, though no one realizes this until he has won the game. God sightings like this still occur today. I have spoken to several people who have met apparently ordinary humans who in some way resembled a god with whom they were involved and who spoke or acted in a significant or helpful way.

If the evidence for possession in the north is unclear, a number of incidents in the sagas are at least suggestive. Embedded in *Gautrek's Saga* we find the tale of King Vikar, who agreed to sacrifice one of his crew to Odin in exchange for a good wind for sailing. Unfortunately, the lot fell on the king. That night, the hero Starkad, who was in the crew, was awakened by one of the other men, who led him to a clearing where eleven men were seated. Starkad's friend was hailed as Odin, and addressed the others by the names of the gods. After debating the fate of Starkad and what to do about King Vikar, they told Starkad to suggest a simulated sacrifice. The next day the supposed royal sacrifice was arranged.

Then Starkad let the fir branch loose. The reed-sprout became a spear and pierced the king through. The stump fell from under his feet, and the calf's intestines became strong withies, and the branch sprang up and hoisted the king into the crown of the tree, and he died there.

("The Tale of King Vikar" 2009, 102)

One possible explanation for this odd story is that Starkad's friend and the others held this discussion while possessed by the Norse gods.

The most suggestive evidence I have found that the Norse might have at times invoked possessory states occurs in the "Tale of Ogmund Bash" (McKinnel 1972, 143), in which a young warrior called Gunnar Half-and-Half substituted himself for the statue of Freyr that was being carried on its annual progress through a country district in Sweden. The people were impressed that the god and his priestess traveled in such weather, and that Freyr could now eat and drink. He also got the priestess pregnant. "That was taken to be excellent, and the Swedes were now delighted with this god of theirs; the weather too was mild and all the crops so promising that nobody could remember the like."

As the story is told, Gunnar did not believe in the god he was representing, and the reader is encouraged to laugh at the gullibility of the country people. But there must have been some tradition of a priest playing the role of the god, or the people would not have accepted the substitution. Furthermore, King Olaf of Norway sent men to bring Gunnar home "because the strongest heathen cults are when living men are worshipped," which suggests that such a practice might have been well known in the past.

This is the only incident I have found in which a god is represented by a priest. It is possible, however, that a tradition of goddess possession might account for the comments made on the position of Germanic priestesses by Tacitus. Einar Haugen suggests that those Eddic poems in the form of dialogues between Odin and another figure were mystery plays in which the priest took the part of the god in order to convey theological teachings and lore (Haugen 1983, 12).

Haugen appears to assume that the knowledge so imparted would have been memorized lore, which the Thul was cued to remember by physical stress and the dramatic scenario. However, the Eddic dialogues could also have been inspired by a ritual in which a priest sought possession by the deity in order to gain new insights and teachings.

Africa and Asia

In cultures that practice possession, the state is generally voluntarily provoked and eagerly desired by the possessed individual and his or her community. In his monumental work on possession, *Possession: Demoniacal and Other,* T. K. Oesterreich shared the general attitude of the educated European toward "primitive" peoples, and felt it necessary to point out that their "child-like autosuggestibility" is natural and not a symptom of pathological hysteria (Oesterreich 1930, 1966). He states that artificially provoked possessions differ from the spontaneous type in that their induction and progress are determined by the ceremonies that precede them. He identifies two varieties of trance—somnambulistic, in which consciousness is displaced completely and the medium remembers nothing of what has taken place afterward, and *lucid possession*, in which the host is to some extent aware of what is taking place but has little or no control over it.

Many of Oesterreich's examples are from Africa or Southeast Asia, and provide useful examples of how possessory states are handled in village cultures, as opposed to the tribal shamanism of Siberia and North America with which we are more familiar. Among the pygmy people of the Malay Peninsula, the ceremony involves burning specific incenses with traditional conjurations. The spirit descends, casts the *poyaung* into unconsciousness, and replies to questions. The Veddas of Ceylon call the spirit of a Yaku, or ghost, to possess the *kapurale* by singing a traditional song of invocation while the shaman dances around the offering:

> As the charm is recited over and over again the shaman dances more and more quickly, his voice becomes hoarse and he soon becomes possessed by the yaka, and although he does not lose consciousness and can co-ordinate his movements, he nevertheless does not retain any clear recollection of what he says, and only a general idea of the movements he has performed . . .
>
> Most sincere practitioners whom we interrogated in different localities agreed that although they never entirely lost consciousness, they nearly did so at times, and that they never

fully appreciated what they said when possessed, while at both the beginning and end of possession they experienced a sensation of nausea and vertigo and the ground seemed to rock and sway beneath their feet. Some . . . said that they were aware that they shivered and trembled when they became possessed, and Handuna [his informant] heard booming noises in his ears as the spirit left him and full consciousness returned.

(Skeat, 133ff)

The possessing spirit may be recognized by self-identification, by its characteristic mannerisms, or by speaking in a particular tone or with an unusual vocabulary. Among the Bataks, for instance, "The incarnated spirit uses a peculiar language, the vocabulary of which is partly periphrastic and partly archaic" (Warneck 1909, 8). Batak *begus* are ancestral spirits who convince their hearers of their validity by giving details of the life of the dead man and taking on his mannerisms and appearance. Nonetheless, the information given is not always accurate—it is "'like stones thrown at night' (i.e. they sometimes hit and sometimes miss)" (Ibid., 89).

As reported by Frobenius, in the Bori cult of the Hausa in Central Africa four priests invoke the spirit, who then seizes someone from the assembled community and fells him or her to the earth. If he comes gently, he is praised. If he is rough, the people insult him. The possessed person is led into the enclosure, where the rhythmic music is continued until he begins to prophesy (Frobenius 1912, xi).

Before the introduction of Islam, possessory practices were part of a religious system featuring domestic sacrifices performed in conjunction with the agricultural year, community rituals, and individual offerings. Initiation, then as now, was performed in order to transform a negative experience such as illness into a positive state that benefits the spirit, the medium, and the community. Initiation is a ritual of affliction performed by associations of the formerly afflicted.

More recently, the Bori cult has been studied by Fremont E. Besmer. His analysis indicates that the cult engages in two types of ritual: the healing rite for an illness caused by a specific spirit which functions as an initiation as a medium for that entity, and rituals performed for the public, part of whose purpose is entertainment (Besmer 1983). In Hausa society, the possessory cult seems to serve as a safety valve and context in which social prestige can be attained by marginal individuals, particularly women who have difficulty fitting into the subservient role prescribed for them in a Muslim culture, and prostitutes, musicians, and male homosexuals, especially transvestites. It has been suggested that in such societies, cults in which women play a major role also have a high percentage of male homosexuals (Beattie and Middleton 1969, xxv). This would also appear to be true in at least some Brazilian Candomblé houses.

The initiatory procedure is similar to that practiced in other parts of Africa, even those with quite different pantheons, as well as that used in the Afro-Diasporic traditions, most closely in the reduction of the initiate to the status of infant for a period of time. In ritual, the spirits are invoked through specific songs and drum beats. Sensory overloading appears to be the main cue for inducing trance. Moving into the trance state is facilitated by sitting or dancing near the musicians, hypo- or hyperventilation, and group pressure or suggestion. According to Besmer's observations, possession occurs in two phases, the arrival of the spirit and its actual "ride." During the first phase, many mediums exhibit symptoms such as heavy perspiration and convulsions. Once the trance state is stabilized and they begin to act in a manner appropriate to the spirit, their handlers help them to assume the spirit's regalia. When the spirit is firmly seated, it greets and is greeted by the musicians and important guests, then dances or otherwise displays the characteristics of the spirit. Some spirits move violently ("treat their horse roughly"), while others move about in a somnambulistic state when not dancing or interacting with the audience.

The technology for invoking and expelling spirits varies among cultures, but it generally seems to be ceremonialized (Oesterreich 1930, 1966, chapter VII). In Africa, the spirit comes to the mount like a wind. Sometimes the dancer wanders about the ring for some time until the spirit "settles down in the saddle"; at other times the mount becomes rigid. Particular spirits or deities are summoned by playing specific tunes on stringed instruments, accompanied by rapping on an overturned cala-bash. In Yoruba tradition, particular chants and drumbeats are used.

The Bataks of Malaya summon spirits by specific rhythms played on a set of five drums with differing tones. Elsewhere in Malaya the *pawang* (a spiritual leader) smudges himself thoroughly, then lies down and draws his sarong over his face. The moment of trance is signaled by a vio-lent convulsive movement. In this state, he performs the various magical actions required for the healing ceremony. This is followed by a second interval of withdrawal, culminating in a serious of convulsive twitchings that leads to a possession by the Tiger spirit, who completes the healing. Among the Besisi, darkness, smoke, muffled singing, and music induce the trance, and smudging with more incense restores consciousness.

In Tonga, as reported by Englishman William Mariner in the early nineteenth century, the priests brought on possession through a period of quiet meditation. The god, once in possession, would eat and drink hugely. In general the experience was controlled, although at times the mount might display extreme agitation. Voluntarily striking the ground with a club induced departure. Experienced priests were apparently able to bring on a possessory state simply by thinking about it. From Tonga, also, we have a report on the subjective experience of lucid possession:

> The best he could say of it was, that he felt himself all over in a glow of heat and quite restless and uncomfortable, and did not feel his own personal identity as it were, but felt as if he had a mind different from his own natural mind, his thoughts wandering upon strange and unusual subjects, although per-fectly sensible of surrounding objects.
>
> (Mariner 1817, 111–12)

Mariner reported that

> the priest, on such occasions, often summons into action the deepest feelings of devotion of which he is susceptible, and by a voluntary act disposes his mind, as much as possible, to be powerfully affected; till at length, what began by volition

proceeds by involuntary effort, and the whole mind and body becomes subjected to the overruling emotion.

At times, the god did not choose to come. False prophecies were interpreted as meaning the gods had changed their minds. When not possessed, the priests were normal members of the community, if anything rather more reflective and observant than ordinary.

(Ibid., 106–08)

Both voluntary and spontaneous possession is also a characteristic practice of village religion in India. In women, the onset is signaled by a circular movement, called the "dance of God," of the trunk from the hips, which can become extremely frenetic. This is accompanied by a half-singing stream of speech in 3/4 time, in which the deity speaks of his love for his worshipper (the possessed woman). During a cholera epidemic, a woman may become Shivashakti, possessed by the cholera goddess, and run through the village prophesying the deaths of the doomed.

Village priests exhibit convulsive movements on the way to the temple, where they become the mouthpiece of the village god. Generally the conversations involve what offerings should be given for healing and the like (Oesterreich 1930, 1966, 349), or instructions to build a shrine for the deity—rather like Demeter's instructions to the king of Eleusis in the Homeric Hymn.

In China, possession was characteristic of the priesthood of the Wu, who seem to have preserved the Chinese branch of Asian shamanism. Marco Polo described a ceremony in which the priests used singing and dancing to provoke their ecstasy until one would collapse in possession. He could then be questioned about a healing and give instructions for the ceremony. The Wu priests were also known to channel the spirits of the dead. The onset of possession for those who served village tong gods was signaled by drowsy staring, shivering, or yawns, followed by hopping and skipping. Even after he was seated, the medium would twitch and shudder. The answers to the questions were sometimes in an oracular language that only his attendants could interpret. When the spirit announced its intention to depart, the process was aided by beating a drum, splashing the medium with water, and burning paper money to thank the spirit. The medium jumped up, collapsed for a few moments, and presently revived, rubbing his eyes, unable to recall what had happened.

A friend who has visited the shrine of Kuan Yin on the island of Mount Putuo in the South China Sea tells me that at specific points on the tour She possesses the monks who guide pilgrims through the site, who then speak Her words and answer questions.

Practice
Exercise 10.1: Trance Analysis 1

What do the different descriptions of possessory trance have in common? In particular,

- What is the context in which it occurs?

- Who goes into trance?

- How is trance induced?

- And what role does trance play in the life of the community?

11

SAINTS AND SPIRITS

*Here I can observe myself, can note with pleasure how the full hem of
my white skirt plays with the rhythms, can watch, as if in a mirror,
how the smile begins with a softening of the lips, spreads imperceptibly
into a radiance which, surely, is lovelier than any I have ever seen. It
is when I turn, as if to a neighbor, to say, "Look! See how lovely that
is!" and see that the others are removed to a distance, withdrawn to
a circle which is already watching, that I realize, like a shaft of terror
struck through me, that it is no longer myself whom I watch.*
—Maya Deren, *Divine Horsemen*

For medieval Christians, possessory experience was by definition
demonic; but in the nineteenth century, a rapidly changing culture loos-
ened the grip of traditional Christianity. When the Spiritualist movement swept through Europe and the Americas it reopened the possibility
of contact with the world of the Powers. Oesterreich does discuss Spiritualism in his work, but strangely enough he has nothing to say about the
Afro-Diasporic religions, which carried African practices into the New
World, mingling them with elements of Native American and European
religion and Spiritualism to create a new tradition based on the practice
of possessory trance.

The Afro-Diasporic Religions

Today, various forms of neo-African religion are enjoying a vigorous existence throughout the Caribbean and South America and have been carried to North America. In Haiti the religion is called vodoun, a form of which is also practiced in New Orleans. In Cuba, it is Lucumi or Santeria, which is probably the version in which it is most widespread in the United States. In Brazil, it takes several forms, including Candomblé, Macumba, and Umbanda. A rapidly increasing number of books and websites attest to the growing popularity of these religions today.

Brazilian psychotherapy, as might be expected, offers a different approach to the treatment of multiple personality disorder as well. When such a case occurs, both spirit possession and past-life evocation are considered as causes. Spiritist practitioners may refer a case of multiple personality disorder to a psychiatrist if they determine its cause was abuse. Other treatments include exorcism (if the entity is malevolent), or merging, in which the alternate personalities are not banished but integrated so they can continue to assist in the medium's work (Golub 1995, 297).

The typical Afro-Diasporic ritual begins with offerings and prayers for the Dead. In voudou, there will be a long series of Catholic prayers (the "Action de Grace") as well. A *fiesta de santo* is a Santeria feast in honor of a single orisha on His "birthday" or a special occasion, such as when someone wants to express gratitude for answered prayers. The possessory ritual itself, in Santeria called a *tambor*, or a *bembé* in Brazil, consists of a sequence of invocations with songs and drum rhythms associated with each Power. During this process, one or more of those present—especially those who have been dedicated to the Power (called orishas in Santeria or Umbanda and the African traditions; loas in vodoun)—are possessed by the deity. The "horse" should not be touched during the process of "mounting." Once the possession is complete, he or she may be assisted to dress in the clothing and ornaments of the Powers, Who then moves around the room, spontaneously giving blessings, healing, or advice, sometimes interacting with other orishas or answering questions. Like the Hindu villager, the Umbandista says, "We pray to living gods, to gods with power, not to empty forms which once existed and which now are cold and weak. We know that our gods are alive because we see them all the time incarnate in the bodies of living men and women" (Bramly 1975, 44).

Writings by those who have attended or participated in these rituals include a number of descriptions of possession, such as this one described by Mother Maria-José, a Brazilian *mae de santo*:

> There are two forms of possession. The first is violent and bru-
> tal; it is extremely undesirable. The medium is sent into con-
> vulsions, and I am forced to quiet the god. The second and
> more common form is progressive and much gentler. It begins
> with an intermediary state, a light, imperceptible trance
> which doubtless corresponds to the moment when the con-
> sciousness begins to blur. At this point, mediums often seem
> to be returning to their childhood . . . Then there's a kind of
> acceleration and the trance actually begins . . . One minute
> the medium is herself and the next moment she no longer
> exists: the god has entered her body. But these moments are
> easy to tell apart . . . [After the trance] She feels good. Very
> good. And tired, of course, especially if the trance has been
> an active one. But she feels good, because her head has been
> emptied and in a sense regenerated. And because the god has
> left behind a great strength."
>
> (Ibid., 45–46)

According to Migene González-Wippler, in Santeria ceremonies the *omo-orisha*, or possessed medium

> loses all consciousness during a possession, and his personal-
> ity disappears, to be replaced by that of the god. A truly pos-
> sessed *omo-orisha* feels no pain and can drink boiling oil from
> his cupped hands . . . The *omo-orisha* seldom has any recollec-
> tions of what has transpired in the course of his possession.
> He usually complains of feeling light-headed, very thirsty and
> hungry afterwards.
>
> (González-Wippler 1984, 55)

Experienced Santeria priests can tell if a possession is genuine by observing the behavior of the mount, and fakers are punished by beating with a leather crop. Although most possessions occur in the context of ceremonies, the folklore of Santeria includes many stories in which an orisha possesses His or Her mount at other times, sometimes in order to discipline the mount or some other person.

Perhaps the best known, and certainly the most lyrical, description of Haitian vodoun occurs in Maya Deren's *Divine Horsemen*. Her comments on the relationship between the human and the divine are especially poignant. The loa are at once inherent in humankind and totally transcendent. The horse is therefore both privileged and ordinary. In Haitian tradition, trance is amnesic. "To understand that the self must leave if the loa is to enter, is to understand that one cannot be man and god at once" (Deren 1953, 249). The separation between the human and divine is maintained by not talking to people about what they did during a possession, and when discussing the actions of the loas, not mentioning which medium was involved.

As described by Deren, there is often a moment of anguish as the divinity rushes in, the terror at a loss of self, which is like a little death. The purpose of the ritual is to make it possible for individuals to achieve those "moments of extra-ordinary dedication." "The serviteur must be induced to surrender his ego, that the archetype may become manifest." This is accomplished by careful training, which reassures the initiate that "the personal price need not be unpredictable or excessive" (Ibid.). Trance is induced by the drums and chants, dancing, and physical contact with those already mounted by the loa, especially if the loa spins the person into a reverse pirouette.

Trance can come on so gradually the horse does not notice, or suddenly, "without warning, like a wind." The officers of the house must have the skills to perceive when this is happening to those who do not wish to trance and either stop the process or bring the individual out gently—"the tender mercy of worldly restoration; so that, to the body which must walk the earth, is retuned the self that is appropriate to such dimension" (Ibid., 256). Emerging from trance can take the form of a violent spasm. After a few moments the medium returns to normal consciousness, although a period of rest may be required before he can function normally once more. Officers of the hounfor (a voudoun temple) must have the control to resist trance when they are working.

Deren's description of a full tambor at the end of *Divine Horsemen* is riveting, in particular her inner conflict over whether to allow herself to trance, and the subjective experience of shifting levels of consciousness, caught in the dance, so that by the time she realizes that it is no longer the persona she thinks of as herself that is dancing it is too late. "This is it!" The moment of recognition gives way to the swooping fall into white darkness. In her notes she discusses the phenomenon in a more analytical style:

> Hypnosis could be described as going inward and downward, whereas possession is accompanied by a sense of an explosion upward and outward. One might say that hypnosis is the ultimate in self-negation, whereas possession is the ultimate in self-realization to the point of self-transcendence.
>
> (Ibid., 321)

For Deren, the experience of possessory trance is both ecstatic and terrifying. It is unclear whether this is a characteristic of the Haitian tradition, or a result of the European fear of losing control. She interprets the grimaces and contortions of mediums being mounted as evidence of anguish. This may be true; however, one must note that such responses are also characteristic of pleasurable or ecstatic states, such as making love.

The role of the Mother of the Gods is to control the trances so that they are neither dangerous nor ineffective. In Santeria, if an uninitiated person is possessed, the Mother persuades the orisha to wait until he or she has been trained. In this tradition, the gods are supposed to descend only upon those who have been prepared to receive them, within a sacred space, in the context of the ritual.

It used to be assumed that the African practices are not physiologically or temperamentally adapted to people of European descent; however, in Brazil people of all racial origins participate, and in the United States Santeria and voudou are moving into the dominant culture. Raul Canizares mentions a number of European-Americans who have not only been initiated but are now running their own houses. He devotes a chapter of his book *Cuban Santeria: Walking with the Night* to the possibility that as it expands beyond its Cuban roots Santeria may become a world religion (Canizares 1999, chapter 14). Practitioners of the Afro-Diasporic religions are beginning to connect with other American and European Pagans and show up at festivals. Some Pagans who are already practicing European-based traditions are becoming dual-trad. The orishas are also on the move, showing up in, and on, the heads of people who have never been to a traditional ceremony.

In British Guyana, indentured workers from India (possibly inspired by local Afro-Diasporic practices) have developed a cult of Kali Ma that involves possession, which now has temples in the United States, Canada, and England. A documentary produced by the Kalimai temple in Toronto shows and comments on the main events of the Kali Puja (https://www.youtube.com/watch?v=ICLCgNO4GAc).

The primary Power is Mother Kali, but some other gods are also called through special drum rhythms, mantras to invoke beneficent aspects, and wild dancing. The mediums, who are mostly men, are called "players." The onset of possession is signaled by swaying, shaking, and wild dancing. The medium signals possession by lifting his arm. To validate the state, a warder strikes him with a wet rope, and he feels no pain. The medium holds a bit of burning camphor in his mouth to purify it before speaking Kali's words, then gives advice, makes healing passes, and gives blessings.

Spiritualism

Perhaps the most successful possessory tradition in Europe and North America is Spiritualism, which works with the Mighty Dead in the form of spirit guides and controls, and the personal ancestors who give messages. Spiritualism got started in the early nineteenth century in the "Burned-Over" district of northwestern New York State, so called because so many new religious movements swept through it. In a time when new ideas had begun to threaten the old certainties, a practice that seemed to prove the survival of the spirit gained many adherents, especially after the Civil War and again after World War I when many people were profoundly traumatized by the loss of so many men.

As defined on the website of the Lily Dale Spiritualist Church in Lily Dale, New York, "*Spiritualism* is the Science, Philosophy and Religion of continuous life, based upon the demonstrated fact of communication, by means of mediumship, with those who live in the Spirit World" (Lily Dale Spiritualist Church, n.d.). Spiritual healers and mediums are available for healing work and readings. The Cassadaga Spiritualist Camp in Central Florida offers message services on Sundays and Wednesdays at which mediums are open to receive communications from the dead who wish to speak to people in the congregation. A Sunday morning church service includes hymns, a guided meditation healing, a lecture, music, and messages (Cassadaga Spiritualist Camp, n.d.).

There have been many attempts to debunk the phenomena that can occur at séances, demonstrating that the unconscious muscle movements of the people around the table can account for table tipping, the movement of the glass or Ouija board, and other methods offered for the spirits to communicate. These phenomena are showy, but perhaps they miss the point, which is to open people up to insight and to create an environment in which they can connect with the spirits of the dead. Today most Spiritualists contact spirits directly or through a spirit guide. Such guides are often from the class of the Mighty Dead, such as Ascended Masters or gods. However, they can also be personal ancestors or archetypal figures, such as an Indian sage or a wise woman.

Spiritualism holds that anyone can learn to communicate with the dead and benefit from that contact. Modern Spiritualist groups provide context and support. However, because everyone has ancestors they can address, and the methods for making contact are easily accessible, people who go exploring on their own may encounter spirits who encourage isolation and delusions of grandeur. As with other individual spiritual work, it is good to do checksums at regular intervals, and have a spiritual director or buddy who can help you make a reality check from time to time.

Spiritism

An unexpected offshoot of Spiritualism is Spiritism, developed by a French educator who wrote under the name Allan Kardec. In the Afro-Diasporic traditions, the dead are always honored first. When Kardec's work reached

Central and South America, it became immensely popular, and elements were incorporated into the African-based traditions, especially in Cuba and Brazil. Kardecist beliefs emphasize reincarnation. In *The Spirits' Book* Kardec explains that spirits advance up the spiritual hierarchy through reincarnation. When not incarnate they are still involved in the moral and physical world, and are particularly concerned with humans.

When Spiritism reached Brazil, its techniques for working with the dead created a point of connection between European spirituality and African religion. The melding of the two resulted in a number of traditions, varying in focus and style (Engler 2009). Candomblé is the most African, or re-Africanized after the late-nineteenth century "whitening," while Umbanda Pura is the most white, both in practice and membership, exceeded only by the Kardecist groups (although all three draw membership from the entire Brazilian racial spectrum) (Ibid., 27). Between are numerous varieties of Umbanda, some of which have also been re-Africanized, Macumba, and Quimbanda (which tends to be rather Gothic in style and includes more ceremonial magic), and which are constantly evolving and changing. Although there is now a federation of Umbanda centers, it has no power to impose orthodoxy.

> Kardecism presents itself as largely independent of place, though its European roots are often associated with past and present status claims, and some works argue that its origin is (mythically) Brazilian. Umbandist texts, again manifesting a spectrum, sometimes point to roots in Africa, sometimes to India, Brazil, Atlantis, or other planets, and sometimes claim a universality free of geographic roots.
>
> (Brown 1986, 1994, 22)

One of the most important activities of an Umbanda *centro* is the *consulta,* in which those who need healing or help with problems can consult with the *caboclos,* the spirits of the indigenous Indians, or the *pretos velhos,* which are the spirits of old Black slaves. At a consulta the orishas are honored, but not called. The mediums sit to receive their spirits, and clients wait until it is their turn to go up and ask their questions (Brown 1986).

In Santeria, exposure to Spiritism resulted in the *misa espiritual,* a practice that exists alongside Santeria rather than being absorbed into it. The misa espiritual

> utilizes the traditional prayers and ritual structure of Kardecian Spiritism, but it also incorporates many elements from Bantú (Congo) religious practice including the use of spirit dolls to represent spirit guides, the smoking of cigars, drinking of rum and other spirits, the use of herbs to cleanse people, the use of perfumes and other potions to cleanse or bless those present, and the channeling and African-style possessions of mediums by spirits including Congo slaves, former priests in either Palo or Santeria, or even possession by the spirits of the dead worked within the ritual context of Palo (Nfumbes).
>
> (Dr. E. June 19, 2012)

Practice
Exercise 11.1: Trance Analysis 2

Which elements do we find in both ancient and Afro-Diasporic descriptions of possessory work? Which elements seem to be culturally determined and which universal?

Exercise 11.2: Speaking to the Dead

Use some of the practices discussed in chapters 8 and 9 to seek contact with your personal ancestors, including cooking a meal for a dumb supper or automatic writing. You may even try experimenting with a Ouija board.

Exercise 11.3: Field Trip

If there is a Spiritualist church in your area, attend a service at which messages are given. If you know someone who is connected to an Afro-Diasporic group, ask if you can attend as a guest at one of their rituals.

12

POSSESSION IN THE PAGAN COMMUNITY

You really can't fake the sense of awe and tangible power that comes from being near one of the Holy Ones when They are inhabiting a person's mortal body, even if it's not a full possession. That's the biggest signal to me whether or not someone is genuinely being ridden.
—Elizabeth, "Possession"

In a training manual on possessory work written for Wiccan elders in 1995, Judy Harrow assumed that such a practice would only be safe in a circle of initiates. Since then, the spread of information and exposure to the Afro-Diasporic religions has introduced many people in the pagan community to the practice, and it is not unusual to find possessory rituals on the programs of Pagan festivals, at least in coastal metropolitan areas.

Terms for various kinds of Pagan possessory practice include possession, aspecting, Drawing Down, assumption of god forms, carrying, horsing, or divine embodiment. In contexts that range from light trance rituals for hundreds to devotionals with carefully selected guest lists, Pagan groups are opening their rituals to the Powers. The Afro-Diasporic traditions are the major inspiration for ritual format and trance induction in large gatherings. A second approach draws from the Western esoteric tradition via Aleister Crowley and Dion Fortune.

Despite popular assumptions, not all Pagans are Wiccan. The Wiccan tradition itself has become a mighty tree with many branches, each with its own identity and ways. What I present here are examples of how *some* Wiccans are working with possessory trance.

As information on the Afro-Diasporic practices has become more widely available, Pagans who are drawn to possessory work look to those religions for examples of how it should be done. Some have worked for a time in an Afro-Diasporic tradition before developing a practice that includes Powers from other pantheons. The Reconstructionist traditions that focus on the deities and practices of a single culture are among the most rapidly growing Pagan traditions, and people are developing possessory practices there too. I have seen or had reliable reports of possessory experiences in Hellenic, Celtic, Egyptian, and Heathen rituals.

Wicca

Drawing Down the Moon and Drawing Down the Sun are part of the Full Moon ritual in which a Third Degree priestess or priest

> essentially sets aside her own human personality to allow the Goddess to interact with the other people in the Circle, thus bringing them a gift beyond words. By assuming the priestess's body and voice, the Goddess becomes visible, audible and tangible to our ordinary senses. She can encourage, challenge, advise, even dialogue with us. She can touch us or even embrace us.
>
> (Harrow and Harrow 1995)

Many of the techniques used are based on ethnographic accounts of the practices of indigenous cultures, refined and adapted to fit the Wiccan tradition's needs. Invoking Divine Assumption is only done within a coven ritual, and is generally limited to initiates.

A single couple may be the designated Carrier and Anchor, or the roles may be rotated among the trained members. The Anchor is responsible for invoking and monitoring the god or goddess and facilitating His or Her interaction with the rest of the group. A specific deity may be called, or the priest/priestess may "open to the possibility and let Them determine Who will come through. They know better than we do Who we might need to hear from" (Harrow 2014).

Those who will Carry prepare by purification and relaxation, and by decorating the Power's altar. The circle is cast and warded, and trance is induced through whichever method—such as drumming, chanting, visualization, or invocation—is customary for the individual or the group. Once the deity is present, He or She speaks to members of the group. Carriers are trained to go out of trance in response to a signal, the circle is closed, and participants ground. Harrow recommends not discussing the trance work for at least a day to let the experience settle.

The Assembly of the Sacred Wheel

One of the few Pagan leaders to have published material about possessory trance is Ivo Dominguez Jr., author of *Spirit Speak*. Dominguez is an elder in the Assembly of the Sacred Wheel, a Wiccan syncretic group whose approach is strongly influenced by the ceremonial Western esoteric tradition. The Assembly includes Aspecting in its rituals for Drawing Down the Moon or the Sun, which Dominguez defines as a lighter trance state than full Divine Embodiment.

The trance work takes place within the context of the tradition's ritual. The Aspecting protocol, described on pages 122–31 of *Spirit Speak*, includes grounding and centering, harmonizing the five parts of the self, calling the balance of goddess and god, naming the Power, opening the portal, doing the work, and returning. Dominguez feels strongly that this kind of work should only be done within the context of a specific spiritual tradition, based on a deep understanding of the subtle bodies and energies involved.

The First Kingdom Church of Asphodel

Located in New England, Asphodel is a polytheistic organization that regularly includes full god possession at its public rituals. They provide attendees with a program that explains which deity is being called and how to interact with Him or Her. The ritual space includes an altar that serves as a focus for the energy and a place to leave offerings, a throne, and another table with food and drink for the Power. The space itself is purified and warded before the ritual begins.

The Power(s) to be called are chosen ahead of time, as are those who will carry Them, so they have time to prepare. The ritual team dresses the medium and helps him or her make the transition into trance. The same team will help restore the medium to normal consciousness when it is time for the Power to go. When it is time for the Power to appear, the medium is escorted by a team of helpers who run interference, facilitate interaction with other participants, fetch food and drink, and otherwise attend to the Power's needs, while the high priest or priestess runs the ritual. Experienced members of the group model correct behavior for newcomers and lead responses. Other members work on setting up and keeping track of gear. For the full discussion of this process, see "Asphodel's Ritual Structure for Public God Possession" (Filan and Kaldera 2009, 309–323).

The Universal Temple of Spirits

The Universal Temple of Spirits (UToS) is based in Pennsylvania. As described on their website,

> The Universal Temple of Spirits is a celebratory group practicing in the Global Spirits tradition. It is a possession-based working. The celebrations welcome all Spirits from around the Globe in love. Rituals are theme-based rather than pantheon-based and incorporate what we have in common as humans: shared food, dance, song, drumming, art, and possession trance. Global Spirits is a harm-none tradition.
>
> ("Global Spirits" n.d.)

The UToS meets once a month and also presents trance rituals at East Coast pagan conferences such as the Sacred Space Conference (www.sacredspacefoundation.org/) and the Free Spirit Gathering (www.freespiritgathering.org/). Theme-based rituals include rites for the Heroes, Spirits of Reflection, and Spirits of Performance. The UToS ritual structure includes an altar set up and a ritual structure we use to set up a safe space and make it more likely for possession to occur. It includes, amongst other things, singing a litany and calling in a Gatekeeper Spirit to "manage" things from the Spirit side. We call the specific Spirits people have invited through drumming, dancing, singing and drawing sacred symbols for them. The Spirit has the potential to possess anyone who is there. Those not falling into trance are on the lookout to assist those who are. We try to entice the Spirit by singing songs in their native language, when possible; making olfactory or auditory offerings (i.e. sprayed salt water for sea Spirits; using metal instruments for Spirits who work with metal). People may carry specific accoutrements for the Spirit as well.

During possession, the Spirit interacts with the participants and other Spirits too, if they are also down. We offer them something they would like, such as a specific food or drink or perfume. They may wish to partake of food and drink, dance with us, offer advice, talk to a specific person . . . The Spirit stays as long as the person possessed and the Spirit do their dance.

We have guardians to help escort the Spirit out, if the Spirit overstays its welcome. If the Spirit shows up when we're calling them, great. If they don't, then we're still honoring them. The process has evolved very little. We have recently included a "clean up" song when we're at a venue where we need to clean up the cornmeal right after we draw the designs.

(Firesong 2014)

The Conjure Dance

The Conjure Dance is directed by spirit worker and shamanic healer Caroline Kenner and presented at the Sacred Space Conference by the Chesapeake Pagan Community. It is inspired by the dance invented by Marie Laveau the Elder in order to bring an end to slavery in the United States that for many years was danced for that purpose each Sunday in Congo Square, New Orleans. Kenner learned about the dance in 2005 at a shamanic workshop led by Sandra Ingerman, who learned it from Martha Ward, an anthropologist and author of a biography of Marie Laveau. Kenner explains,

> In the Conjure Dance, we dance to manifest love, honor, respect, prosperity, peace, and joy. All of the spirits are invited to attend the Conjure Dance, as long as They can interact politely with one another. With a team of helpers, I arrange deity statues from many traditions around the room for the Conjure Dance. I provide a variety of offerings, usually including specialty liquors such as Akvavit and Mead for the Norse Gods, Rum for the Orishas and Lwa, Pomegranate liqueur for Hecate, etc. etc. I provide marshmallow Peeps as symbolic chicken sacrifices, and chocolate kisses, Mardi Gras beads, and phony gold doubloons, King Cake, and blessed spring water bottles at the Conjure Dance. It has become a very important part of my spiritual life, a night that I treasure each year and look forward to with great anticipation.
>
> (Kenner 2014)

Before the ritual, offerings are made to Papa Legba to open the way. Altars are set up on tables around the large room. Drummers support a singer who sings for each of the Powers. New Powers can be added by request, but someone must be available to lead the song. Designated warders move around the space to keep an eye on those who are dancing, offer support to those who are coming

Figure 10: Altar from Conjure Dance 2010

in and out of trance, and facilitate interaction between the Powers and those with whom they speak.

The American Magic Umbanda House

The American Magic Umbanda House (AMUH), located in Northern California, practices a form of Brazilian Umbanda adapted to the local culture. AMUH was founded in the early nineties by Renee Pinzon, who was initiated by her aunt who had learned the tradition in Brazil. The AMUH works with the major African Powers and some of the Haitian lwa. At times up to thirty-three Powers have been honored.

The major ritual form is the monthly bembé. After some songs for the ancestors, a *padé*, or offering, is performed to ask Exu to open the way. After that each Power is called with one or two songs in an order based on Their known preferences, supported by drumming.

> Trance builds on the drums and songs as we focus our minds on the deity and open ourselves to them. Trance is a controlled practice. We do not go into trance at random, but only when the songs of our deity are played during ritual. The trance itself is not wild and uncontrolled. The deities' behaviors conform to their characters and myths. The depth or power of each trance will vary. The three major variables are the Orixas, the medium, and the environment.
> (American Magic Umbanda House 1992, 10)

Newcomers are not allowed to trance until they have attended several events. After that, however, those who are willing may "go out" for up to seven Powers. When all the Powers have been called, Exu is asked to close the gate and after cleanup all join in a communal dinner.

The only public activity of the AMUH is the Pomba Gira Dance at PantheaCon, a very large Pagan convention held in San Jose over the Presidents' Day holiday. After a welcome, the singers launch into a sequence of songs supported by drums. Participants, garbed in everything from ball gowns to lingerie, begin to dance. The majority of participants experience Pomba Gira's sensual energy, while members of the Umbanda House who work with Pomba or Exu are in a light possessory trance. Other house members serve as warders, circulating among the dancers with necklaces and chocolates, ready to help anyone who is overcome by the spiritual or sexual energy to calm down. The ritual walks a fine line between edgy and ecstatic, but the warders at the dance and the staff of the convention are prepared to deal with any problems.

Possessory Practice in the Hrafnar Community

Hrafnar kindred (www.hrafnar.org/) developed out of the first rune class I taught in 1988, many of whose members were already interested in trance work. As the community has grown, subgroups have budded off from the kindred to work with oracular seidh and possessory trance. Although those who work with a particular deity may be overshadowed when invoking Him or Her at a regular ritual, most of their possessory work takes place at special devotional rituals, such as the fifth Wednesday Odin meetings, the Odin party in January, and the Vanir party each May.

When I made my formal dedication to Odin in 1995, I promised him a yearly ritual. By my third anniversary I knew enough people with experience in possessory work to make it a party at which he would be invited to possess any of the participants who were open and ready for

the experience. The invitation list was limited to those who had attended enough of our events to be familiar with the god and the culture.

This was to be a full-dress devotional, and we hung blue and black printed fabric on the walls and draped appropriately

Figure 11: Odin party altar

colored throws and furs over the furniture. Stuffed ravens perched on the curtain rod, and blue lights were strung around the room. Odin's statue was on the mantle between two blue candles, beneath the painting of Iceland. The table held a pipe and tobacco, drinking horns and goblets and bottles of mead, akvavit, Ravenswood wine, and more mead. On another table were some spare black hats, eye patches and cloaks, and the raven drum. Food included a standing rib roast, very rare, along with smoked salmon, black bread and rye crackers, sage cheese, and other goodies. A table at the door to the living room had a pitcher of water, cups, and a dish of salt to ground anyone who needed help. Figure 11 shows one of our Odin altars.

What follows are the notes I wrote to explain what was going on.

Pep Talk

3rd anniversary of my formal dedication. Promised him a yearly party. Purposes tonight include an offering of food and drink and flesh to wear to experience the world through human senses.

Procedure: We'll honor Odin with some songs, the last of which is trance inducing. It will shade into drumming, during which some of Odin's many names will be called. At various points during all this, the god may descend on one or more participants. Up to an hour will be allotted for interaction between aspects of the god and the god and the rest of the participants. Then the conclusion will be announced and the god will be asked to leave. All those mounted will be brought out of trance and the circle will be undone. Afterward, all may share whatever food remains.

Ground Rules: Only those who already have a strong relationship with Odin may horse—we have to limit the numbers as we have a limited number of people available to facilitate. Identify those who are qualified and open to this. If you are not one of the designated horses and feel woozy, move to the edge of the circle, away from the altar, drink some water, ask for help in grounding.

Ask each one what helps hir go into trance and how he/she should be brought out. People in trance are in an altered state and should be handled carefully. The gods come through in various degrees; each one will probably have a different aspect. They should be treated politely. Identify a helper for each horse.

If you are offered alcohol or tobacco you can drink or cup your hands to receive it, let smoke be fanned over you without breathing in. You may offer food and drink, or ask for advice. Remember that communications are coming through a human filter. If he tells you to do something, make your own decision, and if necessary get a second opinion.

Do not allow those in trance to leave the room or do anything harmful to themselves or others, but be diplomatic and gentle in managing them.

When I am in trance, Raudhildr, who has a great deal of experience with this, is in charge. Her decisions take precedence.

Teach songs.

After purifying the space with a smudge made with herbs used by the Anglo-Saxons for magical purposes, the space was defined with the words "Let none enter who fears the point of Odin's spear." The warded space included the dining room and bathroom. Among those who did not intend to offer themselves for trance were several designated warders, and a chain of command established who was in charge.

We called on the dwarves who hold up the four corners of the world to balance the space, and for good measure, intoned the runes. As the horn was passed, each person had the opportunity to toast Odin and state whether he or she was willing to trance for him. Before beginning, I gave each potential "horse" a blessing:

EHWAZ, ELHAZ

Let horses and rider be protected

With the rune of Odin I dedicate you—

(Draw Ansuz and Ehwaz on forehead of each horse.)

We then proceeded to a series of songs in honor of the god, culminating in the one that for most of us was the cue for trance. To further focus the energy, some of Odin's more popular and beneficent bynames were chanted. Several people went into trance in the course of the singing and were offered food and horns of mead. Feasting and interaction between the god and other participants went on for around two hours.

When the energy began to fade, the leader wound things up with the words, "Odin we thank you for celebrating with us here, but the hour grows late, it is time for you to return to Asgard. Leave your horses strong and healthy. Take the offerings you have received with you. Now release them gently, and let them waken to themselves, alert and whole . . ." Warders helped those who were still in trance to sit down and return, taking off hats, eye patches and other regalia, giving them water to drink, and generally "talking them down." The circle was then taken down.

Since then, we have offered this celebration to the god each year. It is open to special guests and people who have been attending our kindred's events for long enough to be familiar with the Norse cultural context. We have also developed an "Odin Party Survival Guide," which we distribute to newcomers ahead of time. I've included an adaptation of this for a multi-deity event in the next chapter.

Another Heathen context in which gods or ancestors may speak through someone in trance is the oracular *spae* rite inspired by the practices of the Viking Age as described in my book, *The Way of the Oracle*. My group in Berkeley offers this rite several times a year, and there are individuals and groups in other parts of the country that are doing the same. We have no evidence that the Norse used spae to contact the dead; however, our audiences come from a culture in which someone in trance is expected to be able to speak to spirits, and there will be a few such questions every time we present the ritual.

The only thing that our procedure has in common with that of the Spiritualists is that the seeress, like the medium in the Umbanda consulta, has reached a state of maximum receptivity as a result of the ritual. When one of the dead is called, she seeks for the spirit. Sometimes he cannot be found. At other times a different spirit steps up to offer advice. There have been occasions when a seeress relayed specific information that no one else could have known, or let the spirit speak through her. In a session at a Apple Valley Winternights Gathering in Virginia (*www.eplagarthrkindred.org/avhg.html*), the seeress took on the speech patterns of the grandmother of one of the querents, repeating a warning "not to answer the door in your underwear," which, we learned after the session, the grandmother actually sometimes used to do.

Since several in our group are also trained in possessory work, when someone asks to talk to a god or goddess, the Power may decide it is easier to answer the question directly, and occupy all or part of the body of the seer. At one session, someone invoked Tyr while the consciousness of the seeress was "in" Hel. Tyr arrived, expressed his displeasure with the setting, the seeress, and especially with his devotee, then left. It was five minutes before the seeress could feel her hand again. Since then, we have requested the querents to first ask the seer if a specific god can be contacted before actually asking their questions.

Practice
Exercise 12.1: Trance Analysis 3

- What do the possessory rituals described in this chapter have in common?

- What are the major influences on current Pagan practice?

- Which ceremonies would you be most interested in attending, and why?

Exercise 12.2: Ritual Design

Based on your reading in chapters 10–12, list the essential elements in a ritual for possessory trance.

13

THE FIELD AND THE PLAYERS

Get your scorecard, scorecard!
You can't tell the players without a scorecard!
—Program sellers at mid-twentieth-century baseball games.

Although large community rituals have attracted the most attention, my correspondence and conversations with people who practice possession indicate that this is only part of the picture. Possession may take place in small groups, and even occur in individual counseling or healing sessions, although unless the client is also experienced in god wrangling, I would strongly recommend that a third person be present. An experienced medium needs little support, but the more people who are present, especially when many of them are untrained, the more structure and staff there should be.

In the previous chapters you will have noticed that some practices appear again and again, whether the ritual is large or small. In Afro-Diasporic houses, ritual structure and roles are determined by tradition. Pagan groups that have had to evolve their own practice have also (through trial and error) identified a number of elements that help make the experience a success for all concerned.

The Action
A possessory ritual may appear to be an ecstatic free-for-all, but as you have seen in the descriptions included in the previous chapters, the

practice in most traditions is based on an underlying structure that can be analyzed as follows.

Preparation

A great deal of physical and mental work must be done before the ritual can even begin, including securing the ritual space, organizing those who will bring what's needed to furnish the altars and feed both the Powers and the people, and making sure there are enough trained staff to watch over everyone. An Afro-Diasporic initiation takes days to perform and requires months of preparation. Any ritual that takes place at a festival or conference, or in any setting other than a permanently designated site, takes some serious planning.

Both the mediums and the place in which they will work must be prepared to host the Powers. Some Powers may impose dietary restrictions during the days before the event. Kuan Yin, for instance, may ban meat and alcohol. They may request specific garb or offerings, which will have to be obtained. Mediums should meditate to connect with the Powers. Linda of Oya says,

> I prepare for trance with any deity by doing altar work. This is a session where I light a candle, make an offering and sing a chant. I also usually wear the necklace of the particular power. Altar work is a negotiation. You promise to do something for the power, and the power in turn promises to respect whatever limits you have set. If the power doesn't respect these limits, you withdraw permission for possession for that particular power.
>
> (Linda of Oya 2014])

You will also need to set the stage. When the ritual is focused on a single Power you can follow the principles of Giovanni Pico della Mirandola and go all out in decoration. At an Afro-Diasporic initiation or orisha birthday party the "altar" may take up an entire wall, draped with fabric in the orisha's colors, furnished with sacred items and images above an array of food offerings that extends partway across the floor.

Cleanliness is next to godliness. The site for the ceremony must be physically and psychically clean. Even if you are in a hotel with a house-keeping staff, check the floor. Make sure everything you are going to use is clean and in good repair. Those who are expecting or open to possession should take whatever steps the Powers they are working with require, such as a ritual bath with herbs appropriate to the Power.

Once the place is physically clean, it needs to be purified by sprinkling with salted water or using incense or smudge. Move around the space, paying special attention to any places where you feel unsettled or negative energy, especially if you are working at a Pagan festival or convention where the space has been in use nonstop for other rituals. Pagans who normally work in their own dedicated or personal

Figure 12: Altar for Exu birthday party

space may not understand the need to clean up their psychic leftovers. Even if there is nothing wrong with the energy, it can be disruptive.

It is also a good idea to reach out to the local landwight or the spirit of the house or hotel, explain what you are doing, and ask it to help keep out any inappropriate influences. If people are opening their heads to the spirits, make sure only the invited spirits can come. Wicca is in origin a magical tradition, and it assumes that one needs to ward the circle. Reconstructionist groups, on the other hand, in their ordinary practice may see no need for such protections. But even if the ritual is as informal as inviting a friend over for a beer, some of the participants will be psychically open, and the ritual space should be protected.

Information, Please
Even when all present are experienced and trained, it helps to focus the energy with some kind of introduction. At a large event with guests or newcomers it's essential. The behavior of both people and Powers in a

rite in which the Powers are being asked to do some specific work such as answering questions or healing will be different than when they are being honored with a party.

Participants need to hear who is doing what, what to watch out for, and who to go to if there are any difficulties. If the ritual will be "open floor," in which anyone who has expressed their willingness is allowed (if the Powers so choose) to go into trance, they should be given an opportunity to say yes or no. Everyone also needs to know who the designated mediums are, which Powers are being called, and any points of etiquette that should be observed. Think about your audience. What elements might need explanation? Identify the warders or support staff, explain how food is to be handled, and point out the location of the bathrooms.

Launching the Rite

Sometimes, the preparations are themselves a ritual. Writer and voudou and Santeria practitioner Lilith Dorsey says,

> In Haitian Vodou and New Orleans Voodoo sacred blessings with waters, fires, incense, chants, rhythms, vevés and food are all part of the advance ritual, what my godkids and I like to call "the ritual before the ritual" which is often more important.
>
> (Dorsey 2014)

In the Afro-Diasporic religions, a ritual begins with a welcome to Eshu/Exu/Legba, the messenger of the orishas and opener of the way, a step often adopted by eclectic possessory groups that include African Powers. Some Wiccan covens salute the Mighty Dead at the start of all their rituals. The African traditions may also begin by honoring the ancestors. The rationale for this seems to be that the ancestors will be protective because they are closer to us and have a personal interest.

Invocation/Induction

The ritual gets going with the invocation of the Power(s). This alerts participants to focus their thoughts on the Power being called and their energy on the medium, signals the medium to begin opening to trance, and of course it gets the attention of the Power. A verbal invocation may be sufficient for a medium who has been doing her own inner work, or it may be followed by drumming and/or song. The more experienced the medium, the more preliminary work he or she has done, and the more support he or she has from others, the more quickly the transition into trance will occur.

When more than one Power is being called the invoking songs will be sung in a prescribed order. The words and music identify not only the Power being called, but in some cases the aspect or "path" of the Power. The medium may already be dressed in the ritual costume of the Power, or he or she may be helped to change clothes as a way of seating the possession after it has occurred.

Interaction

The "meat" of a possessory ritual is of course the interaction between the Power(s) and the people. My experience has been that although many of the Powers enjoy a good party at which they get to experience the pleasures of eating and drinking and moving in a physical body, what they really like is to work. This is one of the major reasons for possessory practice.

Depending on how you have structured the ritual and the preference of the Powers, people may come to consult where They are enthroned or They may work the crowd, pausing to give advice or perform healings. When a Power is being called into a single designated medium, as in Drawing Down the Moon, She may answer a question or deliver a message to the entire group.

When only one Power is called, invocatory singing or drumming may stop after the possession is complete. When working with a number of Powers, divide the time allowed for interaction into equal segments, time the songs, and work out how long you can spend on each. Powers may depart as soon as the time allotted is done or remain to interact with each other or the people. Who remains, and for how long, is decided by the person running the ritual.

Devocation and Closing

Sometimes, the only thing harder than getting a Power to possess a medium is getting Him or Her to leave. It is the job of the warders or leader to make sure that everyone who was "out" has returned to being the person on their driver's license before the circle's guardians are thanked and the wards are taken down. Specific ways to do this will be discussed in part four. The mundane activities involved in cleaning up the space will also help people return to consensus reality.

Recovery and Aftercare

Intense spiritual practice consumes energy. If the Powers take the offerings with them as they are supposed to, even mediums who ate and drank (sometimes in great quantity) while they were possessed will find that they are still hungry. The ritual may be followed by a feast appropriate to the Powers and the tradition, but even if it is only a few PowerBars, the mediums need some kind of food that includes both carbohydrates and protein.

The meal is also a good time for debriefing. Problems can be identified for further discussion later, and participants can ask for help to interpret advice from a Power. However, in some traditions, when the actions of a Power during ritual are discussed, the carrying medium is not named.

Although very few rituals go completely according to plan, most glitches require no more than a few notes on what to fix next time. Sometimes, however, an issue will arise that requires thought and care. If a medium has not done sufficient altar work and negotiation with the Power, he may not take the alcohol with him. A guest who has received harsh words from a Power may need comfort and counseling, and the group may need to consider whether the message or action was in character for the Power or "horse talk." (For more on this, see part four.) In other cases, even when the message was valid, misunderstandings may cause gossip in the community that will require damage control.

The Players

From the above it should be clear that in anything larger than a private consultation, for the Powers to interact with the people in ritual requires a team. The size of the team depends on the size and expertise of the group. If six people, all of whom are experienced mediums, gather for a small devotional, all you need is for one person to stay "sober" at a time. A big public ritual will need warders, god wranglers, and a setup crew to keep things under control. In part four we'll look at what the medium does and how he does it. First, however, let's consider the people who make it possible for the medium to do the job.

Ritual Leader

Mae de santo or *mambo*, high priest or coordinator—even when the group works by consensus, somebody has to have final authority. In a Brazilian Candomblé house, the *mae de santo* is the leader of a sizeable community with senior priestesses, priestesses in training, and mediums under her. Whether the group is large or small, the leader coordinates the action, introducing the events, deciding when to shift from one Power to the next, when to take breaks, and when to conclude. Determining which Powers are to be called may be a group decision, but there must be someone who can take undisputed action if there is a problem, from dealing with a neighbor who has come to complain about the drumming to ejecting or calming a Power who is endangering the medium.

The ritual leader should not only be thoroughly familiar with the ceremony, but with all the Powers to be called. She should be trained in possessory work and ideally should have carried the Powers herself so that she knows them from the inside. She should know the likes and dislikes of each Power on the program. She should also know how each of her mediums goes into trance, or make sure that there is someone on the team who does, and even more important, whether there are any specific things that should be done or not done when it is time to bring the medium out again.

Warders

The support staff, variously titled warders or guardians, can help with everything from purifying and guarding the ritual space to keeping an eye on the mediums and other participants and if necessary, protecting the group from disturbance by outsiders. Warders are the leader's eyes and ears, and they bring any problems they cannot deal with to his or her attention.

Crowd warders should know how to help anyone who is not supposed to go into trance to stay "sober." At the end of the ritual, they make sure that everyone is grounded. The first step is to get the person out of the ritual area or away from the drums. A drink of water or a pinch of salt restores body awareness and helps people to ground, except for ocean deities, who may just laugh at you and start talking about the sea. If salt does not work, try "sour salt" (citric acid), which is not, so far as I know, sacred to any of the Powers. It can be purchased at Middle Eastern grocery stores.

God Wranglers/Servitors

God wranglers, or servitors, are assigned to the mediums. If the god wrangler is someone with whom the medium works, he or she can take over inducing the trance and helping the medium recover afterward. When the body a Power is using needs the bathroom, a warder or god wrangler should act as escort, especially if the facilities are outside the ritual area. The warder also makes sure the Power does not do anything dangerous or inappropriate, such as running away or stripping. My feeling is that warders should keep the Power from leaving the circle, although Thenea Pantera, a writer and blogger practicing the Mediterranean Syncretic traditions, comments that, "If no one follows the deity, they'll get bored and either release the horse, or return to the circle. Unless it is Artemis, and you are in the woods. Then, all bets are off, and you had better hope that your horse isn't the fastest runner" (Pantera 2014).

In a large public ritual, it may be wise to assign a god wrangler to each Power to make sure food and drink are offered and to facilitate interaction with other attendees. For instance, some Powers may want people to keep their distance until asked to approach, while others like working the crowd. A god wrangler can also advise people on how to act and react or interpret the Power's actions and words.

For a more on a warder's work, see Appendix II of *Trance-Portation*.

Batteries

A battery is a group of drummers marching in a band, the family of drums used in African practice, or a device that stores and provides power. For our purposes, I am going to use this term for those who raise energy in a ritual. This can include drummers, singers, and the people attending the ceremony who join in the choruses and clap their hands. The more excitement generated by those attending, the more easily and strongly the Powers will respond.

In neoshamanism, "sonic driver" is the term for an instrument that raises, focuses, and directs energy, and induces trance through sensory over-loading, which consists of any kind of music or percussion that has a neural effect. Drums, rattles, bells, or any kind of rhythm instrument can be used. The Eastern traditions use chanting to alter consciousness. African traditions have a rich legacy of songs and drum rhythms for specific Powers.

Music has a powerful effect on the psyche. Playing recordings of evocative orchestral tone poems or traditional music from the culture in which you are working will go a long way toward moving everyone present into the right frame of mind. Any sound cue, including original songs, to which a medium has been trained to respond may be used to induce trance.

Cooks

If music can invoke the spirit of a culture, so can food. Every holiday has its traditional menu, from champagne and ham at New Year's to beer and hot dogs at the baseball game. The African religions have cookbooks with recipes for each orisha (as well as warnings regarding which foods and drinks should *not* be offered to a given Power). Reconstructionist groups are developing a research-based consensus regarding what to serve their gods. One custom, for example, is making sure that none of the bones have been broken if you roast a leg of goat for Thor. As you work with a

Power, identify appropriate offerings. This can lead not only to an exploration of ethnic cooking but also new skills, such as brewing mead.

Before the ritual, mediums and attendees prepare by cooking for the Powers and putting offerings on the altars. If the offerings are perishable or need to be served cold, someone should be delegated to bring them out just before the Power is called. Equally important is the food to be served after the ritual, which restores spent energy, supports group bonding, and completes the process of returning everyone to consensus reality. Casseroles that can be prepared ahead of time and kept warm or reheated allow the cooks to participate in the ritual.

The People

Whether the "congregation" consists of one lovelorn person who needs advice from Freyja, a room full of Santeros at an initiation, or a hundred curious Pagans at a festival, other than the medium, the attendees are the most important people at the ritual. A Power may shadow or share consciousness with a devotee in order to enjoy a particular experience, such as a special meal or shopping, but levels of possession at which the consciousness of the medium is in the "backseat" or absent require the presence of at the very least a god wrangler, and ideally enough people to make the visit worthwhile. Sometimes the Power has something to communicate and would like an audience to hear it. At other times the energy of the people calls the Power in the best aspect to meet their need.

THE POSSESSORY RITUAL SURVIVAL GUIDE

This generic outline for a "survival guide," based on the one used by the Hrafnar community and written by Lorrie Wood, can be sent or given to newcomers attending their first possessory ritual. It should be focused and adapted to fit your needs.

Possessory Trance

Possessory trance, in which a god or other spiritual being displaces the consciousness of a medium and interacts with the people, is found in some form in every human culture, from Classical Greece to the Afro-Diasporic traditions such as Santeria and voudou, and is occurring more and more often in Pagan contexts today.

In (*name the group sponsoring the ritual*) we hold rituals that include possession for (*describe the kinds of rituals and purposes*). Today's ritual is (*name and purpose*).

Purpose

In our tradition, the purpose of a possessory ritual is to honor the Powers being invoked, to enjoy being in their presence and to feel their energy, and (*if the ritual is "open floor," add that you are offering guests the opportunity to experience some level of deity possession if they so desire*).

Who's Who

- The Power(s) we are calling are (*name, or list in order on a sign on the wall*). You are welcome to look at the altar(s). Consult with one of the ritual staff if you want to make an offering. Food on an altar may only be taken by the Powers or servitors, although They may share it with others.

- Ritual leader: Our leader (*title*) is (*name*). If he/she is unavailable, (*name or name*) are in charge.

- Attendees: This will be most of you at the rite, interacting with those in trance, raising and enjoying the energy.

- Warders: These are people who have received training in how to handle mediums in trance, get them into and out of trance, protect the medium from doing anything that will hurt or shame him/her, run interference between attendees and overly active Powers, and help people who don't want to trance to stay "sober." They will be identified at the beginning of the ritual.

- Mediums: These are the people *in* trance. They can be identified by the fact that they don't look like their normal selves, are dancing especially beautifully, have put on some garment or jewelry that represents a Power, etc. Be aware that the Powers don't particularly care about the gender of the medium.

Before You Arrive

Remember to eat before the ritual. Wear clothes in which you can move easily, and a cap or scarf to cover your head. *(Specify if guests should wear white, neutral colors, clothes in the colors of the Power being honored, or if they should avoid any particular colors.)*

During the Ritual

Those who are experienced in possessory trance may shift quite quickly into the persona of a deity. Others may take longer. The depth of each trance varies, as can the ability to speak. The shift is signaled by changes in body language, taking off the head covering, putting on the regalia, etc. A number of people may "go out" for the same deity simultaneously, often exhibiting different paths or aspects. They eat and drink, interact with those who are not in trance, or simply sit or dance and share consciousness with the deity. After awhile, the singing may stop, but the interaction continues. Eventually there will come a time when the energy has ebbed and the rite is done, and at this point the Power is asked to depart from anyone who is still carrying. When he or she goes, the medium may be disoriented and is helped to ground and return to normal consciousness.

We are not slaves to our gods, but partners in the work we do. Yet, even as many humans may have good ideas that contradict one another, so do the gods. If you are given any direction that does not have the immediate ring of truth, and does not *continue* to have it for several days after, you are no longer being affected by that Power's intense charisma, and/or if it's any direction more significant than "what flavor of ice cream would you like?" *Get a second opinion. You are the person who chooses your actions.* Second opinions can include, but are not limited to, rune or tarot readings, seidh oracles, or even asking another medium in trance for the same god who wasn't in earshot at the time. Sanity checks with knowledgeable, experienced humans once the event is over are good, too.

If the Power offers you something to eat or drink, you may accept or not. Accepting does not usually mean that you are also agreeing to act as a medium during the event, much less enter that god's service. A god that wants more from you will generally say so. In any case, *it is always all right to say no*. You can also ask what the Power wants. If it is expensive, ask him/her to help you find the money. If you don't want to drink something that is being proffered to you, you can touch a drop to your forehead.

Deities don't care about the gender, ancestry, creed, sexual orientation, or physical ability of the medium. Some possessory traditions hold that only amnesic possession is valid, but this is not universally accepted. *You* are the best judge of the validity or value of the trance of the person, or Person, talking to you. Remember that:

- They may be at any level of trance.

- What they say and how they appear will depend on what aspect of the deity they are carrying as well as the medium's experience and skill.

- The deity will have access to some or all of what the medium knows, as well as access to "what he is when he's at home." How much of each are available at any moment will depend, again, on the medium's experience and skill level.

- Regardless, the deity will be speaking through the medium's "software." They will use the vocabulary they have to hand to the best of Their ability, but sufficiently alien concepts will not be conveyed very well. Any of these may distort the message.

To Avoid Trance

- Consider wearing a skullcap or other brimless cap. In particular, attendees and warders with training in the several Afro-Diasporic traditions will recognize a white head covering as a signal that you don't want to let anyone in.

- Drink water, paying particular attention to how grounded it makes you feel.

- Leave the ritual space.

- Ask a warder to help you ground.

If the event is open floor, you may also include the following.

Preparing for Trance

Trance can refer to any of several altered states of consciousness. Light trance states include the following:

- A feeling of "presence," usually over one shoulder or in the back of the head, near where the spinal column enters the skull.

- Holding an internal conversation with that presence.

- Sharing consciousness with another entity.

These can be safely done solo. The states below should not be attempted alone and/or without close experienced supervision:

- Piggy-backing (you are a passenger in your body and the other entity is driving).

- You feel perfectly in control, but the "you" that is in control is not the "you" on your driver's license.

- You feel you are going to remember everything and could stop this at any time—but why would you want to? After the ritual you hear about a lot of things you did that you don't remember or only remember when prompted.

- The self that you recognize as yourself is completely evicted: "You" are sent Elseworld and have a journey or other visionary experience.

- The self that you recognize as yourself is completely silenced: "You" don't remember a thing from the moment you go out until you are called back again.

If you are planning/hoping to go into trance, during the days before the event, meditate on the Power. Negotiate ground rules—specifically, any limitations on what your body can handle. If the deity drinks, He should take the effects with Him when He goes—although do be advised that a slight amount of "god tipsiness" can be a natural and pleasant after-effect of these affairs. When you arrive at the event, tell the warders what you have agreed.

Symptoms of oncoming trance may include (but are not necessarily limited to)

- A repeated song sounding *really* good to you

- Finding yourself swaying to the music or losing your balance

- Feeling dizzy or strange

- Finding it natural to put on the deity's regalia

- Really wanting some of the deity's favorite food or drink

If you *want* to go into trance, the warders will have the following concerns:

- If you are experienced enough to know what your limitations and signals are, be sure the warders know. They should especially be made aware if the signal is something that may be construed as intimate, e.g., blowing in the ear.

- The warders should *especially* know if you have any life-threatening conditions or allergies.

- Some people in trance become nonverbal and, indeed, it is a perfectly valid and rewarding experience to simply sit in communion with the power in question.

- Our warders are trained to look for signs of obvious and *inappropriate* distress. For example, tears can also be an expression of joy—or catharsis.

- However, do not be surprised if anything short of this becomes short-circuited for the duration of your experience; deities in possession often are able to deal with things that the medium would never touch.

If you appear to be on the verge of entering trance, and in need or desire of a little extra nudge, the warders can also assist with this—as may any Power on the floor that is already in possession of a medium. A Power may

- Pull off your hat (if you're wearing one)

- Spin you around (thus disorienting you)

- Offer you something to drink

- Talk you into the trance, assisted by runes, energy manipulations, etc.

This is expected to be a consensual act. If you do not consent, disengage and inform a warder *at once*. If you *do* consent, the deity may be more firmly seated by any of the following:

- Putting on His or Her regalia

- Eating or drinking offerings

- Being recognized as such by others

At the end of an event, the deity may be unseated, and the medium restored, by any or all of the following:

- Being politely but firmly requested to go

- Removing regalia

- Being given water to drink

- Being addressed by the medium's magical name (if known) and then their mundane one

- Being asked mundane questions

- Being doused with water (in emergencies, and only by the most experienced warders)

I do not recommend that you experience trance if any of the following situations pertain to you:

- You feel uncomfortable, fear being vulnerable, etc.

- You don't feel comfortable with the deity.

- You are taking medication or are ill.

- You have suffered from involuntary personality dissociation.

- You are currently in an emotional crisis.

Practice
Exercise 13.1: Design a Ritual

Using the outline in this chapter and what you learned in previous chapters, write a devotional possessory ritual for one of the Powers with whom you have been working. Include the following:

- Time, place, setting, and number of attendees

- Ritual roles and who could fill them

- Decorations, food, garb, and regalia for the Power

- A procedure for setting, purifying, and warding the space. This can consist of the usual sequence for your tradition.

- Prayers and songs for invoking the Power

- A procedure for devoking the Power

- A procedure for opening the circle and concluding the ritual

INVITATION TO THE DANCE

To dance is to be out of yourself. Larger, more beautiful, more powerful.
—Agnes de Mille

By this time you may be wondering when we are going to stop talking *about* possessory work and actually *do* it. In part four we will explore the nature of possessory trance, the concepts that support the ability to go into trance, and exercises and practices that will help you work at the level of trance you desire.

When I first began exploring possessory trance I had to find my own way. In the more than twenty years since then, I have talked and corresponded with many others who follow this spiritual path, some of whom have been doing possessory work in Pagan or Afro-Diasporic contexts (or both) for thirty years or more, who were kind enough to respond to a questionnaire on the subject. Their insights and perceptions expand and balance what I have learned from my own research and experience.

14

LEVELING UP

Level up: To progress to the next level of . . . stats and abilities, often by acquiring experience points in role-playing games.
"I leveled up after defeating the dragon."
—Wiktionary.org

Each possessory tradition has its own definitions and assumptions; however, several concepts seem to be fundamental. The first is that the possessory experience includes more than one state of consciousness. Which one manifests depends on the ritual structure and expectations of the tradition, the training and qualities of the medium, and the needs of the situation. A second is that all of these states involve a (usually voluntary) dissociation from the primary person-identity. In gaming, levels are hierarchical, and leveling up is considered an advantage, but in my opinion the value of a possessory experience should be judged by how well it serves the medium and the community.

Levels of Trance

Emma Cohen defines "executive possession" as having the following features:

> the presence of an incorporeal intentional agent in or on a person's body, that . . . temporarily effects the ousting, eclipsing or mediation of the person's agency and control over behaviour, such that . . . the host's actions are partly or wholly

attributable to the intentions, beliefs, desires and dispositions of the possessing agent for the duration of the episode.

(Cohen 2008, 9)

In the African descended traditions, verbs such as "horsing," "carrying," "hosting," "receiving," "to fall," "to dance for," "to be out," "to go under," or "be gone," may all be used for possession by a Power. Terms such as "channeling" and "mediumship" are used in New Age and Spiritualist circles. In neoshamanism, the technique is called "merging." In some groups, "shadowing" refers to a state in which the Power is perceived as being near the medium rather than within. In Wicca, the major possessory activity is called Drawing Down the Moon (for the Goddess) or Drawing Down the Sun (for the God). The WildWood Tradition recognizes four states, or stages: Enhancement, Inspiration, Integration, and Possession ("Trance Possession" n.d.). The First Kingdom Church of Asphodel lists Aspecting, Shadowing, Channeling, and Possession (Filan and Kaldera 2009).

Ivo Dominguez Jr. of the Assembly of the Sacred Wheel defines Divine Possession as a state in which "the Great One that has been called interleaves itself into the subtle bodies of the practitioner like two decks of cards being shuffled into one" (op. cit., 115). Aspecting is a term also used by the Reclaiming, Feri, and other Pagan traditions. As practiced in the Assembly of the Sacred Wheel, it integrates the various parts of the Self to bring through the Power. For a full discussion of Dominguez's protocol for possessory states, see chapter 6 of his excellent book, *Spirit Speak*.

Gardnerian elder Don Frew explains,

When I give talks on deity possession, I usually say that the experience can involve any combination of six variables, each of which is a scale:

1. How present are you? From fully present and aware to somewhere else to unconscious.

2. How present is the deity? From a general feeling of inspiration to being told what to do or say to full-on possession.

3. How much in control are you? From fully in control to relinquishing control but able to intervene to having no control at all.

4. How focused is the encounter? From a general feeling descending over a group to entirely on one person.

5. Who is the possession for? From allowing a group access to a deity through the one possessed to entirely for the spiritual enlightenment of the one possessed.

6. How does the deity manifest to others? From displays of power without speech to imparting knowledge.

I have experienced or witnessed possession experiences with many different combinations of these variables.

(Frew 2014)

There has been a lot of debate regarding what constitutes an "authentic" possessory trance. In the African-derived traditions the assumption is usually that only somnambulistic trance, in which the medium is unable to remember anything that has happened, is real. For Maya Deren, overwhelmed by trance in a voudou ritual, it is "the white darkness." As a medium from Belém, Brazil, describes it, "I don't know where my spirit goes. I don't know. I only know that I switch off. I don't remain in me" (in Cohen 2008, 9).

On the other hand, in groups derived from European magical traditions where the medium initiates the release of consciousness, he or she is expected to retain some awareness and control. According to Ivo Dominguez Jr. in *Divine Embodiment*, it is "a state of being created by will and with consent in which an individual anchors into themselves some portion of the energy, information, and essence of a discarnate being of greater stature and/or greater evolution than that of the incarnate individual (Dominguez 2008, 100). Judy Harrow reports that in the ritual, a priest invokes the Goddess into the priestess/medium, and recalls the medium "when She seems finished with what She had to say." She usually remembers much of what went on (Harrow 2014).

River Devora, who has experienced possession in Heathenry, Santeria, Espiritismo, hoodoo, and spirit work, says,

> When I am in full possessory trance . . . I generally have little to no memory of what happened. Sometimes I may have snippets of memory, though generally the memories are incomplete, not in sequential order, and I don't remember how things piece together. Sometimes I am blacked out altogether, sometimes I may have a feeling of being held or absorbed into the heart of the Power (this is more true with the deities with whom I have oathed relationships). Occasionally I have had my own journeys and experiences in the spirit world happening tandem with the Power who is possessing me in the material world, but this is fairly rare.
>
> (River Devora, 2014)

On the Road

While the image of the horse and the rider has an archetypal appeal, today a more meaningful image is that of the car and the driver. In the early nineties, Don Frew characterized some kinds of possession as "riding in the back seat of a car—you can see and feel what's happening, and even speak up, but someone else is driving" (Frew 2014). This simile has spread through the pagan community, evolving into a continuum of related images.

The version used by the Global Spirits community is:

- "Spirit is in the trunk": Spirit may be unaware of the interaction. This phase isn't generally considered trance possession . . . the person puts on the accoutrements of the Spirit in order to coax the Spirit to possess them. Some may call it aspecting. The person is in full control, but they have a connection with that Spirit, so they are consciously tapping into that Spirit's energy, to look/act as they believe the Spirit would. It is still completely the person, though.

- "Spirit is in the backseat talking to me": This is channeling. Spirit can speak to you but has no control over your body. You can consciously choose to follow, ignore, or pass on to others the advice being given by Spirit.

- "Spirit is in the passenger seat": Spirit can grab the steering wheel and guide your driving. Sometimes this appears as not a possession of the head, but as a possession of a part of the body, such as a limb dancing in a particular way.

- "Spirit is in the driver's seat, you are in the passenger's seat": Spirit has control of your body and your head. You can still grab the steering wheel and get control to an extent, though. You can see what is going on and influence it. The two passenger seat states feel very much like a dance with Spirit.

- "Spirit is driving, you are in the backseat": Spirit has control of your body and head. The voice speaking to the people is that of Spirit. You can still see some things that are going on, but can't control what is happening. You can tell Spirit "no, not that" or "yes, go over to that person there." Spirit may choose to follow or ignore or intentions. "Backseat" feels like a coach on the sidelines of a game.

- "You are in the trunk": Spirit has complete control of your head and body. You don't have any recollection of what is going on.

Sometimes the Spirit in the passenger seat gives you directions, and while some people come to and wonder what happened to the last few hours, others may spend the time talking to the gods in the Otherworld. As Lina puts it, "Sometimes it's like watching your car speed away—and hoping you will both get off at the same exit." I think that it is a mistake to apply value judgments to different levels of possession. Lucid possession (like lucid dreaming, in which one is aware that they are dreaming) allows the medium to benefit from the expansion of consciousness; but if possession is amnesic, knowing that one has served the community by becoming a vehicle for a Power is the only reward. (Firesong 2014).

Given that possessory trance involves voluntary dissociation, it should be pursued only by those who have taken the lessons in part one to heart and are comfortable with their identity and boundaries. Those with a history of schizophrenia or dissociative disorders or who are currently taking heavy medications or in an emotionally vulnerable state should probably not participate either as a medium or attendee.

Opening the Head

The purpose of training is to open the head (and body) to trance, but what actually happens when we do? When I give classes on trance work, we sometimes refer to the training process as "cracking the head." In the Afro-Diasporic traditions, initiation may include actually making an incision in the top of the head and inserting sacred herbs. Opening up to possessory trance is not usually that dramatic, but studies have shown that learning to use your mind in new ways will in fact cause physical changes in your brain. Chanting or regulating one's breathing affects the prefrontal cortex. Depending on the kind of spiritual practice, comparative brain scans will show increased energy in the thalamus, frontal lobe, anterior cingulated cortex, or parietal lobe. The observed changes seem to be accompanied by improved mental health and ability to cope (Newberg and Waldman 2010).

But these studies have mostly focused on people who are practicing apophatic prayer. What about people who not only do not deny the senses, but invite the Divine to share their experience? If such a practice does not unbalance the psyche (and as we saw in part three, centuries of possessory practice in traditional cultures suggest that it does not), what is it about the ordinary human mind that allows this to happen?

In an article titled "Cultural Variations in Multiple Personality Disorder" (Golub 1995), Deborah Golub points out that the ability to dissociate is fundamental, ancient, and cross-cultural. Whether dissociative phenomena are interpreted as religious experience or mental dysfunction seems to depend upon when and where they are occurring. In the days before multiple personality disorder or dissociative identity disorder became psychiatric diagnoses, William James described hysterics as incipient mediums. This would certainly fit with the practice of many possessory cultures, in which certain illnesses are considered indications that the patient must be initiated into the cult of a particular deity.

However, possession by a deity and a dissociated identity are not the same. While the same psychobiological capabilities may make them possible, some form of culturally accepted altered consciousness occurs in almost all human societies, belief in possession in most of them, and trance in at least half, whereas multiple personality disorder is a diagnosis that is found mainly in industrialized Western society and is comparatively rare. Psychiatrists are still arguing about whether or why this is so. It has even been suggested that some diagnoses of dissociative identity disorder are therapy-induced. Are people in first world cultures conditioned not to believe in spirits, or is it only when psychological integrity has been damaged by trauma that they become vulnerable to involuntary trance? Does multiplicity only become dysfunctional when it clashes with the dominant culture's view of reality?

I have not found any studies that measure the neurological effects of possessory trance. The closest anyone seems to have come is some EEG research done in the eighties with patients with multiple personalities. The most interesting results are from F. W. Putnam's work with "evoked potential" responses, which are electrical changes that occur at particular spots on the cortex when the subject is exposed to a strobe light. The studies found that not only do different individuals respond with different patterns of spots, but that the various personalities, or "alters," of a patient diagnosed with dissociative identity disorder responded differently from each other. The patterns for these alters resembled those of normal individuals with similar personalities, whereas the patterns of people who were role-playing such personalities did not (Kelly and Kelly 2007, 172).

Felicitas Goodman argues that
> on the neurophysiological level, we are dealing with two
> manifestations of the same human capacity. In the case of the

vodun dancer, in traditional possession, the map (*of activated spots on the brain*) is created under the effect of the ritual and then dissolves at the proper time. That is, possession constitutes a manipulation of brain processes that can be learned.

(Goodman 1988, 21)

I have long suspected that something of the sort might be so. I would venture to predict that if one were to try this experiment with three subjects in trance for Odin (who would find the process fascinating), the EEGs would show a clear similarity.

Receptivity

The level of a possessory experience may be determined by factors such as the purpose and parameters of the ritual, the amount of energy raised by the other participants, the intensity of their need, and the will of the Power. But I have come to believe that the most important single factor is the receptivity of the medium.

Western magic, like Western culture, emphasizes control—"Love is the Law, love under will" (Crowley 1938, I, 57). In possessory work, on the other hand, when we call on the gods we say "please." Giving up control of one's body is an offering to the Power, a surrender as intimate as taking the receptive role in the act of love. The analogy between allowing a lover to penetrate one's body and allowing a Power to fill one's soul is obvious. In a sexual relationship receptivity is also usually a female role.

For this reason, although there is no physical reason a man cannot receive a Power, in cultures in which women's status is low and the status of a man depends on his strength the majority of mediums are women and gay men. This is certainly true in some groups in Brazil, where Ruth Landes was told,

No upright man will allow himself to be ridden by a god, unless he does not care about losing his manhood. His mind should always be sober, never dizzy or "tonto" from invasion by a god. Now, here's the loophole. Some men do let themselves be ridden, and they become priests with the women; but they are known to be homosexuals.

(Landes 1994, 37)

Men can perform divination, play the drums, or run the temples, but a straight man who feels himself about to "fall" may run out of the terreiro to avoid going into trance.

This was also true in the Viking Age, but may not have been so in the period that preceded it. In the introduction to his history of the Norse kings, Snorri Sturluson describes the magical skills of the god Odin, many of which require entering trance. He finishes by stating, "But the use of this magic is accompanied by so great a degree of effemination (*argr*) that men were of the opinion that they could not give themselves up to it without shame, so that it was to the priestesses that it was taught" (Sturluson 1990, 7).

According to Sørenson, "The man who is *argr* is willing or inclined to play or interested in playing the female part in sexual relations . . . When the feminine form of *argr, örg,* is applied to a woman, it [means] . . . that she is generally immodest, perverted, or lecherous" (Sørenson 1983, 18). By extension, the term is used for any behavior considered inappropriate for the Viking male. It is my belief that as Scandinavia was assimilated into medieval Europe, Christian concepts of the inferiority of women lowered the status of everything identified as feminine.

As a feminist I feel obliged to reject the imagery of being over-powered and abducted, even though being "carried away" is part of the ecstasy. Possessory work should not *need* to use the vocabulary of a rape culture. As a Heathen I find myself seeking new terms for a power differential that is not dependent on gender identity. What I can say is that the Powers are very big, and we are small. The relationship is inherently unequal, and no human can comprehend, much less contain, more than a portion of one of the Powers.

When meditating on this problem with Kuan Yin, I got the following insight:

Remember that you also have Buddha nature. You have the
Divine within you. You cannot be spiritually raped if you

expand and open to the divine essence that is yours and let it rise to meet the essence of the god. Yes, that is brilliant! A connection of equals—the expanded essence of your Self joining with the limited part of the god that you can perceive. That is a much more equal dance, yes? (warm laughter) You must become bigger, that's all.

My response was, "That's easy for You to say," but it is worth considering. Working with the Powers is indeed a mind-expanding experience. Those who practice yoga know that persuading the joints to move and the muscles to stretch takes time and patience. I think it is the same with the soul. If we develop a relationship with a Power based on knowledge and respect and then work to increase the capacity of our souls, our receptivity will become an offering rather than a sacrifice.

Practice
Exercise 14.1: Altered States

Look at the following list and note which experiences you have had. (Don't be too concerned about matching the description exactly—we all perceive things in different ways.) How, and in what context, did this happen? What was the result, and what did you learn?

Have you ever:

- Played the role of a god, goddess, or other Power in a play or ritual?

- Played the role of a Power and felt your voice and body language changing?

- Connected with a Power and relayed his or her words (in quotes)?

- Spoken in the persona of a Power while on an internal journey?

- Received information or "heard" commentary internally from a source you identified as a Power?

- Felt the presence of a Power very near you or in your head?

- Felt a stimulation or buzz in part of your cortex when meditating on or thinking about one of the Powers?

- Found yourself twitching during a chant or invocation?

- While giving a reading or counseling someone, received and transmitted information that did not come from your own knowledge or feel like your own ideas?

- Received from a Power or spirit a message that was intended for someone else?

- While aware that you were in a human body and remembering its person-identity, identified your Self as one of the Powers, with that Power's tastes and opinions (e.g., thinking that cigarette looks really good even though you have never smoked)?

- Taken the role of a Power and been told afterward that in addition to the things you do remember, things happened in the ritual of which you have no memory?

- Been aware of nothing between the start of a ritual and waking up after it ended?

Exercise 14.2: Shadow Play

Sit down and get comfortable. Call to mind the Power you have been working with. You may focus awareness by contemplating an image or singing the song you have made for Him or Her. Now close your eyes and visualize the Power standing nearby. Build up the image in your awareness. If there are words, note the message.

Now ask the Power to come closer. See Him or Her sitting next to you or standing just behind you. Open your awareness to a sense of the Power's presence until you can feel it as a pressure beside you. Lean into it; savor the sense of being close.

Practice by thinking of your Power at other times. Open your awareness to His or Her presence while walking, eating, or watching a movie you think the Power would enjoy. Pay attention to your physical sensations and offer them for the enjoyment of the Power.

Exercise 14.3: Moving Meditation

This exercise is one that I learned in the American Magic Umbanda House. It requires a group of people and some music. Participants form a circle and begin to sing a song for one of the Powers. If you do not have a song, choose a piece of music with a good rhythm that is appropriate to the Power's character or culture. As the music is sung or played, sway to the rhythm, clap, and think about the Power. As you feel the energy of the Power, move into the circle and stop singing. Dance or sway, letting the Power's energy move you. After a little while, step back into the circle and let someone else have a turn.

15

THE MIRROR AND THE MASK

Look in the mirror. Are you sure you're you? Are you sure you
didn't slip out of yourself in the middle of the night, and someone else
slipped into you, without you or you or any of you even noticing?
—Charles Yu, *How to Live Safely in a Science Fictional Universe*

As we saw in part one, the Self can be viewed as a community of parts. Paul Bloom's research in developmental psychology suggests that at quite an early age children begin to realize that person-identity transcends what happens to the body the person is in (Bloom 2004). This intuitive dualism not only enables us to believe in life after biological death, it makes the idea that a different spirit could inhabit the body comprehensible as well.

Most of the experienced mediums with whom I have spoken feel that possessory work includes many types of trance. Some people find a level at which they feel comfortable and stay there, while others work at different levels with different Powers or may experience multiple levels at different times or during the course of a trance. Mediums learn to reach these states through training and conditioning, which will also help "natural" mediums to control when and how they go into trance.

Before you begin the exercises that will lead to possession, take stock of where you are now. Review the work you did in part one. Exercise 15.1 at the end of this chapter will help you to evaluate the relevant aspects of your background and articulate your present needs.

The Severed Head

In the introduction I talked about what happened when Odin appeared so unexpectedly in my living room. As a result, I realized that I needed to know not only how to support possessory trance in others, but what it was like from the inside. At the time, I had made enough progress in

chipping away at my shields to no longer consider myself a "cement head." I could visit the Powers in "Their place," but I was not making much progress in getting them to come to mine.

That summer I visited Celtic scholar and author Caitlin Matthews in England. She had recently taken Sandra Ingerman's workshop on soul retrieval and volunteered to demonstrate. But first, she said, I would have to come up with a question. Since possessory trance was on my mind, I asked her to look for a reason why I was having so much trouble learning to do it. I recall how puzzled she sounded when her journey led to a head made of marble. Not wanting to bring back a severed head, she looked around until she found

Figure 13: The Severed Head. Painting and plaster head created by the author's mother in the late 1930s.

treasures from which to construct a body and brought them back to me. When the drumming stopped, we sat up and she asked if this had made any sense at all.

I was laughing. At home I had two pieces of art that my mother had created before I was born. One was a painting of an imprisoned lady holding out her head The other was a plaster head of the goddess Diana. (see figure 13). I realized that my mother, who eventually became a Christian Science practitioner, had programmed me to think of spirituality as something that ends at the neck. I don't know if the change was caused by understanding this or by internalizing the completed soul image that Caitlin brought back to me, but I began to make progress from that time on.

Channeling

One experience on the possessory spectrum is channeling, in which a medium voluntarily allows a spiritual being to speak through him or her to transmit teachings, do healing work, or receive or offer guidance.

Not only did Dion Fortune write nonfiction books on occultism and spiritual thrillers, she also dictated over ten million words while in trance. As described by Fielding and Collins (1985, 73–81), her method required a warded and sealed room and a three-person support team. She worked lying on a couch positioned east–west, and put herself into trance by taking a few deep breaths and visualizing a succession of symbols. At a certain point she lost consciousness of her physical surroundings and journeyed to an inner-plane temple where she met her Guides, who took over her voice and consciousness. The response of the other people in the circle, addressed to the Guide, activated a full connection, and the Guide would then proceed to dictate spiritual teachings or answer questions.

In this kind of work, the material transmitted may come in the form of feelings, ideas, or a richness of impressions, which the channeler then translates into words. Guides choose channels with the vocabulary to express the kinds of material they are interested in communicating. The richer the channel's mind is in knowledge and experience, the more words the Guide has available to express his thought impulses. As Dion Fortune put it,

> The communication brought through a medium depends to a
> large extent upon the capacity of the medium to act as a suitable channel. There are two aspects to this: one is the grade of
> the medium, which reflects the medium's own evolutionary
> development; and the other is the degree of education and

general culture of a medium. If a medium is ill-educated and has few symbols available for the mind, then the inner-plane communicator can only work with what he has. Someone has described the process of an inner-plane communicator trying to work through a poor medium as being analogous to Michaelangelo trying to build his famous statue, David, out of tins of soup.

(Fielding and Collins 1985, 151)

In chapter 8 you began to work with taking dictation. In Exercise 15.2 at the end of this chapter you will find suggestions for developing a trance practice in which only your voice is used.

Masks

Most human cultures have some kind of masking tradition, bringing mythic figures to life and freeing ordinary people from status and inhibition. Masks were used in Paleolithic rituals. They cover the faces of modern children every Hallowe'en. They hid the faces of the actors in Classical Greek plays. For a vivid recreation of this tradition, see Mary Renault's novel, *The Mask of Apollo*. A mask, like any other object that has been used in ritual, takes on some of its energy. A mask that portrays a god becomes, at the very least, a powerful cue to invoke His persona.

Figure 14: The mask of Odin

After the soul retrieval helped me over some of my inhibitions, I began to make progress with possessory work for the goddess Heide, but I was not getting very far with Odin. Although I knew that in possessory traditions the gods pay no attention to the age or gender of the medium, I couldn't believe that anyone would accept that Odin was speaking from the body of a middle-aged woman if my own face could be seen.

The following spring, when another Odin priestess, Freya Aswynn, came to visit, we discussed the problem and decided to make masks. We painted and decorated plain plastic masks from the local theatrical supply store (see figure 14). Since the original mask was featureless, I chose a minimalist style, painting the mask a metallic silver. I glued some black cloth behind the left eye hole so that in use only one eye would be seen, and added a beard. I consecrated the mask with a bind rune of Ehwaz, the Horse rune, and Naudhiz, for Need. Inside the mask I inscribed several of the bynames of the god.

Freya took her mask home. I hung mine over my Odin altar for a while and "fed" it with a little mead. Then I called on a friend to help me, put it on, and waited as she called the god. My body was still my own, but I found that if I sat in a chair wearing the mask, the god gave me words.

In Exercise 15.3 you will find suggestions for working with a mask.

The Goddess in the Mirror

One variety of possessory work is taking on a god form, a practice in which the image of the deity, formulated through intense focus and visualization, overshadows and surrounds the priest or priestess. One way to do this is through contemplation. In Buddhist Vajrayana practice, seekers gaze at a *thangka* image of the *yidam*, or meditation deity. They visualize themselves becoming the deity, internalizing the qualities of the Buddha (Lipton and Ragnubs, 1996). Something analogous can be done with a mirror.

In the early eighties, my Pagan spiritual focus was Darkmoon Circle, an eclectic women's spirituality group which I founded with Marion Zimmer Bradley, and which still meets today. One of the rituals we came up with was the "Come As Your Favorite Goddess" rite. One by one, each woman in the circle, dressed to represent a different goddess, took her place behind the altar. As the others sang "Goddess, heed us now, beloved Lady _____, bless us!" the woman whose turn it was would visualize the chosen goddess overshadowing her.

When the singing had gone on long enough, she lifted her hands to give a blessing. Sometimes all we got was whatever the priestess felt was appropriate. At other times, the words of the goddess were relayed as they came into her head. Occasionally, we had that sense of Presence where the skin gets goose bumps and you know that something more than human is here. Then we might see the figure of the woman overlaid by the image of the goddess as we received Her words.

In 1983, Marion gave me the following poem.

Trance Formations

Through the smoke of incense
And across the candle flame,
I look at the woman in the mirror,
I look until her face blurs and she is not myself.

Across the incense smoke
The woman in the mirror looks out at me
And I become
The woman in the mirror.

Across the candle flame
I look at the woman in the mirror
And her face blurs
About her head I see the halo and hood
The blue crescent glows on her forehead
The ornaments of a priestess circle her brows.
I see the priestess in the mirror.

And across the incense smoke
The priestess in the mirror looks out at me
From beneath her sacred garlands;
The blue crescent burns upon my brow,
And I become
The priestess in the mirror.
Standing beneath the sacred garlands,

I behold the priestess in the mirror
Through the Delphic clouds of the laurel smoke,
And again her face blurs,
The garlands become a shimmering aura,
The robes of the priestess merge into folds of air
Never woven on earthly looms,
I see the Goddess in the mirror.

I see the Goddess in the mirror.
Who is this Goddess?
Shall I call her Ceridwen, Isis, Nuit?
Innana, Ashtoreth, Astarte. . . .
White Buffalo Calf Woman, Grandmother of the Human Race?
I see the horns spread wide on her brow
The crescent moon shadowing her face,
Where she stands upon the wide pillars of the world,
I behold the Goddess in the mirror
And I become. . . .

In fiction, it is often possible to convey the essence of an experience more vividly than in any training manual. This is certainly true in *Moon Magic* when Dion Fortune describes a ritual in which the priestess assumes the form of Isis.

I saw something moving in the mirror, and knew that the Goddess was formulating. A light haze began to spread over its surface. I have to conceive of the Goddess as behind me when She formulates, so I left my chair and went and stood at Malcolm's feet with my back to the mirror . . . I began to give magnetism to the Goddess and Her form built up as I visualized it, and then power began to come through into it—power from that for which Isis stands; power from the moon and the moon-side of things, and the thing for which the moon stands. The image became alive in its own right. Then, strangest form of obsession, it slowly superimposed itself upon me, and, already fortified by the accession of Malcolm's magnetism, I received it, so that I became Isis for the time being (this is the old temple-working, not generally known), and Malcolm found himself face to face with the Goddess who both was and was not me.

My consciousness seemed to be in abeyance in the background, somewhere behind the form of the Goddess, and yet I was She, and shared Her consciousness.

(Fortune 1978, 185–86)

This sounds very close to the technique for the Assumption of God Forms described by Ivo Dominguez Jr. on pages 111–13 of *Spirit Speak,* which contains some excellent material. If your training is in one of the ceremonial magical traditions, you will probably find that the approach to possessory trance described in that book will work well for you.

Practice
Exercise 15.1: Self-Evaluation Before Training for Possessory Trance

1. What is your general state of health? Do you have any chronic or cyclical problems or conditions (especially heart, blood pressure, diabetic, menstrual or menopausal symptoms, etc.) that affect your mood, energy, or focus? Are you on any medications?

To work as a medium requires both psychic and physical strength, especially for full-body possession. Carrying a god takes a lot of energy, and some Powers engage in vigorous activity that may stress the body. Certain conditions, or the medications used to treat them, can get in the way of a clear connection.

2. Have you been in counseling? What kind and for what?

Before you can safely allow another being to use your voice or body, you need to be very clear about who you really are. Those who have been diagnosed with mood, post-traumatic stress, or personality disorders could suffer harmful aftereffects from voluntary dissociation. People who have had psychotic or bipolar problems should definitely avoid this kind of trance work. Other issues, such as anger management, might make a difference in the kinds of Powers you are able to work with.

3. What is your experience with altered states?

- What traditions of trance or meditation have you practiced? How long?

- Which ones did you find most compatible, and which seemed unsympathetic? In each case, can you identify why?

Analyzing your experience with trance will help you identify the skills you bring to the work.

4. What do you know about the following?

- Relaxation and breath control—these skills can help the medium to still the mind so that a Power can get in. For exercises that will help you to develop them, see chapters 1–3 of *Trance-Portation*.)

- Visualization—a useful method for developing your relationship with the Powers. For exercises that will help you to perceive, focus, remember, and articulate what you see in a vision, see chapter 4 of *Trance-Portation*)

- Self-hypnosis—adapt this to cue possessory trance.

- Solo journeying—one way to connect with a Power. For exercises, see chapters 5 and 8 of *Trance-Portation*.)

- Shamanic healing—a useful experience in working with spirits.

- Mythology—list the pantheons and cultures you know well, and those you know well enough to identify deities and symbols. You should only attempt to contact/answer questions about deities of whom you have some knowledge. A good resource is Joseph Campbell's *Masks of God*.

5. Have you ever had an involuntary psychic experience? Has it happened more than once?

Some people are drawn to possessory work because they have had such experiences, and others because they would like to. If you are the former, analyzing what happened will help you predict how you are likely to react to formal training.

6. How do you react to alcohol and drugs? Have you ever taken any psychoactive drug or hallucinogen? How did it affect you?

Although drugs are not necessary to reach an altered state, they can propel you into one. Drug experience may give you an idea how you might react to trance.

7. Have you ever had a life-threatening accident or illness? Did you have any weird experiences during the crisis? Did it change your attitude toward life?

Such experiences are common in shamanic traditions. They may also point you toward spiritual work of other kinds.

8. What is your religious background?

- How did the faith you grew up in view the relationship between humans and God?

- Did it provide training in prayer or other spiritual skills?

- Did it teach the gifts of the Spirit or other ecstatic practices?

9. Do you have a strong affinity with/devotion to specific gods or goddesses? How did you encounter them? How often do you contact them, or how do they contact you?

Those who have strong relationships with deities are more likely to be able to carry them.

10. Do you belong to a circle, kindred, coven or other spiritual group? Does it practice trance work or meditation? If so, what kinds? How often? For what purposes?

Although developing a relationship with spirit requires individual work, trance possession requires other people with whom the Power can interact. To safely do the work, you need a team.

11. Are any other group members working with this book? Will your group support your efforts to master these skills? Is this group part of a wider community that a possessory team might serve?

In order to give answers, you need people who will ask questions and a support team.

12. Would you characterize yourself as god-hungry or god-bothered? What are your goals in beginning this training? Why do you want to learn how to do possessory work? In what context do you see yourself using this skill?

This is the critical question. Try to visualize yourself acting as a medium. Who are you serving? What will you get out of it? What will they?

When you have answered these questions, consider whether you are ready to take on a demanding spiritual practice. In particular, evaluate your health. If you have concerns about any ongoing conditions or problems, now is the time to deal with them.

Exercise 15.2: Channeling

The essential skill in mediumship is the ability to release consciousness and control. This is easier if you are lying down, are speaking rather than trying to type, and are supported by people who can watch over your body, boost your energy, and keep you focused. You will need a comfortable bed in a room that can be kept at an even temperature and where you will not be interrupted.

Prepare by practicing the breathing exercise in chapter 2 until you can maintain a state of relaxed clarity in which all the distracting thoughts can be shunted aside. Find one or two friends to work with you, and create a ritual structure that includes cleansing and warding the space. Develop an induction sequence based on the instructions for journeying in chapter 6 that will take you to the temple of your Power.

Ground and center, stretch to release tight muscles, and lie down. A light blanket will keep you comfortable—it can get cold between the worlds. Your guide will instruct you to deepen your breathing and enter the contemplative state, leaving time between instructions, and ask for confirmation from you as you reach each stage. The guide will then direct you to begin your journey to the temple. Maintaining verbal communication will keep your voice active even as awareness of other parts of your body fades. When you have found the Power, the guide will ask the question that has been decided on. Your response may begin as a relay—"He smiles, and says, 'That's an interesting question . . .'"—but as the interaction continues it will probably become easier and easier to simply say the words as you hear them. You may find yourself carrying on another conversation with the Power in your head as you speak Her words, your consciousness may go somewhere else, or you may be aware of nothing at all until your guide calls you back and instructs you to start homeward once more.

Exercise 15.3: Masks of God

Make a mask for your Power. Use paint, appliqué fabric, etc. to build the features into something resembling the image you see in your mind. Decorate with the colors and symbols you discovered in your research. Finish with fixative or another preservative. Inside, write the Power's name.

When the mask is ready, bless and dedicate it. Hang it over the altar of the Power to absorb energy, and for a week offer it a little of the Power's favorite drink every evening. Talk to it as you would to the Power.

Then, with the support of one or more friends, set up a ritual. Prepare the space as usual. Position a mirror where you can see the mask from your chair. Put on a ritual robe or appropriate garment, sit down, and start singing the songs that bring your Power most strongly to mind. When the moment seems right, put on the mask. How does that feel? Turn to look into the mirror. Who do you see?

You may simply sit, enjoying the sense of shared identity, or the Power may get you up and moving. Your friends should ask questions, to which you respond from the point of view of the Power. Presently, it may become something more. When the energy begins to fade, your friends should get you to sit down, ask the Power to depart, and take the mask off.

16

HORSE TRAINING

*So that when he came at last to this one [death], he could offer the
goddess a smooth and steady partnering . . . humbling parallels
involving the training of mules offered themselves to his mind.*
—Lois McMaster Bujold, *The Curse of Chalion*

Everyone who gets involved with the Powers has a story. While I am sure
my own experience is not universal, it is the one for which I have the most
data. Fortunately I still have the notes describing our early experiments.

After the soul retrieval described in chapter 15, I began focused
work with Heide, seen by some as a witchy aspect of the goddess Freyja
and by others as a separate Power. Since she usually presents as a mature
woman and in my own meditations identified herself with the primal
seeress of the *Völuspá*, I thought that we had enough in common for me
to carry her not only comfortably, but credibly.

Although the soul retrieval had broken down my initial resistance, I
had a lot of anxiety about opening up to possession. I thought I might feel
safe enough to let go if, drawing on the analysis of soul parts described in
chapter 3, I put each part of myself under the protection of a deity. This is
certainly not the only way to open up, but for someone who is being held
back by anxiety it can be helpful. I worked this list into the induction at
the end of this chapter, aiming for a connection with Heide.

10/29/91

Taped and tried out complete induction sequence, allow-ing about a minute for each stage. Physical relaxation fairly easy; releasing *hamr* interesting = feeling of lightness, possi-bly what I actually released was my shielding; mind-blanking fairly easy; release of *önd* produced strong sense of tingling in the crown chakra and a kind of disorientation which may relate to Raudhildr's comment on sensations associated with spinning around; at this point things became somewhat confused, difficulty with precise visualization/identifica-tion. There was an intermittent sensation that the locus of consciousness had shifted to slightly above and to one side of the back of the head. Something happened, but I'm not sure precisely what or who. Impression is that the aspect I got was more Gullveig than Heide, almost a Lilith personality, sensual and amused rather than grim and hag-like. Next steps, internal journeying to learn more, devise better procedure to close up again—reverse of induction.

My friend Raudhildr and I practiced in this way for several weeks, did a dry run, and then a ritual to bring Heide through for the kindred.

11/13/91

I'm glad I had practiced and meditated beforehand. It was still a less complete change than I would have liked, much less total possession, but at the very least I was able to escape my inhibi-tions and let the power of the goddess flow through. In seidh trance, I lose awareness of my body to the point where limbs sometimes go to sleep, and retain control of my face and lips only. I float in darkness until someone asks a question, when the visions form. This, time, however, I felt more energetic than usual, leaned forward, gestured, moved around in the chair. I/we felt quite capable of getting up and dancing. The responses tended to pick up on some metaphor in the ques-tion, or find one from Norse myth, and use it to give an answer.

The content was delivered in a style which my characters use in my books sometimes, but which I would not feel comfortable using in my own person. We took questions from about eight people; when I became aware that all the talking was getting to the throat I/She finally gave in and got out, which was relatively easy and painless, except that I immediately began coughing furiously. It wasn't like being talked out of trance, where the need is to regain control of the body. It was more like being asked to leave a party where I was having a good time. Whether or not this was possession, it was certainly a step forward for me. I felt, basically, as if I were fully conscious and in control—but the Self in control was not the usual me.

During the year that followed, a small group from the kindred met every month or so to work on inducing and managing trance. Many of the sessions involved calling Odin into Niklas. The following is a good example.

2/5/92

Odin seemed to have too much energy to sit quietly, nor was he completely in synch with Niklas's body. When seated, he tried to fold his legs cross-legged, which was not really practical in the chair. There were frequent spasmodic leg movements, and in fact the effect was very much like watching someone riding a lively and restive horse. Some of the jerking may have been Niklas trying to regain some control. We attempted to stabilize by gripping his knees, stroking leg or hands, sending reassurance through the body, and also helping Odin to keep his balance. He wandered about a lot, sometimes steadily, sometimes not. We supported him or scurried ahead moving chairs or cushions out of the way.

Several times, Odin rose on his toes so that he literally seemed to grow taller—was this an attempt to expand the human body to contain a being of larger size? (Reminds me of the moment when Demeter reveals herself in the Homeric

Hymn, expanding so that her head brushes the lintel and causing everyone to go pea-green with fear! Apparently the gods are around 7' tall). Niklas is actually a tall man, but his body was not quite big enough for the god. Odin's expression is quite different from Niklas's, somehow sterner, sharper, hard to describe because my eyes unfocus when I look directly into His, and in the darkness of the eye patch I see stars. His posture is very erect, His body language is commanding, His grip extremely powerful. The impression is definitely of being in the presence of a vivid and powerful personality. There is an atmosphere of danger, but it is exhilarating.

After a year of practice both our mediums and our community had gained experience. We noted that the time and complexity of preparation needed for a medium (even me) to get into trance grew shorter as support and energy from the team increased.

12/92

I need a few minutes to work myself through each stage of release (this may get speedier with practice). Awareness of approaching deity precedes union. Allow time to say hi before jumping into bed. This is facilitated if others maintain chant or repeated god-name. Internally and externally perceptible symptoms of possession include quickened breathing, not panting, but slightly accelerated, deeper breaths; Tourette's-like nodding and shaking of the head, which may be followed by hand movements; sense of pressure first at back of head, extending over crown; dilated eyes. A period of shared consciousness in which an internal dialogue is going on may be succeeded by a state in which self and Other are unified into a conscious joint identity which is perceived as being different from my normal personality.

In January 1993 I was invited to attend a bembé at the American Magic Umbanda House:

1/23/93

P went off instantly when Exu was called, and maintained possession through the entire event as gatekeeper. Most of the orixas [orishas] the group works with have a "child" who acts as senior medium, maintaining trance for a longer period, but all of them are horsed by several people simultaneously. Most of the regulars horse more than one deity, some of them seemed to do most. Those who do more than four in one session are called "trance sluts." The ability to do this safely is considered a result of experience.

I was prepared for Iansa or Iemanja; however, this is not what happened—perhaps the gods' way of convincing me it was not wish fulfillment. B got Ogum, and then, as expected from his previous experience, Oxossi. When Oxossi came by and spun me around, I did too. What was happening was confirmed and intensified by the reaction of the other people giving me implements of the god etc. I think this sense of being supported and protected allows the trance to deepen.

My perception of the personality involved was that of a very old Indian woman. For a time I/we squatted on the floor, moved around that way, blessing the floor/earth and people's feet with the feathers. Eventually We got up, did some Indian style dancing, took an ear of corn and went around blessing people with it. At the end of the Oxossi songs, they doused me with water to bring me out.

When we got to Oxum, I was minding my own business, enjoying the energy, when I felt the solar plexus rush, and we were off again. This state was characterized by wild laughter and a compulsion to dance, using some belly dance movements. Oxum immediately got rid of my hair clip. The main hazard here is getting fed honey, which gets all over one's face and in the hair. This one did not surprise me so much, as I have worked with Freyja, who is a very good match for Oxum . . .

B did a brief Gedé, then Obatala was invoked, and he went off fast and deep, and was seated with a horsehair whisk and a cloth over his head. I was standing, holding onto his chair, and presently started the head jerkings I have come to associate with onset of the Norse deities. Eventually, though my posture was erect and I wasn't falling over, this became pronounced enough so that someone noticed and gave me a chair, a veil, and a cup to hold. Eventually I got up and moved around, blessing people.

Afterward I was tired and very hungry. Ate a plateful at the bembé, and a lot more that evening. A little spacey still, with a tendency to head twitches whenever I think about it too much. The bembé is a very supportive environment. Once I convinced myself that it was okay with the house for me to do this, that in fact they wanted me to, it was much easier than when I work alone.

In the months that followed, almost every time I attended a bembé I would go into trance for a new Power. I felt as if I was on display in a spiritual supermarket where the Powers were shopping. With all this practice, getting in and out of trance became steadily smoother. Instead of going through the lengthy release-and-protection induction, I simply released personal awareness with my breath, relaxed, and let myself be filled by the image of the Power or the song. Putting on a veil or being given a tool belonging to the Power "seated" the change. Being in a warded environment with people who knew how to handle possessory trance supplied the necessary security. The cues were provided by the ritual.

I was still, however, unable to go into trance for Odin. When I took my dog for his last walk of the evening I would meditate on this problem. My notes from one of these evenings illustrate the difficulty:

After folk magic class we watched the last scene of *Rheingold* as an example of a storm summoning spell. While watching Wotan, I noticed the usual head twitchings of trance coming on and Odin started talking in my head. The conversation continued, with comments on the action in the opera and discussion of my book, while I was getting everyone out of the house and walking the dog. By this time it was clear the god really wanted to come in. Walking, it actually felt as if I were a horse being ridden by someone with good, steadying hands, as when I used to imagine being both horse and rider as a child.

A few months later, Freya Aswynn came to visit and we made the masks described in chapter 14. Throughout that year, members of my kindred explored different ways of working with the Norse gods, and I regularly attended the AMUH bembés. The following year, Freya came to visit once more. We set up a small devotional ritual for Odin, talking about the work we had been doing and singing His songs.

At one point I got up and began to dance around, beating the drum as I sang. I felt the energy rising, and suddenly a Voice in my head that said, "Finally, I've got her to *move*!" At that moment, Odin came in fully with a great shout of laughter, and I was gone.

Since then, my relationship with Odin has extended and deepened. Although He requires exclusivity from some of His devotees, He has encouraged me to work with a variety of other Powers. During the months that followed I found myself picking up all the female Powers with whom He is linked—Freyja, Skadhi, Gunnlodh, and eventually Frigg Herself, however He also encouraged my contact with other pantheons, perhaps to make it easier for Him to communicate with them.

After I had been working with the AMUH for a year, my primary deity in the house was identified as Nana Buruku, the "grandmother of the gods." Like Heide and Hecate, with whom I have also worked, Nana Buruku is old and wise, an easy ride. These are my notes on an early experience with Her:

11/8/93

I have been horsing Nana regularly since July. The first time I was sitting on the couch, not expecting anything, and suddenly went out like falling down a long blue well. Eventually someone threw a veil over me and I sat there trying to figure out what was going on.

Since then, she has come regularly, and the house now expects it. I begin to go almost as soon as the chant starts—walk a few steps forward and then stand swaying until someone gets me into a chair. The aspect that seems to come through me is a rather jolly old lady, very grandmotherly. She seems quite delighted to be honored—says nobody ever pays attention to old ladies. She sometimes hops and jiggles a little to the drumbeat. She likes to have a plate of cookies handy to share. Sometimes stays through the songs for Aganju and Xango, who she really likes and calls "a good boy."

At the retreat this weekend, the house tried out the consultation ceremony, in which the orixas are invoked and seated and consult instead of partying. I felt tired and a little wonky beforehand, as usual, wondering if it was going to work, but went out almost immediately and was seated. Once this had happened, however, I/She felt quite alert, and interested in what was going on. She got several visitors, which I remember only vaguely, and had a long time to sit and think. What came through in these ruminations was concern and outrage at the idea of old women in old folks' homes, and then a deepening meditation on primal earth, with insights about fossils, and a desire to tell folktales. When we got to the fossil level Mama thought she'd better pull me out before things became too pre-human. Afterward I felt very energetic.

As I did more work with the Powers, I found that although I usually had only the most vague memories of the Power's interaction with other people, I could often remember conversations that the Power and I had been having in my head at the same time. One exception was that although I might not retain what a Power said to one of His other devotees, to share in the rush of love the Power felt for His child colored my later perceptions of that person, no matter how annoying he or she might sometimes be.

As it became clear that Nana was going to be one of my "regulars," I began scouring the Internet and the libraries for information. An affinity based on similarity became even clearer:

9/10/94

As I read more about Nana, especially the Ayizan aspect—if they are the same—I begin to understand better why she is coming to me. [In Haiti, Nana does not possess, and some consider Ayizan Her manifestation in the physical world.] The priestess aspect is in fact what I am doing with my life, and the Mother of Memory relates to the resurrection of old myths and storytelling. The other Orixas also perform these functions, but Nana is the one who does it as an older woman, a role which I am trying to prepare for. I would like to be the Völva when I grow up.

By the spring of 1995, the mother of the house had begun to suggest that it was time for a head washing. The problem was that one ought to be initiated to one's head deity first, and it was clear that my primary Power was Odin. My connection to Him had developed so gradually that a formal dedication had never seemed necessary. The best solution I could think of was to call Odin in for a talk with Mama and let them fight it out.

I am told that He came through in His finest and most charming form. One friend reported that my aura flared with a surge of blue-white light when He arrived. She also said it was really disturbing to see my body with a personality that wasn't me. In the discussion that followed, Odin told Mama that *He* didn't need a ceremony, but that for me to feel right I should get a valknut tattoo. After that, I could go on with other initiations. I got the tattoo the following April, accompanied by runic chanting by Kveldulf Gundarsson and Freya Aswynn, and in October had my head washing for Nana.

Since then, I have developed a relationship with several other Powers in the African pantheon, as well as with several deities from other traditions. With a little time to research and prepare, I am able to enter a medium-level trance for almost any deity that someone needs to talk to. While doing research for an article about Kuan Yin, I discovered that She is one of the more aggressive and active Powers around. When I opened the door, She grabbed me, and I have been working with Her ever since—especially to do healing.

My process has also become much more streamlined. Although I only go for a deep trance in a community situation where I can depend on experienced support, to direct some energy from a Power for a specific purpose, I sometimes use a modified induction as follows:

1. Articulate the purpose, such as sending healing energy to someone who needs it.

2. Light a candle on the altar, or simply face it.

3. Play atmospheric music, or sing a song for the Power.

4. Close my eyes, breathe deeply, and release tension and self-awareness.

5. Focus on the image of the Power.

6. Sway to the music until I feel the buzz through the back of my head. My head shakes back and forth as if to release energy, and my whole body twitches. The energy releases with a stamp or drumming by one foot, and sometimes a burst of laughter.

7. Settle back down, filled with the personality of the Power, who remembers the purpose for which She was called, turns to face the direction of the patient, and projects Her energy.

8. When it is done, if there is no other work, the Power relaxes, awareness fades, and I recognize my own identity once more.

Do I achieve "full possession"? The depth of trance can vary, even within a ritual. Certainly it is more rewarding for *me* when I can remember what things look like from the perspective of Odin or Kuan Yin. A more relevant question is whether what I am doing is *useful*. The deepest states are called forth by the greatest need—not mine, but the need of the Power to communicate, and the need of the community to hear.

Practice
Exercise 16.1: Body and Souls

Reread the section on soul parts in chapter 2. Drawing on the mythology and culture of the Power you are working with, identify guardians and (if possible) culturally appropriate names for

- The physical body

- The astral or etheric body

- The emotional body/unconscious/memory (right brain)

- The mental body/mind (left brain)

- The breath/spirit/divine spark

- The higher self/god link (your patron deity)

Review the work you did in part one and chapter 6 to create an induction that will meet your needs.

While you are doing this, develop awareness of each part through practices such as the following:

- Accept and learn to love each aspect of the physical body in turn, including your appearance and the way you move. Evaluate your health; let your body tell you what it needs.

- Learn the boundaries of your aura. Practice moving internal energy, practice moving the etheric body outside of the physical (astral projection), and visualize looking at your body from another part of room.

- Observe emotional states and note what triggers them. Identify memories that move you, identify elements of your family and cultural inheritance that have emotional impact.

- Observe your mental monologue. Identify habits of thought. Meditate and work on the state of no-mind.

- Practice breathing. Focus on each breath. Note the effects of breathing at different speeds.

- Learn to sense each "soul" and develop a cue associated with it (an image, a verse, or a command). Spend three to seven days on each one.

- Write an induction for releasing each "body" into the protection of a guardian and read it onto a tape. Leave a space in the middle to experience the connection with your deity. You can use the induction I developed as an example. Practice doing the exercise with the tape until you have internalized the process, then increase the speed until you can release each "body" in smooth sequence, and in reverse order, restore awareness equally smoothly. You may also practice by having a friend read the induction.

Induction for Releasing and Protecting Soul Parts Using Germanic Imagery

If you are using this induction to lead someone besides yourself, change all instances of "my" and "I" to "your" and "you."

My* body's likeness now I leave,	
The lovely lyke that Lódhurr gave	
Lá and læti and litr too	(bindrune: Elhaz + Othala)
I give to be guarded	(assume comfortable position,
by the holy gods.	relax muscles)

My holy hide I will not hold,	
hail, hamingja, help me journey	
as hamr spirit shape I shed,	(bindrune: Elhaz + Uruz)
guard it all ye holy gods.	(release awareness of body)
Huginn and Muninn now I summon	
to master mind and memory;	
emotion's energy is ended,	(Elhaz + Berkano)
thoughts, I thank and thrust away.	(Elhaz + Tyr)
Dis and fylgja shall preserve them,	
guard me all ye holy gods.	(clear consciousness of all thoughts and emotions, float in calm clarity)
The önd that Odhinn gave flows out,	
breath I bid bear spirit skyward	
While lyke and hide & hugr & minne	(Elhaz + Ansuz)
are guarded by the holy gods.	(regularize breathing, and move into a deeper level of trance)
With Hoenir's help,	
_____ (Name of deity) I hail,	
Ecstasy all else excelling	
Possess the place that I have opened,	(godrune or Ehwaz)
Now I call thee to come in!	(visualize deity, meet, match energy, let deity take over)

On the tape, allow up to five minutes to experience the connection with the Power. Ask that you be allowed to remember whatever information is conveyed to you. If you are doing this with a guide, that person can ask questions and note the answers.

When you are done, reverse the process to return to ordinary consciousness.

(Name of deity) the hour grows late—	
I bid you bless and let _____ (me/name of medium) go.	
Hoenir, help the returning spirit,	
Safe into the head once more.	
Holy Odin, bless the breath,	
As önd flows in and out and in again . . .	(breathe in and out at a normal rate)
Huginn and Muninn here I hail	
To bring back thought and memory.	(think about who you are)
This place is _____ (identify location)	
And I am _____ (name)	
Now the holy hamr I hold,	
Wrap it warm and safe around me.	(focus awareness on the energy field around your body)
My body's likeness I reclaim,	
The lovely lyke that Lódhurr gave,	(focus on heartbeat, senses)
Lá and læti and litr.	(wiggle fingers and toes)
Sigh and stretch, my form resuming,	
Hale and whole I am restored.	

Drink some water or taste some salt if you are still a little spacey. Then write down what you remember.

17

FILLED WITH THE GOD

The Greeks understood the mysterious power of the hidden side of things. They bequeathed to us one of the most beautiful words in our language—the word "enthusiasm"—En theos—an Inner God. The grandeur of human actions is measured by the inspiration from which they spring. Happy is he who bears within himself a god, an ideal of beauty, and who obeys it.
—Louis Pasteur

In the preceding chapter I described my own journey, but no single experience is universal. While writing this book I corresponded with people who do possessory work in a variety of traditions. Their insights give us a more inclusive picture of what it means to be a medium.

People participate in possessory rituals for many reasons. For the mediums, rewards include exercise for the body and soul and satisfaction in having been able to serve the community and the Powers. For the people, it is the opportunity to feel the energy of the Powers and to receive counsel, inspiration, and sometimes healing.

Coming to the Work

People become trance mediums in many ways. Kathleen, who has been doing possessory work for thirty-two years, had out-of-body experiences as a child. As a young woman, she "got tapped at a séance rather heavily." The next year she joined a coven, and later on a voudou house. She learned to control her trance work by watching others, and she was also taught by a "mentor" on the inner planes. As a teenager, Thenea Pantera suffered from possession by a discarnate spirit, who was finally banished only when she began to work with the Greek gods.

Some people are recruited by their gods. In college Camilla Morgaine experimented with channeling techniques learned from books, then did Drawing Down in her coven. After a personal crisis, she met the Morrigan in dreams, and eventually found a friend to work with, channeling online. River Devora, a Heathen and Santeria practitioner, says,

> Others have to learn because they are given no choice.
>
> I declared I believed in all deities and wanted nothing to do with any of them, since deities seemed to me to be large opportunistic entities who used people to effect change according to their own agendas, with little regard for my safety, comfort, or consent. I felt violated and disposable. The random possession slowed way down once I stopped attending events but didn't stop entirely. At some point during that time, an entity calling herself a faery showed up in my life as an ally and teacher. She encouraged me to reconnect with the human pagan community, and half helped, half bullied me into connecting with deities, first with Freyja, then a Saami goddess named Juksakka, and eventually with Odin as well as others from a variety of pantheons. I did a yearlong intensive training with Juksakka, which included learning how to safely and consensually navigate trance possession. She eventually handed me over to Odin, who got me working with the rest of the Norse pantheon. The bunch of Them pushed me towards Santeria. I initiated as a priest of Ochun in July 2011.

Someone who needs to learn about possessory trance can look for a group that works in an Afro-Diasporic tradition or a Wiccan coven that trains its members in Drawing Down or Aspecting. Unfortunately, although the number of such groups is growing, in many places there are none or they are not open to new members, or you do not wish to leave the tradition you already have. Afro-Diasporic groups are becoming more inclusive (just as people from many ethnicities are being drawn to neopagan traditions), but to understand the Powers you must study their cultures. People in the Reconstructionist traditions are developing practices that are rooted in the cultures of Greece, the North, or the Celtic lands. Another source of training is through internal connection with a helping deity or spirit. The kind of relationship you developed with your god while working through part two will help you to negotiate a useful process.

Inducing Trance

Whether you're trying to open up and let a Power come in or close the head and keep it out, I believe that the most effective way to train and control trance is by working with cues and conditioning. With such training, not only will you open up more quickly, but in the absence of those signals you are less likely to be possessed.

In a traditional culture, the medium is supported by the knowledge that she will be surrounded by people who understand what is going on. She grows up associating certain colors, symbols, drum rhythms, and songs with Powers whose myths and nature she also knows. By the time she is permitted by initiation or custom to "go out" for a Power, she has internalized the process. In the Afro-Diasporic religions, the ritual provides specific cues that signal the medium to shift awareness. Singing, clapping, and swaying to the beat of the drums, the other participants raise the energy level to carry her through. The Power being invoked is summoned by their need.

The same kinds of cues bring through Powers from other cultures. By creating an altar, you learned to associate certain colors and symbols, and by writing prayers and songs, how to call the Power. Now, simply seeing the images or hearing the music should bring the Power vividly to mind. When these things are presented in a ritual context in which trance is both permitted and expected, they will act as signals to open up to the Power.

Physical consciousness-altering techniques include percussive sound, movement, and hyper- or hypoventilation. The music of a trance dance opens the psyche to release what is within the dancer. The music at a possessory event opens one up so that a Power can come in. A touch from a Power who is already being carried by another medium can be enough to tip the balance.

Mediums often go through a threshold state in which they waver, simultaneously drawn by trance and resisting it. Some common symptoms of approaching trance are loss of balance, uncoordinated or repetitive movements, or sometimes, standing very still with an unfocused gaze. The support team needs to be ready to catch the medium if she starts to fall, but otherwise should not interfere until the transition has been made. The violence of the transition may depend on the resistance of the medium, the energy of the Power, and perhaps the cultural expectation regarding how such things occur.

As the possession settles in, posture, body language, accent, and expression all change. The energy and aura are different for those who can see. When you know Whom you are dealing with, the possession can be solidified by addressing the medium by the name of the Power, and offering His or Her garments or sacred tools. The possessed medium may be led into another room to put on the full costume of the Power before returning to the ritual. Depending on the culture, tradition, and preference of the Power, He or She may dance, sit, and talk to participants or move around. Eating and drinking the offerings can help to bring the Power fully into the body of the medium.

With experience, you will learn to recognize the symptoms of oncoming trance and work with them. You will also be able to tell the warders or other participants how to support and help you. As the following reports show, some reactions are fairly common, while others are specific to the medium.

> I feel as though I am lifting out of my body, that I am suspended for a fraction of a fraction of a second, then I come back to rest lightly around or in my body. Sometimes I feel as though I am separate yet part of my self. Other times I'm in the "backseat," or in the trunk, but I can still hear what's going on. A really good trance (or so they tell me) is when

it feels very dreamlike, where I feel as though I have taken a drug that's relaxed me so everything is hazy, wonderful, beautiful, and "wow, man, far out . . ."

I've noticed that at these times, time does weird things, and I may tend to forget things that happen (unless someone mentions it, then I have a hazy recollection of the incident mentioned). A good trance will leave me very tired afterward, so I plan on having a quiet day the day after bembés. Sometimes, usually when I'm with the Umbanda people, I will slide into light trance and not realize it. Sometimes the Spirits are just "peeking in."

Kathleen (Wicca, Voudou, Umbanda)

My main clue that I have a "visitor" is hearing thoughts that are not my own—thoughts that "taste" like somebody else's. Usually this is in the form of commentary, but sometimes it's a sensation or a wave of emotion. Then comes the "knocking," which feels like waves of vertigo [and is] potentially intense enough to knock me off my feet, but usually just enough to make me dizzy or stumble. It can feel like the air immediately around my head is somehow thicker or more humid than the rest of the air. If I resist and They insist, my body may start shaking until I either give in or fight it off, but that's rare. If I don't resist, I start taking on Their mannerisms and vocal tones as They settle in.

Ember Cooke (Heathen, Umbanda)

The earlier levels . . . feel like mild nausea to me and dizziness. Awareness seems to be significantly lessened when I am speaking in another language, especially one I don't speak—LOL. Afterward I can remember small pieces of what went on, [but] it almost seems like the more actively I try to remember, the more fleeting the experience becomes.

In most instances when I have observed someone going into genuine trance, they have fallen to the ground and experience some shaking, shrieking, speaking in tongues or a language they aren't fluent in, and perform extreme feats and the like. I support them by having items they may request handy and also having what we refer to as a spiritual first aid kit including Florida water, crystals, cascarilla, etc.

Lilith Dorsey (Voudou, Santeria)

The focus is to get myself out of the way, at which point I know I'm looking, or moving around and speaking. I then have the feeling like I'm floating, rising above my body. I'm aware of what has been asked and responded. When I come back I'm fully aware of everything that was said, then it just drifts away.

Kwauo (unnamed path, hoodoo, Umbanda, Spiritualism)

Once I am getting ready to do a shamanic session, the spirits start coming into my head thick and fast, and sometimes I have a Tourette's-like twitch when spirits are coming in too suddenly or too big for me to handle gracefully. I sing a series of songs to the spirits in order to become entranced. The spirits reiterate my cosmology. By the time I begin singing and rattling, I am already partly entranced. With my songs, the spirits know it is time for us to work.

Caroline Kenner (shamanic healer)

I feel something that's almost, but not quite, like being light-headed or inebriated. My behavior shifts in a way that we term "wonky," or "god-drunk." It becomes progressively harder to focus on things that require rational thought and concentration, e.g., cooking, although simple tasks that are obviously leading towards a possessory event are okay because they lead me further towards where I eventually intend to go. At most of these steps, I can ground out and attempt to put that feeling, and my increased awareness of the power, "back in the box." This will get harder as the moment draws closer . . . When all of the background cues are in place, and it's time to actively hand over control, I try to find a moment to run through my active cues (breathing and so on), bringing that power to an active co-awareness in my mind. We do a lot of singing in Hrafnar, which is one of the ways I know it's "okay to go."

Lorrie Wood (Heathen)

Negotiation and Consent

Possessory trance may be ecstatic, but it is not always comfortable or easy. Like any relationship, the connection between the medium and the Power may require negotiation. Working with a Power in such an intimate way can activate deep issues relating to vulnerability and control. Just because you have become a medium does not mean you have no boundaries. In fact, once you have learned to welcome Them in to your place, it may become even more important to be able to shut the door.

As you develop your capacities you will learn what you need. Some mediums require warning from the gods or the community well before a possession ritual. Most only allow possession by Powers with whom they are familiar, and to whom they have given informed consent. For many mediums, the patron Power or a spirit guide of some kind acts as a gatekeeper and protects them from possession by unwanted entities. Firesong, of the Temple of Global Spirits, offers the following advice:

I don't want to be a "Spirit bitch" and just let anything ride me. I check the energy out before it comes in. In general terms, though, it is voluntary or involuntary, depending upon the person and the Spirit. It is a dance between them, so that is very individual for them and also depends upon other factors, such as the setting, whether the Spirit has an important message and "needs" to come in, and how experienced the practitioner is.

Considering the misunderstandings that can occur between two humans who love each other, it should not be surprising that we can have problems working out a functional relationship with a possessing

Power. The gods may love us, but They are not human. They don't always understand our limitations and they have Their own agendas, which sometimes take precedence over the needs of the medium. As Thenea Pantera puts it, "To me, possession is a lot like sex—it doesn't work the same way with any two people, and if you don't tell your partner what you need, you won't get it."

Part of the altar work done in preparation for a possessory ritual includes negotiating the ground rules. The Powers often prove their presence by great feats of strength. African and Norse Powers, especially, like to drink. I myself have put away a significant amount of alcohol while in trance and come away quite sober. On the other hand, inexperienced mediums or those who have not spent sufficient time in preparation sometimes return to ordinary awareness to find themselves leaning over a toilet bowl.

The fact that these things are possible does not mean they don't put a strain on the human frame. The Power may need to be reminded to take care of the horse. I suspect that a possessing Power could probably eat things to which the medium is allergic, but I would still recommend that she negotiate avoidance of those foods. If the medium has a weak ankle, the Power can be asked to avoid dancing. One medium told Exu that He could smoke any number of cigars, but if the medium were ever left with "ashtray mouth" He wouldn't get any more.

> Carrying Freyja merely requires that She be present, interested in riding, and that I not be so anxious or hyperfocused on something mundane that I can't just choose to get out of Her way. Heck, when it's been urgent, even the process of choosing to get out of Her way hasn't been necessary. She just drops in, does what She needs to do, and leaves, consent already having been established.
>
> Ember Cooke (Heathen)

> Hermes is a bit unpredictable. Sometimes he is in the mood for formality, and other times not. He likes the traditional Greek prayer formulae, mostly because it is traditional, and

he gets nostalgic about it. Sometimes, however, he'll say, "I'm already here. Why are you still calling me?" Sometimes he will make it clear to me what he wants, and other times he'll make me play a guessing game with him about how I should approach him. Sometimes he wants an offering, sometimes he will ask that I tell him a story, and other times he'll just decide that he's going to do what I am doing no matter what.

I usually start by calling out, mentally, "Hey, Hermes." If he doesn't answer, or I don't hear him, I'll light some incense and try again. I'll keep adding on components: wine, meat, hymns, chanting epithets . . . until he shows up. Once he's arrived, I'll fully explain what I'm trying to do and why I'd like him to help. He'll either say "yes" or "no." Most of the time, no is conditional. In other words, he has no strong internal reason to help, and he sees an opportunity to get me to do something that I would not ordinarily do. With Hermes, it is very rarely a firm "no." He loves to bargain and haggle.

Thenea Pantera (Mediterranean Syncretic traditions)

The lighter levels of possession, in which the medium is "in the driver's seat" can intensify and empower a ritual. In Greek drama, the actor became a channel for the power of the god's Persona when he put on the mask, but he still spoke the words of the play. It is my experience that gods don't read scripts. When the Powers come fully in They say what they please; however, in many traditions this freedom is bounded and supported by a ritual structure that may be quite formal. In some groups, dangerous exploits are a proof of authenticity, while others set careful limits on what the Powers are allowed to do if They want to be invited back again. And sometimes the requirement for consent falls before the will of the Power.

Dispossession

So far, our focus has been on how to get the Powers to come in. But eventually we have to let Them go. I have many memories of an almost postcoital sadness upon returning to awareness that I was only myself once more. Here are some steps to devoke a Power:

1. Assist the medium to sit or lie down, as deities have been known to "drop" people rather unexpectedly when they go. Since the muscles are completely relaxed, one falls "bone-lessly" and is not hurt, but it can be disturbing to bystanders.

2. Remove the Power's garments or tools, say thank you, and ask Him/Her to return again when called. Depending on the tradition, tell the Power to return to an appropriate dwelling (Ile Ife, Asgard, etc.), or command Him/Her to leave, in the name of a psychopomp from that tradition.

3. Call upon the medium's guardian spirit to bring him back; if he has a magical name, call it.

4. Call the medium's mundane name, tell him where he is, and tell him to remember the circle and the ritual. If necessary, talk about work or family.

5. Restore physical awareness; instruct the medium to move hands, feet, breathe, sigh, etc. Sprinkle him with water, get him to drink water, or place salt or sour salt on the tongue.

If necessary, assist the medium to a place away from the ritual area where he can collapse in comfort for a little while.

Thenea Pantera was told by a Guatemalan shaman that

strongly brewed, piping hot black coffee is highly disruptive to etheric energies. It is like a cup of banishing juice. If you don't want to be possessed, have a cup on hand, and slowly sip it until the ritual is over. Be aware, however, that coffee cleans out your aura. Once you stop sipping, the usual gook that might get between you and the deity won't be there anymore. So, it's a double-edged sword. Have enough coffee to last for the duration of the event.

How to Avoid Trance

Although the main focus of this book is to help you learn how to get *into* trance, there are times when knowing how *not* to go into possessory trance is equally important. In Brazil, a requirement for admission to the higher ranks of the priesthood is the ability to stay "sober" and in control. Once I learned how to go into trance for Odin easily and deeply, I found that I had become almost too open. If the Magic Fire Music from *Die Walküre* suddenly played on the radio, I would get twitchy. When I heard them calling the god at a Wiccan ritual I would have to explain to Odin that they were not invoking *Him*, and certainly not through me.

People who are natural mediums have this problem all the time. The first need is to dampen sensitivity in general. The second is to find ways to keep Powers, whether you are already connected or They would like you to be, from taking over your head. The following suggestions, most of which are also useful when you are trying to get a Power to leave someone else, may help. Mediums should make sure that the god wranglers know what will, and especially what will *not*, work to get them out of trance.

Leave

Avoid situations which are likely to induce trance. If you are at a ritual and feel an inappropriate or unwelcome Power knocking on your head, leave the room, or at least get as far as possible from the altar or the drums. If the Power does not release a medium when requested, get him or her out of the ritual area.

For a long-term problem, try to withdraw your attention. Thenea Pantera observes, "Professing your undying hatred for a deity does not serve to distance you from them, nor does passionately expounding upon your desire for them to leave you. Forgetting to interact with them, however, certainly will."

Distract

If you are conditioned to respond to specific songs or music, play or sing something completely different. Use the person's legal name. Distract yourself or the possessed person by talking about something entirely mundane. A discussion of income tax is almost guaranteed to bring someone down.

Set Up a Barrier
If you are going to be in an evocative environment or possession is happening in a variety of situations, wear a head covering that is tight enough to feel like a restriction. Silk is especially effective. As you put it on, state clearly that its purpose is to keep any Being other than yourself out of your head.

Reconnect with Your Body
Practice grounding until it takes only a moment to root yourself in the earth. Eating or drinking can also reconnect you. A pinch of salt or citric acid crystals will shock you back to awareness of your physical body. Pouring water over the head can help, as can applying ice cubes to the back of the neck or getting into a very hot or very cold shower. Blowing in the ear will get some people back, whereas it makes others crazy. If the same method is used consistently, it will become a cue to return. In the American Magic Umbanda House we used to keep a tub of water handy and if a Power refused to leave, we would threaten to plunge the medium's head in, the idea being that the survival reflex would force the Power to go. So far as I know the tub was never used.

Invoke a Higher Authority
If you are working with or are dedicated to a specific Power, ask Him or Her to act as gatekeeper and keep others from bothering you. If you are not, look for another Power who might have the authority or connection to exercise control, and make an offering, asking for help.

Negotiate
If a Power keeps trying to get through to you, especially at inappropriate times, He or She may have something important to say. If you know someone who works with that Power, ask for advice. It this person does possessory work, talk to the Power through him or her. Otherwise, you

will have to do it yourself. Arrange a time when possession can take place in a controlled environment, with the support of one or more trained—or at least steady and responsible—people who can invite the Power in. Find out what is wanted and negotiate an agreement, then tell Him or Her to go. You may have to agree to let the Power in at regular intervals. This will relieve the pressure and let you live a more normal life the rest of the time.

Practice
Exercise 17.1: An Attitude of Prayer

Visualize the Power you are working with in motion. Note characteristic gestures or postures. It is said that if you put yourself in an attitude of prayer you will find that you are praying. Imitate the movements of a god or goddess, and you will find that She or He is moving you.

Exercise 17.2: Dress for Success

Put together an outfit in the style and colors appropriate for the Power, or something that can be put on over a simple robe or plain clothes. Hats and veils are particularly useful.

Exercise 17.3: Throw a God Party

The best way to develop skill in possessory trance is to do it. Early experiences should take place in small private sessions rather than large public rituals. The minimum number of people for such a session is two—the medium and a god wrangler to set up the ritual, invoke, and interact with the Power. A few more participants can raise more energy. It is said that the more paths or aspects of a power are represented, the more coverage there will be, but a single medium will get a more intense, if narrower, possession. If two people are working with the same Power, you can invoke Him or Her for both at once. The possession may be weaker, but sharing the experience may ease some of the performance anxiety. Part of your preparation will be to find out what kinds of feast food would please your Power, and bring it.

If you are working through this book with a group, after you have done two or three dry runs in which one Power is invoked, try a God Party, in which the Powers that members of the group have been working with are invoked one by one. For this you will need the full support team described in chapter 13. Each medium may also bring one or two friends to act as helpers and to give the Powers someone to talk to.

The ritual structure outlined below can be used for both small and larger rituals. If several different Powers will be invoked, the leader should think carefully about the order in which to call them, especially if they are from different pantheons. In one of my classes, students chose the Sabbath Bride, Inanna, Horus, Isis, Freyja, two Freyrs, Lugh, Thor, Frigg, and the Baron Samedi. The spectacle of Baron Samedi waltzing with the Sabbath Bride was particularly surreal.

Outline for a Possessory Ritual

Set Up Sacred Space
Purify or smudge the space, establish the circle, and honor the spirits of place (especially if you are working outdoors).

Consent and Protect
Formally ask if the medium or mediums are willing to be possessed by the Power(s). State the ground rules and boundaries for behavior.

Honor the Power(s)
Focus the ritual by stating your purpose and making a formal prayer to the Power to come. The medium may make a personal prayer. If several powers are being invited, call each one after the previous one has been seated. If you have enough god wranglers, you may devoke Them after They have had a little time to receive offerings and interact, or give Them the option of remaining.

Transform
Put on regalia.

If necessary, lead the medium through a trance induction for relaxation/release.

Call on the Power to come in through spontaneous invocation by the group, and/or a specific chant. Continue this process until whatever body language, signals, etc. are characteristic of this medium indicate that the deity is "in." Offer the Power His or Her gear or tools, if any, and appropriate food or drink.

Interact
Coordinate whatever work, such as answering questions, is needed.

Dispossess
When the work is ended or the medium tires, formally thank the Power and ask Him or Her to release the medium. Have a chair ready in case the Power leaves suddenly. Remove any regalia. Call the medium back in whatever manner is appropriate to that individual, such as calling magical and then mundane names, sprinkling with water, brushing the head, giving salt or citric acid, etc. If more than one Power is involved, several helpers can work at the same time, or a single leader can release each Power sequentially. If needed, take mediums to a quiet place to rest after the ritual.

Return and Aftercare
In reverse order, thank and dismiss any other Powers that have been invoked and open the circle. Give the medium food to ground and restore energy. Debrief with the group to identify what worked well and what needs to be improved.

18

A TOUR OF THE ISSUES

Dangerous? And so am I, very dangerous: more dangerous than anything you will ever meet, unless you are brought alive before the seat of the Dark Lord. And Aragorn is dangerous, and Legolas is dangerous. You are beset with dangers, Gimli son of Gloin; for you are dangerous yourself, in your own fashion."
—J. R. R. Tolkien, *The Two Towers*

Religion can be a tricky business. A lot of people have ended up in trouble because they started listening to gods, but (unless they start a religion) they usually only harm themselves. When the Powers speak *through*, instead of *to* us, they want an audience. As a community-based practice, possession affects not only the possessed medium but also those around her. Every group that engages in possessory work has stories about times when something went wrong—but knowing how to deal with a possession can also save someone's sanity. Let us look at some of the issues that can arise.

You're Doing It Wrong

My friend Ben Waggoner once joked that in Heathenry the only two rules are "you're doing it wrong" and "you're not the boss of me." People who do possessory work might say the same.

In traditions with a lineage the procedures for doing possessory work have been written or handed down, but practice may vary from one group to another even within a tradition. Possession occurs in every culture, and success is its own proof of validity. We may consider another group's practice irresponsible, but until we have an EEG test that will measure the extent to which a Power is "in," we cannot truly judge whether or not their possessory practice is "real."

A similar response might be made to accusations of cultural misappropriation. Dissociation is a basic human ability. There is plenty of evidence that the African Powers can and will speak through people who have no ethnic connection to Their cultures. Many Reconstructionist groups have found that the European gods are equally unprejudiced. The Powers care more about the inside of the head than the outside of the skin, and political correctness is a poor reason to deny them.

Whether someone's practice is ethical or responsible is another question. Like electricity, which can also cause harm when not handled carefully, the Powers are, well, powerful. Just because they are spirits does not mean they are "safe." It is irresponsible to open the door to the Powers if you don't know what to do with Them when they arrive. Each group and tradition must work out the prohibitions and parameters that will enable people and Powers to get along.

Uninvited Guests

One reason for learning how to deal with possession is because it can happen spontaneously to people who neither seek nor understand it. This is especially likely at Pagan festivals, where ritual energy and contact with others who share your beliefs can cause people who are short on food or sleep to lose whatever shielding they have. People who have no boundaries are vulnerable to beings Who are looking for a home, or a ride.

One of my most dramatic experiences with involuntary possession occurred at a Heathen moot. An ex-military man whom we'll call Rollo had come to the event. It was his first Heathen gathering, and as often happens, he was overwhelmed by the discovery that he was not alone in his love for the Norse gods. He spent most of the moot helping in the kitchen and unburdening himself to Raudhildr, herself an experienced priestess, who was in charge of the cooking. Unknown to her, when he was not in the kitchen he spent a lot of time fingering the oath ring he wore on his arm and singing a song he was putting together to the tune of "Men of Harlech" with the words "Men of Odin."

By the time he had put himself into trance by repeating this song he was wide open, and as we were cleaning up the kitchen preparatory to leaving, suddenly what we had was a very angry Balder. Raudhildr sent out a call for the psychic SWAT team, and we went into action. One person got the ring off Rollo's arm and put it into a dish of salt to mute the energy. Others got him to sit down and drink something and began to talk to him. I tried asking if he had any pets, but that just invoked his Bear fetch, so I switched to rent and income tax. We got the man focused enough so that we could take him off to the local Denny's and feed him, and eventually he was grounded enough to drive and reached home safely, where we were able to connect him with an experienced Heathen priest.

Someone with a really open head can get possessed at any ritual whose organizers put real energy into calling a Power. What started out as a ritual play can turn into something more. At other times, the designated medium is not the only one who gets jumped. In Santeria, the usual rule is that only initiated mediums may trance, and only in their own houses. Anyone else will be assisted to leave the floor. At a possessory ritual that is announced as "open floor," the organizers should ask those who do not want to go into trance to identify themselves. Of course the warders will also be watching those who do trance, but a buddy system in which friends who know each other's reactions can take care of each other is also a good idea.

To deal with an unexpected possession, first make sure the afflicted individual is physically safe, calm, and if necessary, restrained. The next step is to talk to the possessing entity and find out what, or Who, It is and what It wants. If the entity presents Itself as one of the Powers, find someone who knows that tradition to check It out.

Sometimes, a Power has a message and after delivering it will leave. If the Power has decided to become a part of someone's life, help the person find a group that can train him. People may also be opened up to apparent or real possession by drugs or mental illness. Pagan clergy need to distinguish between physical, mental, and spiritual problems, and refer people to the appropriate professionals. The methods suggested for depossession in the preceding chapter can be used to banish an involuntary possession.

Guests Who Don't Leave

"Possession sickness," a state of involuntary, frequent, or continual possession by a discarnate spirit or Power, can have serious effects on one's ability to live a normal life as well as inhibiting or stunting development of the primary personality. In some cases, however, the host may welcome the connection.

I know of at least two instances in which someone's person-identity was replaced by one of the Powers. In one case, a teenager who had to take responsibility for her family when her mother died coped by letting the Norse goddess Frigg take over for a number of years. It required some hard work in therapy to reclaim her own identity. In another case, a ceremonial magician who was skeptical of ecstatic practices in general picked up Hermes at a ritual. A number of improvements in his life occurred thereafter, and he continues to willingly share his consciousness with the god.

Breaking Boundaries

One question that any group doing possessory work must answer is whether boundaries can be imposed on the Powers, and if so, what they should be. Herskovits writing about Haitian voudou, says that

> a release of psychic tension is undoubtedly afforded those who become possessed . . . Nevertheless it must be emphasized . . . that this form of worship of the loa is neither unrestrained hysteria nor drunken orgiastic satisfaction of the sex drive. The behavior of the participants . . . often seems uncouth, vigorous, violent and even dangerous, when it is merely the expression of a different tradition.
> (Herskovits 1937, 177ff, in Deren 1953)

The Powers are not "tame lions." When Odin drinks down a horn of mead in one long swallow or Gédé makes lewd suggestions They are acting in character, but They may not be observing community norms. In their journey from Africa to the Americas, the orishas have learned how to adapt to new conditions. Coming to North America from the Caribbean, they can probably do it once more. Gods who have not been invoked in this way for centuries (if ever) have to be brought up to date on the ways of the modern world. An increasing sensitivity to the role of power dynamics in sexual interaction may require that we limit physical contact to a PG-13 level at a ritual. We laugh about telling Aphrodite she can't have a hand-woven gown dyed with real saffron, or refusing to sacrifice a horse to Freyr, but if what comes through in possession are authentic deities, They may not understand *why*. Nor do they always understand why we keep saying, "Be kind to the horse" when They start to display Their power.

How do we balance the need to be true to the Power with our concern for the well-being of the human? A medium possessed by Ogun once moved an iron grate from the fire with his bare hands. An Exu bit off the top of a bottle that had not been opened for Him and crunched it up. When someone offered Coyote a desiccated baby bird He assumed it was something to eat. He liked the cachaça with which the priestess tried to disinfect His mouth even more. The possessions were validated by the fact that none of the mediums concerned were harmed. But what if they had been?

For legal as well as ethical reasons most Pagan groups that do possessory work try to keep the activities of the Powers they invoke under control. Clothing must remain on, physical contact is limited, and consumption of alcohol is limited by negotiation with the medium. In the previous chapter we talked about negotiation and consent. But what happens if the Power breaks the agreement?

In our community, possession can sometimes occur in our oracular rituals. When someone has a question for a god or goddess, the seer can journey to find the deity and relay the answer, or, if she is trained in possessory work, the god may step in and answer it. We try to make sure that this only happens when the seer consents, but if the guide does not enforce the negotiated agreement the results can be traumatic. I am grateful to Ember Cooke for sharing the following:

I sat seidh at a large festival several years ago. I had established that I am not an Odinswoman. I was willing to take questions for Him, and relay His answers, but I was not consenting to His possession. I took the chair, confident that everyone was clear on these parameters. The third question was for Odin.

What I remember is an image of a dirt path through woods. My view is at ground level, as though I am buried to my neck, bodiless, or prostrate. I am looking straight across the path. There is a marker, a line. Sometimes in my memory I see it clearly; sometimes I just know it's there. The Old Man comes walking down the path. As He approaches in His soft leather boots, He slows but does not pause at the line at all. He does not look down to acknowledge me or the line He is crossing.

The next thing knew I was filled to overflowing with an immensely compassionate Allfather. He answered questions. I sat behind, silenced. I was amazed at the depth of His love for the querents, for humanity in general. But not for me: I wasn't there. *I was nothing.*

I felt a slow panic setting in. I could hear a strange silent screaming in my mind, and I knew it was my own voice. I felt the strain of my personal warder behind me—my lover, an Odinsman—trying to hold the chair. I couldn't tell if he knew something was wrong, but I knew he was having trouble too, and that I needed to tell him what was wrong, and I couldn't.

When He released me, I was exhausted and shaken, and I couldn't express what was wrong. I felt scraped raw across the inside of my spirit, violated by a strangely compassionate god. It was all I could do to not sob in front of a room full of querents. All the warders could do was gentle aftercare. Treat me like a rape victim with no physical evidence to collect and no real recourse with the offender. An offender they all loved dearly. I tried to summarize the experience to them afterwards:

"I felt like I was drugged and given to someone else's lover."

Consent only matters with the gods because They choose to let it matter. If a deity insists on possessing me, there's ultimately very little I can do about it without help from another deity. On the one hand I accept that in the same way I accept that natural disasters are outside my control. On the other hand, if I think about that too hard for too long, it can trigger a panic attack.

The vast majority of my possession experience has been positive. I've even carried Odin in consenting, positive ways since then, although it took years of work. But if I ever had any doubts this work could be dangerous, painful, and terrifying, that what we are dealing with is real, outside entities with Their own agendas, those doubts were obliterated that night.

What you do about this kind of experience depends on the group culture. Some groups not only recognize that the Powers *can* do this, but accept it as Their right. In the Heathen tradition we are allowed to argue with the gods. According to *our* group culture, Odin should have been told to get out, and if that didn't work, we should have brought the medium out of trance. I cannot guarantee, however, that doing so would have been any less traumatic than letting Him finish his work.

It is important that everyone involved play by the same rules. Firesong reports an incident in which

> we called in a really difficult Spirit, who was requested by a temple member. I did not think this was a good idea in the first place, but the member (Person A) was well versed in trance possession and had been working with that Spirit for several years. Person B (a relatively respected person by some) came, who was a possession practitioner, but in retrospect, not accepting at all of how our temple works and extremely disrespectful of us. Person C attended and . . . didn't mention to anyone what a fragile state she was in. Person B reportedly became possessed by the Spirit and put a lighter to the hand, (considered very mild compared to activities allowed by other trance groups, but

not encouraged by our temple) of Person C. Person C at the time said it was fine but later said that she was partially possessed and not able to speak for herself. The Guardians took her "it's okay" to be all is well, even though usually they would have stepped in and gotten the Spirit to leave.

Afterwards, Person C felt violated by Person B. We had discussions about it later. Ad nauseum. Eventually people worked out what their part was in the snafu and how we were to avoid it in the future. Person A worked out that they embellished how they were to call the Spirit in the first place: Their mistake was that they got direction but didn't follow it. Person C admitted to being in such a difficult place that she should have excused herself. The Guardians knew that they should have stopped the possession when it went beyond what they would normally consider safe boundaries.

The problem with Person C is an example of the need to put limits not only on who should be allowed to carry specific Powers, but who can interact with Them. People attending possessory rituals should be warned that this will be an intense experience and that the Powers don't pull any punches. If someone is known to be in a fragile state, they should not attend.

At a possessory event for Odin a young woman knelt down to look at the runes on his spear. From across the room, a medium carrying Freyja began to berate her on the grounds that Heathens do not kneel to their gods. The girl, who was in a vulnerable state, was extremely upset, a condition that in the days that followed turned into a major breakdown. This led to a great deal of self-examination and discussion. Was Freyja speaking, or was it horse talk? Should the companion of the person with the problem have been keeping an eye on her? Should we change our procedures?

Our response was a renewed commitment to make sure all newcomers read our policies and procedures for trance work before being allowed to participate in events, to enforce the rule that possessory events are invitation only, and that before attending people must have been to enough regular kindred events to become acquainted with our gods and customs, to give the events more structure and more warders, and to only allow trained and prepared mediums to trance. We also stated,

> However, this doesn't mean we are asking our gods to be less than themselves. The rating of these events will still be, roughly, PG-13 . . . among these expectations for warders, mediums, and the powers is that correction of attendees' behavior shall be done discreetly whenever possible. Going forward, those intending to carry a god (or similar) will be expected to spend some time in the days prior to the event in meditation/communion with the power in question, to better prepare them to carry the invited god with grace and clarity.
>
> (Lorrie, Hrafnar Thul)

Deception and Self-Deception

Given that actors, con men, and drama queens can all play roles, how do we guard against intentional or unintentional fakery? In some Afro-Diasporic traditions, Powers prove their presence by acts that would cause pain or injury to anyone who was not possessed. Of course just because someone is possessed doesn't guarantee the Power is telling the truth about His or Her identity. The leaders should know enough about the Power to identify uncharacteristic behavior.

One symptom of an incomplete or faked possession is "horse talk"—opinions or directions that reflect the known opinions of the medium rather than being characteristic of the Power, or are clearly intended to bring some benefit to the medium. In general, Powers will be too focused on their own agendas or the people to whom They are talking to even mention the medium, and if They do, They will refer to "the horse" rather than saying the medium's name (which tends to break the possession). An exception would be when the medium has requested friends to ask the Power questions on her behalf, or when the Power takes advantage of the opportunity to express concern for or disapproval of His devotee.

Those who think a possessory ritual is an excuse to work off their repressions through aggression or inappropriate sexual behavior should be restrained by whatever means necessary. If they are not causing a problem, Filan and Kaldera recommend that they simply be deprived of the attention they are so obviously seeking. The real danger here is that the Power will take the simulated possession as an invitation to claim the individual, or be insulted and punish him (Filan and Kaldera 2009). For a more extensive discussion of these problems, I recommend their book, *Drawing Down the Spirits*. They have a great deal of experience doing possessory work in public settings and have dealt with a wide range of issues. Their discussion of the impact that encountering the Powers can have on inexperienced attendees at a Pagan ritual is especially valuable.

Validation

One of the issues with any kind of spiritual communication is figuring out whether it is authentic and what it means. When the message comes through a medium in possession, it can have a glamour that transcends its actual meaning. But you should be able to judge it by the same standards you would use for any other communication.

Does the message make sense? Some Powers are less articulate than others, or They do not yet have a contemporary vocabulary. On the other hand, confusion may indicate that the possession is not firmly seated.

Is this the sort of thing we would expect that Power to say? If the message diverges too much from the community's understanding of the character of a Power, it will be rejected. The lore and ethos of the group act as a filter so that even in full possession, a member is likely to present things in an expected way. However, it is always possible for a different aspect than usual to appear. This is why the group's leaders must know as much as possible about the Powers they call.

Is this the sort of thing we would expect that medium to say? Especially if the message is harsh, an accusation of horse talk may be made. Even when possessions are "tested" by physical challenges, personal contamination is always possible. If you know that the medium has a strong opinion on something, it will be easier to tell if her opinion is coloring the message. In Africa, an instruction received through a medium is confirmed by casting the cowries. In Hrafnar we remind people that

Everything you hear at a possessory event comes through several filters, including the medium's and your own. Just because a god tells you something does *not* absolve you of responsibility for your actions. If something does not "ring true," get a second opinion. But I will add: Neither are the mediums wholly absolved of responsibility for the integrity of their work.

(Lorrie, Hrafnar Thul)

Compatibility of personality certainly makes it easier to develop a connection. It may also, however, make it harder to distinguish between the opinions of the medium (or his or her higher self) and the Power.

Evaluating the influence of the tradition or community on the opinions expressed by the Powers they invoke is harder. In Haiti, life is harsh, and so, often, are the Powers. Even within a tradition, different groups work with different aspects. In Brazil there are houses whose entire focus is on the "family" of Exus, whereas others put His offerings out in the street to get Him out of the way. Some divergence is natural—look at all the variation in lore from different periods and lands. Groups in the same tradition can avoid becoming too inbred by practicing what Lorrie Wood calls "spiritual exogamy"—sharing information and debating the meaning of the lore. On the other hand, finding that the Powers have given the same messages to people who have had no contact supplies validation. It is always impressive when a possessing Power picks up a conversation that the questioner started with that same Power in meditation or on another medium, or provides information neither the questioner nor the medium knew.

Personal and Group Dynamics

One of the hazards of possessory work is the temptation to believe that this practice somehow makes you superior. Although you may carry a Power and feel that He or She is as close to you as breath, always remember that you yourself are *not* the Power. Maintain healthy boundaries and avoid ego inflation. You should also be wary of transference by others who are attracted to the Power you are working with. Everyone likes to be admired, and it is tempting to bask in the glow cast by a charismatic deity.

Make it clear to everyone (including yourself) that although working with and for the Power is a large part of your life and you strive to manifest His or Her virtues, they must develop their own relationships and not contact the Power solely through you. This will work better if you are not the only one in the group who can carry that deity. Acting as priest or priestess of a god for your community is a responsibility and a privilege, not a reward. You have been given this connection to serve the Power and the people, not to glamour them into serving *you*.

One concept on which most of my questionnaire respondents agreed is the need to avoid creating a hierarchy. Firesong recommends that service as a medium should remain independent of any "honor or initiation step." This comment from Morgan Daimler sums it up pretty well:

> Many of us, myself included, are called to serve. Service doesn't make you special; it makes you useful. The fact that people don't like to acknowledge is that we are all extremely temporary to the gods and spirits. Our mortal lives are moments in their far broader reality. Do we have value to them? I'm certain we do, even on an individual level, but that value is not eclipsed by their wider need to accomplish certain things and keep an eye always to greater goals. I won't ever pretend to understand the wheels within wheels of Odin's plans—I know I have a value to him and serve a purpose, but I am also keenly aware that when I am gone someone else will take my place. . . . No matter how knowledgeable, how powerful, how skilled, or how well a person serves the Gods, their time is limited and the importance of their power, knowledge, skill, and service in their life is not measured by how special they think they are, but by how they affect the lives of other people and how well they serve their purpose. And that, ultimately, is only truly measured and judged by time.
>
> (Daimler 2013)

Like any other powerful practice, possessory work can be hazard-ous. Performing great feats of strength can harm the medium whose level of possession is not as deep as she thinks—but they also prove that the Power is truly present. Letting the Power lay down the home truths that leave someone in tears may also be the only way to get that person to hear them. As Odin once put it, "If all you want is a pleasure party, you need one set of rules. You need warders and invitations to make sure no one gets hurt. If you want to make spiritual progress you need another set of rules—warders and invitations, yes, but also training and goals." If we only allow the Powers to mouth platitudes we might as well be put-ting on a play. Providing a trained support staff and limiting the size and attendees at some rituals will help keep things under control, but each group has to decide where to draw the line.

CONCLUSION

I would believe only in a God that knows how to dance.
—Friedrich Nietzsche

So where do we go from here?

We live in an era of religious transition: "More than one-quarter of American adults (28%) have left the faith in which they were raised in favor of another religion—or no religion at all" (Pew Research 2007). The traditional mainline Christian churches are losing members most rapidly. Evangelical Christianity is doing better, perhaps because it encourages people to develop a personal relationship with God. The other contemporary religious movement that does so is Paganism. Surveys of religious preference often do not offer Paganism as a choice, but Adherents.com estimates Pagan numbers at around 1 million. If we add to that the estimated 300 million people in indigenous faiths, 100 million traditional and diasporic African, and the 15 million Spiritists, we have a possible total of over 400 million people worldwide who are following traditions in which some form of possessory practice might occur ("Major Religions of the World Ranked" 2007).

So what is the future of possession in our communities?

Some Wiccan covens have moved from a more archetypal view of deity to work with specific manifestations of the Goddess and the God. But Filan and Kaldera observe that

> Deity-possession, in particular, seems to have appeared in Reconstructionist and Reconstructionist-derived groups at

a faster rate than it has grown in Wiccan-derived eclectic groups, although the majority of strict Reconstructionist groups are still wary of the practice. This is significant, considering that "recon" groups . . . are moderately recent as part of the Neo-Pagan demographic and still very much a minority . . . The rise of Reconstructionist groups may create a higher percentage of individuals who are actually bothering to learn the ways in which those deities were honored in the past, thus strengthening those deities' connection with this world through their worship.

(Filan and Kaldera, 2009, 93–94)

It does make sense that the Powers may connect more easily with groups that are deeply involved with the culture from which they come. I have heard from or about groups and individuals working in the Greek, Egyptian, Celtic, and Germanic cultural traditions who accidentally or on purpose have found themselves hosting gods. However, there are problems. Wicca is a mystery tradition which people join because they want to learn magic. The need for training is assumed. In the folk cultures on which most Reconstructionist traditions are based, magic is performed by specialists. Lorrie Wood observes,

Possessory work within the several Heathen communities is complicated in several ways . . . there are many places where it is a socially limiting move to be known as someone who engages in almost anything magical, with the possible exception of runic engraving. While it has been a common trope throughout the current modern Heathen revival of the US and Western Europe to pledge oneself to one or another among the gods, it is *not* common, by contrast, to speak well of any sort of relationship where the gods *talk back* . . . even in a group where magical practices are at least tolerated as the work of specialists, and it's even plausible that a god may grant some guidance or direction, possessory work *as such* remains a contested practice, a fringe of a fringe.

As River Devora points out, "If specific polytheistic religions within the umbrella of paganism incorporate trance possession as part of their practices, this will shift the demographic of folks who choose to become part of these traditions. This is neither good nor bad necessarily, but it will alter who is drawn to these traditions." In some cases, as when a god speaks through a seeress in the oracular ritual, possession contributes to another specialist activity that is more accepted in the Heathen community. Reconstructionist pagans have to decide whether to maintain possessory work as a fringe practice for trained subsets of the community (as we have done in Hrafnar) or to incorporate it into regular activities. River goes on to say,

> I do think trance possessory practices have a role to play in reconstructed polytheistic traditions, as folks like me find our way into these traditions precisely because the gods are speaking through us (whether we want them to or not). So whether these practices "should" or "should not" exist is a moot point: the Gods and spirits want to be known to their followers in this way and are making themselves known. The more important question is how to create safe and meaningful frameworks in which these practices can exist, in ways that work for the mediums, the possessing entities, and the communities impacted by these interactions and relationships.

Ember Cooke comments, "I don't believe possessory work is required for contemporary Pagan practice. However, it is part of a larger mystical tool set that is particularly helpful to hard polytheists who are building relationships with the individual Powers in their lives."

Eclectic Pagan possessory events like the rituals sponsored by the Global Temple of the Spirits or the Conjure Dance, in which Powers from many cultures are called, are another option. Their structure follows the time-tested model of the Afro-Diasporic tambor, but their community draws from a variety of other Pagan traditions. Staff are experienced in managing trance, but can they know enough about all of the cultures from which these Powers come to evaluate and interpret what They do?

It's a complicated question. Some Powers, like Brigid or Isis, move easily between cultures. Others, like Odin, have expressed a specific interest in making alliances with the deities of other pantheons. My current opinion is that such rituals, when responsibly managed, can offer a supportive environment for those who are called by the Powers but have no group within which to carry Them, and introduce newcomers to the concept of possessory trance. I would hope, however, that if someone wants to bring a Power that the organizers do not know well, he or she will bring their own god wrangler.

As more groups explore possessory trance, we will need to think more about where our mediums come from and what their role in our communities should be. Some say that trance mediums are born, not made. Some hold that unless the Powers give you no choice you should not be doing this work at all. Certainly being naturally open makes the connection easier, but there is also something to be said for taking down the barriers one by one so that you know what and where they are. The many levels of possessory trance are valuable in different ways. My feeling is that what matters most is whether the trance meets a need in the community. Jennifer S. comments,

> I think at the very least pagan groups should consider the question of their position on mediumship and if they allow it *now*, before confronted with a situation where someone is impelled to deliver some message. Then groups can be clear on which ones will listen to and accept and maybe train mediums and which won't.

Firesong feels that "Money should not be a major manipulative factor when it comes to possessory work. Yes, costs need to be covered, but getting rich off of trance possession is a bad idea. Contemporary Pagans often do not mix money with practices, so this is a bonus for them."

Ember says that possessory trance

> should not be treated as an addicting, intoxicating substance. It should not be treated as a special ability that makes some

people more important than others. It should not be treated as an opportunity for bad behavior. It should not be treated as a freakish habit, the practitioners of which should be shunned. It should not be treated as an opportunity to boss the gods and spirits around—even the ones who are small enough for us to have that kind of power over them. It should be treated as an opportunity for hospitality and relationship building with entities we respect and love. It should be treated as an offering and an obligation to the gods and the community. It may even be treated as a joyful, pleasurable experience for the medium and those with whom the experience is shared. It may be treated relatively lightly, or with a frank practicality, but it should never be treated callously, or as insignificant.

We are just beginning to understand what a Pagan possessory tradition can be. Integrating it into our culture will take work. Why should we make the effort? I believe that the Powers are reaching out to us because we are Their children, and together we need to save our world. This practice is one way to begin.

You may work all your life to invent a babytalk or pidgin, to convey concepts *you* will never yourself fully understand, because of never yourself speaking the mature language that would result in a generation or three. I'm sorry about that, but I don't have anyone incarnate who can teach you this stuff fully; it simply *isn't in the culture.* Your people are groping, and we're all eagerly helping (though sometimes at cross purposes with each other). Out of this, eventually, better understanding will come. But. Not. Today . . .

Tell them that we are partners. We don't want servants. Worship is nice, but it's more like fluffy candy than a decent meal. Nor do we want people to use as magical tools . . . Tell them that partners make mistakes and may need forgiveness. Tell them that we need to know about you and your hopes and fears. Tell them that we are not omnipotent. Nor, though

I see far, and have agents, am I omniscient. Much have I striven for wisdom, but omniscience is beyond me.

(Odin "Possessory Work," Source Five)

ACKNOWLEDGMENTS

Possessory practice is a group activity, and this book could not have been written without the insights and input of the many people who have shared their experiences and energy with me through correspondence and ritual, and the inspiration of the Powers Who work with us. I would like to thank the students in our trance classes, especially those in the most recent group, along with Lorrie Wood and Hilary Ayer who helped me to teach it. Thanks also to the American Magic Umbanda House and Hrafnar kindred, to Dr. Kevin White for reviewing the manuscript from a psychiatric point of view, and to Odin, for getting me into this in the first place.

WORKS CITED

Addey, Crystal. 2010. "Divine Possession and Divination in the Graeco-Roman World: The Evidence from Iamblichus's *On the Mysteries.*" In *Spirit Possession and Trance: New Interdisciplinary Perspectives.* Edited by Bettina Schmidt and Lucy Huskinson. New York: Bloomsbury.

Allen, James P. 2003. *The Oxford Essential Guide to Egyptian Mythology.* New York: Berkley.

American Magic Umbanda House. 1992. "Introduction to the American Magic Umbanda House." Oakland: CA.

Barnes, Steven. February 5, 2014. "Origins of Lifewriting #3: We Create Story. And Story Creates Us." www.facebook.com/notes/steven-barnes/origins-of-lifewriting-3-we-create-story-and-story-creates-us/10151914744343663.

Beattie, John, and John Middleton, eds. 1969. *Spirit Mediumship and Society in Africa.* New York: Africana Publishing.

Besmer, Fremont E. 1983. *Horses, Musicians, & Gods: The Hausa Cult of Possession-Trance.* South Hadley, MA: Bergin & Garvey.

Blalock, Jessica A. 2003. "From Odin to Freyr." *Idunna* 57 (Fall 2003): 20–21.

Bloom, Paul. 2004. *Descartes' Baby: How the Science of Child Development Explains What Makes Us Human.* New York: Basic Books.

Bourguignon, Erika. 1976. *Possession.* San Francisco: Chandler & Sharp.

Bradley, Marion Zimmer, personal communication, 1983, by permission of the MZB Literary Trust.

Brook, Peter. 1981. "Lie and Glorious Adjective: An Interview with Peter Brook." *Parabola* 6(3) (Fall, 1981).

Brown, Diana DeGroet. (1986) 1994. *Umbanda, Religion and Politics in Urban Brazil,* Columbia University Press.

Bujold, Lois McMaster. 1996. *Memory.* Riverdale, NY: Baen Books.

———. 2003. *Paladin of* Souls. New York: HarperCollins.

Burt, Ramsay. 2013. "Katherine Dunham and Maya Deren on Ritual, Modernity, and the African Diaspora." Academia.edu. https://www.academia.edu/985349/Katherine_Dunham_and_Maya_Deren_on_ritual_modernity_and_the_African_Diaspora.

Canizares, Raul J. 1999. *Cuban Santeria: Walking with the Night.* Rochester, VT: Inner Traditions.

Cassadaga Spiritualist Camp. N.d. "Church Services." *Cassadaga Spiritualist Camp.* http://www.cassadaga.org/church_services.htm.

Cohen, Emma. 2008. "What Is Spirit Possession? Defining, Comparing, and Explaining Two Possession Forms." *Ethnos* 73(I) (March 2008). users.ox.ac.uk/~soca0093/pdfs/CohenEthnos08.pdf.

Cole, David. 1975. *The Theatrical Event: A Mythos, a Vocabulary, a Perspective.* Middletown: Wesleyan University Press.

Cooke, Ember. January 9, 2014. Personal email communication.

———. March 4, 2014. Personal email communication.

Cross, Tom Peete, and Clark Harris Slover, eds. 1969. *Ancient Irish Tales.* New York: Barnes & Noble Books.

Crowley, Aleister. 1988. "Liber Astarte." In *Gems from the Equinox*, selected by Israel Regardie, Las Vegas, NV: Falcon Press.

———. 1992. *Magick in Theory and Practice.* New York: Castle Books.

Crowley, Vivianne. 2000. *Jung: A Journey of Transformation: Exploring His Life and Experiencing His Ideas.* Wheaton, IL: Quest Books.

Cutler, Norman. 1987. *Songs of Experience.* Bloomington, IN: Indiana University Press.

Daimler, Morgan. November 12, 2013. "Why None of Us Are Special Snowflakes." *Living Liminally* (blog). lairbhan.blogspot.com/2013/11/why-none-of-us-are-special-snowflakes.html?m=1.

Deren, Maya. 1953. *Divine Horsemen: The Living Gods of Haiti.* New York: Thames and Hudson.

Deussen, Paul, and A. S. Geden. 2010. *The Philosophy of the Upanishads.* New York: Cosimo Classics.

Devora, River. February 24, 2014. Personal email communication.

Dominguez, Ivo Jr. 2008. *Spirit Speak: Knowing and Understanding Spirit Guides, Ancestors, Ghosts, Angels, and the Divine.* Rochester, VT: New Page.

Dorsey, Lilith. January 19, 2014. Personal email communication.

Dr. E. June 19, 2012. "Espiritismo Cruzado." Santeria Church of the Orishas. santeriachurch.org/espiritismo-cruzado/.

Dumézil, Georges. 1958. The Rígsþula and Indo-European Social Structure. *Gods of the Ancient Northmen.* Edited by Einar Haugen, translated by John Lindow. (1973). Berkeley: University of California Press.

Dumézil, Georges. 1974. La Religion Romaine Archaique, Paris.

Eliade, Mircea. 1964. *Shamanism: Archaic Techniques of Ecstasy.* Translated by Willard Trask. Princeton, NJ: Princeton University Press.

Elizabeth. August 8, 2012. "Possession", *Twilight and Fire*, 8/8/12 Pagan Blog Project: Possession (A Rant). twilightandfire.wordpress.com/2012/08/08/pagan-blog-project-possession-a-rant/.

Engler, Steven. 2009. "Umbanda and Hybridity." *Numen* 56. stevenengler.ca/wp-content/uploads/2013/04/Engler.2009.hybridity.pdf.

Erdoes, Richard. 1985. *American Indian Myths and Legend.* New York: Pantheon.

Espin, Orlando O., and James B. Nickoloff. 2007. *An Introductory Dictionary of Theology and Religious Studies*. Collegeville, MN: Liturgical Press.

Fatunmbi, Awo Fá'lokun. 1991. *Lwa-pele: Ifa Quest, the Search for the Source of Santeria and Lucumi*. Bronx, NY: Original Publications.

Fielding, Charles, and Carr Collins. 1985. *The Story of Dion Fortune*. York Beach, ME: Samuel Weiser, Inc.

Filan, Kenaz, and Raven Kaldera. 2009. *Drawing Down the Spirits: The Traditions and Techniques of Spirit Possession*. Rochester, NY: Destiny Books.

Firesong. January 18, 2014. Personal email communication.

Fontenrose, Joseph. 1978. *The Delphic Oracle: Its Responses and Operations*. Berkeley, CA: University of California Press.

Fordham, Michael. 1985. *Explorations into the Self*. London: Karnac Books.

Fortune, Dion. 1962. *Applied Magic*. London: Aquarian Press.

———. 1978. *Moon Magic*. York Beach, ME: Samuel Weiser.

Fraser, Mikki. October 14, 2013. "Godphone Question." *Sacred Iceland* (blog). sacrediceland.wordpress.com/2013/10/14/godphone-question.

———. October 22, 2013. "God-Owned or God-Slave?" *Sacred Iceland* (blog). sacrediceland.wordpress.com/2013/10/22/god-owned-or-god-slave.

Frew, Don. February 11, 2014. Personal email communication.

Frobenius, Leo. 1912. *Und Afrika sprach . . . Wissenschaftlich erweitete Ausgabe des Berichts über den Verlauf der dritten Reiseperiode der deitschen innerafrikanischen Forschungsexpedition aus den Jaren 1910 bis 1912*. Vol. II. In Oesterreich 1966.

Gay, Peter, ed. 1989. *The Freud Reader*. New York: W.W. Norton.

"Global Spirits." N.d. Global Spirits. http://www.globalspirits.org/.

Glossary of Kabbalah and Chassidut. www.inner.org/glossary/gloss_c.htm.

González-Wippler, Migene. 1984. *Santería: African Magic in Latin America*. Bronx, NY: Jamil Products Corp.

Golub, Deborah. 1995. "Cultural Variations in Multiple Personality Disorder." In *Dissociative Identity Disorder*. Northvale, NJ: Jason Aronson Inc.

Goodman, Felicitas D. 1988. *How About Demons*. Bloomington, IN: Indiana University Press.

Goodwyn, Erik E. 2012. *The Neurobiology of the Gods*. New York: Routledge.

———. 2014, *The Heathen Psyche*. Lulu.com.

Greer, John Michael. 2005. *A World Full of Gods*. Tucson, AZ: ADF Publishing.

Haberman, David L. 2001. *Acting as a Way of Salvation*. Delhi, India: Motilal Banarsidass.

Harrow, G., and J. Harrow. 1995. *Carrying Deity*. Private publication.

Harrow, Judy. 2003. *Devoted to You*. New York: Citadel Press.

———. 2014. Personal email communication.

Haugen, Einar. 1983. "The Edda as Ritual: Odin and His Masks." In *Edda: A Collection of Essays*. Edited by Robert J. Glendinning and Haraldur Bessason. Winnipeg: University of Manitoba Press.

Hodges, Richard. 1995. "The Quick and the Dead: The Souls of Man in Vodou Thought." *Material for Thought* 14, November 1995.

Hopcke, Robert H. 1995. *Persona*. Boston: Shambhala.

Homer. 1937. *The Odyssey*. Translated by H. D. Rouse. New York: Mentor Books.

Iamblichus. 1911. *Theurgia*. Translated by Alexander Wilder. London: William Rider & Son. www.esotericarchives.com/oracle/iambl_t2.htm.

Erigena, John Scotus. 2011. In *Patrologia Latina,* translated by G.B. Burch, in *Great Thoughts, Revised and Updated*, George Seldes, New York: Random House.

Jung, Carl Gustav. 1959. *The Archetypes and the Collective Unconscious*. Princeton, NJ: Princeton University Press.

———. 1953. *Two Essays on Analytical Psychology*. London: Routledge, Kegan Paul.

Kardec, Allan. 1857. *The Spirits' Book,* Book II. Translated by Anna Blackwell, Federação Espírita Brasileira. caminodeyara.files.wordpress.com/2013/01/the_spirits_book_allan_kardec.pdf.

Kathleen. November 29, 2013. Personal email communication.

Kelly, Edward F., and Emily Williams Kelly. 2007. *Irreducible Mind: Toward a Psychology for the 21st Century*. New York: Putnam.

Kenner, Caroline. January 27, 2014. Personal email communication.

Kornfield, Jack. 2001. *After the Ecstasy, the Laundry: How the Heart Grows Wise on the Spiritual Path*. New York: Bantam.

Kipling, Rudyard. 1959. *Kim*. New York: Dell.

Krasskova, Galina. April 20, 2009. "Terms of Service." The Gods Mouths (blog). godsmouths.blogspot.com/2009/04/terms-of-service.html.

Krishnananda, Swami. 1982. *The Philosophy of the Panchadasi*. Rishikesh, India: The Divine Life Society.

Kwauo. February 1, 2014. Personal email communication.

Landes, Ruth. 1994. *City of Women*. Albuquerque, NM: University of New Mexico Press.

Lewis, C. S. 1956. *Till We Have Faces*. London: Geoffrey Bles.

———. 1962. *That Hideous Strength*. New York: Collier Books.

Lewis, I. M. *Ecstatic Religion: A Study of Shamanism and Spirit Possession*. London: Routledge, 1989.

Lily Dale Spiritualist Church. N.d. "Our Religion." *Lily Dale Spiritualist Church, NSAC*. lilydalespiritualistchurch.com/.

Linda of Oya. January 14, 2014. Personal email communication.

Lipton, Barbara, and Nima Dorjee Ragnubs. 1996. *Treasures of Tibetan Art: Collections of the Jacques Marchais Museum of Tibetan Art.* New York: Oxford University Press.

Loewe, Michael, and Carmen Blacker. 1981. *Oracles and Divination.* Boston: Shambhala Publishing.

Luck, Georg. 1989. "Theurgy and Forms of Worship in Neoplatonism." In *Religion, Science, and Magic.* Edited by Jacob Neusner, Ernest S. Frerichs, and Paul Flesher. New York: Oxford University Press.

Luhrmann, T. M. 2012. *When God Talks Back: Understanding the American Evangelical Relationship with God.* New York: Vintage.

Lynch, Beth. 2013. "So You Wanna Be a Godspouse? (Some Plain Talk)." Wytch of the North (blog). wytchofthenorth.wordpress.com/2013/01/01/so-you-wanna-be-a-godspouse-some-plain-talk/.

MacCana, Proinsias. 1970. *Celtic Mythology.* London: Hamlyn.

Mahabharata, The. Translated by Kisan Mohan Ganguli. www.sacred-texts.com/hin/maha/.

"Major Religions of the World Ranked by Number of Adherents." Adherents.com. www.adherents.com/Religions_By_Adherents.html. Last modified August 9, 2007.

March, Jenny. 2009. *The Penguin Book of Classical Myths.* New York: Penguin.

Mariner, W. 1817. *An Account of the Natives of the Tonga Islands in the South Pacific Ocean.* Edited by John Martin. In Oesterreich 1966.

Miller, Geoffrey. 2003. "Anubis." In *Devoted to You,* edited by Judy Harrow. New York: Citadel Press.

Morales, Frank. "Brahman of the Vedas: A Unique Concept of the Absolute." About Religion. hinduism.about.com/od/basics/a/brahman.htm.

Newberg, Andrew, and Mark Robert Waldman. 2010. *How God Changes Your Brain.* New York: Ballantine Books.

Nicholson, D. H. S. and A. H. E. Lee, eds. 1917. *The Oxford Book of English Mystical Verse,* #239. Oxford: Clarendon Press.

Ocelfa, Silence. December 8, 2013. Personal email communication.

Odin. "On His Nature and Purpose." Odin Speaks. www.odinspeaks.com/nature.html.

———. "Possessory Work." *Odin Speaks.* www.odinspeaks.com.

Opsopaus, John. 2002. A Summary of Pythagorean Theology. web.eecs.utk.edu/~mclennan/BA/ETP/I.html.

Oesterreich, T. K. 1966. *Possession: Demoniacal and Other.* New Hyde Park, NY: University Books.

Pantera, Thenea. March 17, 2014. Personal email communication.

Pascal, Blaise. 1909. *Thoughts.* Translated by W. F. Trotter. Harvard Classics Vol. XLVII, Part I. Collier & Son. www.bartleby.com/br/04801.html.

Paxson, Diana L. 1995. "Hyge-craeft." *Idunna* 28 (Autumn 1995): 24–32.

———. 2008. *Trance-Portation: Learning to Navigate the Inner World.* San Francisco: Weiser Books.

———. 2009. "Eighty-One Names of Odin." *Idunna* 81 (Fall 2009): 7–11.

Pew Research. Religion and Public Life Project: Religious Landscape Survey. August 13, 2007. religions.pewforum.org/reports.

Pinch, Geraldine. 2004. *Egyptian Mythology: A Guide to the Gods, Goddesses, and Traditions of Ancient Egypt.* New York: Oxford University Press, 2004.

Plato. *Cratylus.* Translated by Benjamin Jowett. classics.mit.edu/Plato/cratylus.html.

———. *The Apology.* Translated by Benjamin Jowett. classics.mit.edu/Plato/apology.html.

Plutarch. 1936. *De Defectu Oraculorum.* Loeb Classical Library Edition, Vol. V.

Pratchett, Terry. 2003. *Lords and Ladies.* New York: HarperTorch.

Price, Neil. 2000. *The Viking Way.* Uppsala, Sweden: Uppsala University Press.

Ramprasad Sen. 1982. *Grace and Mercy in Her Wild Hair: Selected Poems to the Mother Goddess.* Translated by Leonard Nathan and Clinton Seely. Boulder: CO: Great Eastern.

Raphael, Edwin. 1992. The pathway of non-duality, Advaitavada: an approach to some key-points of Gaudapada's Asparśavāda and Śaṁkara's Advaita Vedanta by means of a series of questions answered by an Asparśin. Iia: Philosophy Series. Motilal Banarsidass.

Reddington-Wilde, Maureen. 2003. "Part III: Beltaine—Aphrodite." In *Devoted to You: Honoring Deity in Wiccan Practice,* edited by Judy Harrow, 157–226. New York: Citadel Press.

Renault, Mary. 1988. *The Mask of Apollo.* New York: Vintage Books.

Roman, Sanaya, and Duane Packer. 1987. *Opening to Channel,* Tiburon, CA: H. J. Kramer & Co.

Rose, Winifred Hodge, 2006. "Heathen Full-Souls: The Big Picture" /Idunna/ 67, Spring, 2006.

Saraswati, Swami Satyananda. 1984. "The Five Koshas," Satsang in Toulon, France, June 9, 1984. In *Yoga Magazine,* April 2008. www.yogamag.net/archives/2008/dapr08/5kosh.shtml.

Scannell, T. 1910. "Latria." In *The Catholic Encyclopedia.* New York: Robert Appleton Company.

Shimomissé, Eiichi. 1998. In case 23 of the Mumonkan, The Gateless Gate. www.csudh.edu/phenom_studies/mumonkan/mumonkan.htm.

Simon, Tami. 2011. "Shamanism and Spiritual Light." Interview with Sandra Ingerman. *Cultivate Life!* 49 (April 6, 2011). www.trans4mind.com/cultivate-life-magazine/issue-049/Sandra-Ingerman.html.

Skeat, W. W. 1902. "The Wild Tribes of the Malay Peninsula." *Journal of the Anthropological Institute of Great Britain and Ireland* XXXII.

Smith, Daniel B. 2007. *Muses, Madmen and Prophets.* New York: Penguin Press.

Spence, Lewis, 1921. *An Introduction to Mythology.* New York: Moffat, Yard & Co.

Sørensen, Preben Meulengracht. 1983. *The Unmanly Man.* Translated by Joan Turville-Petre. Odense, Norway: Odense University Press.

Śrīmad Bhāgavatam. Translated by His Divine Grace A. C. Bhaktivedanta Swami Prabhupāda. Bhaktivedanta Book Trust International. Bhaktivedanta VedaBase: Śrīmad Bhāgavatam. srimadbhagavatam.com/.

Steger, Michael F., Patricia Frazier, Shigehiro Oishi, and Matthew Kaler. 2006. "The Meaning in Life Questionnaire: Assessing the Presence of and Search for Meaning in Life," In *Journal of Counseling Psychology* 53(1): 80–93.

Sturluson, Snorri. 1978. *Edda.* Edited and translated by Anthony Faulkes. London: Everyman.

———. 1987. "Skaldskarpamál." In *Edda,* translated by Anthony Faulkes,.

———. 1990. *Ynglinga Saga.* Translated by Erling Monsen and A. J. Smith.

"The Tale of King Vikar." 2009. In *The Sagas of Fridthjof the Bold,* translated by Ben Waggoner. The Troth, Lulu.com.

Teresa of Avila. 2008. *The Book of Her Life.* Translated by Kieran Kavanaugh, O.C.D. and Otilio Rodriguez, O.C.D. Indianapolis, IN: Hackett Publishing.

Underhill, Evelyn. 1961. *Mysticism.* New York: E. P. Dutton.

Uždavinys, Algis, ed. 2004. *The Golden Chain: An Anthology of Pythagorean and Platonic Philosophy.* Bloomington, IN: World Wisdom.

McKinnell, John, trans. 1972. *Viga-Glum's Saga, with the Tales of Ogmund Bash and Thorvald Chatterbox.* Canongate, Edinburgh: New Saga Library.

Waggoner, Ben. 2010. "Tales from the Flateyjarbók V." *Idunna* 85 (Autumn 2010): 34–38.

Warneck, J. 1909. *Die Religion der Batak.* Göttingen.

Watkins, Calvert, ed. 2000. *The American Heritage Dictionary of Indo-European Roots,* 2nd ed. Boston: Houghton Mifflin Co.

Wawn, Andrew. 2000. *The Vikings and the Victorians.* Rochester, NY: D. S. Brewer.

White, David Gordon. 1996. *The Alchemical Body: Siddha Traditions in Medieval India.* Chicago: University of Chicago Press; 18.

"Trance Possession & Drawing Down The Gods." WildWood Tradition. www.wildwoodtradition.net/index.php/tradition-lore-a-mythos/trance-possession-and-drawing-down-the-gods.

Williams, Charles. 1953. *The Figure of Beatrice.* New York: Faber & Faber.

Wodening, Eric. 1998. *We Are Our Deeds: The Elder Heathenry, Its Ethic and Thew.* Lulu.com.

Wood, Lorrie. March 18, 2014. Personal email communication.